P9-CRO-368

event *planning*

event
planning

The Ultimate Guide to

Successful Meetings

Corporate Events

Fundraising Galas

Conferences, Conventions

Incentives and Other

Special Events

Judy Allen

JOHN WILEY & SONS CANADA, LTD

Toronto • New York • Chichester • Weinheim • Brisbane • Singapore

Copyright © 2000 by Judy Allen

All rights reserved. No part of this work covered by the copyrights here-in may be reproduced or used in any form or by any means—graphic, electronic or mechanical—without the prior written permission of the publisher.

Any request for photocopying, recording, taping or information stor-age and retrieval systems of any part of this book shall be directed in writing to the CANCOPY, 6 Adelaide Street East, Suite 900, Toronto, Ontario, M5A 1H6.

Care has been taken to trace ownership of copyright material con-tained in this book. The publishers will gladly receive any information that will enable them to rectify any reference or credit line in subse-quent editions.

John Wiley & Sons Canada Limited
22 Worcester Road
Etobicoke, Ontario
M9W 1L1

Canadian Cataloguing in Publication Data

Allen, Judy, 1952–
  Event planning : the ultimate guide to successful meetings, corporate events, fundraising galas, conferences, conventions, incentives and other special events

Includes index.
ISBN 0-471-64412-9

1. Meetings – Planning. 2. Congresses and conventions – Planning.
3. Special events – Planning. I. Title.

AS6.A44 2000   658.4'56   C00-930535-1

Production Credits
Cover & text design: Interrobang Graphic Design Inc.
Printer: Tri-graphic Printing Ltd.

Printed in Canada
10 9 8 7 6 5 4

This book is dedicated with all my love to my family: my father and my mother, Walter and Ruth Foote, my sister, Marilyn, my two nieces, Natasha and Jasmine. You are all so very special to me.

And to Honey Sherman, Louise Cornblum, Michelle Levy, and Mary Shechtman. They are all extraordinary ladies who work tirelessly in their efforts to raise funds and lend their support to worthy causes. Through them, I became involved in fund-raising galas and saw first-hand, a need I could fill by writing this book and sharing my experiences in event planning. This served as a beginning, and the book was then expanded to encompass my background in worldwide meetings, corporate events, conferences, conventions, incentives, and special events, in addition to gala fundraisers.

CONTENTS

Preface   xi
Acknowledgements   xiii

Chapter 1: The First Steps: Initial Planning & Budgeting   1
How Much Can You Spend?   2
The Purpose of the Event   4
Initial Planning   8
Visualization   11
Budget Breakdown   14

Chapter 2: Organization and Timing   17
Critical Path   17
Function Sheets   20
Timing Is Everything   24
The Time of the Day and the Day of the Week   28
Date Selection   31

Chapter 3: Location, Location, Location   37
Site Selection   37
Location Requirements   43
Hotels and Convention Centres   46
Restaurants, Private Venues, Catering   49
Location: Q&A   49
Theatres   62
Tents   64
Contracts   70
Gala Openings in New Venues   71

Chapter 4: Transportation   **73**
  Limousines   73
  Motor Coaches   76
  Parking   78
  Transportation: Q&A   80

Chapter 5: Guest Arrival   **97**
  Weather Considerations   97
  Arrival & Weather Considerations: Q&A   99
  Fanfare   111
  Fanfare: Q&A   112
  Registration: Guest Pass Security and Ticket Pick-up   121
  Registration: Q&A   122

Chapter 6: Venue Requirements   **131**
  Staging, Audio-Visual, Lighting   131
  Staging, Audio-Visual, Lighting: Q&A   135
  Room Requirements: Q&A   144

Chapter 7: Who's It All For?   **149**
  The Guest List   149
  Invitations   152
  Media   158
  Media: Q&A   158
  Children At Your Event   160

Chapter 8: Food and Beverage   **163**
  Menu Planning   166
  Staffing   202

Chapter 9: Other Considerations   **207**
  Entertainment   207
  Entertainment: Q&A   208
  Photographer   215
  Photographer: Q&A   216
  Themes and Programs   223
  Final Touches   231

Conclusion   **235**
   It's a Wrap   235
   Applause! Applause!   236
   Your Next Event   237

Appendix A: Sample Cost Sheets   **239**

Appendix B: Sample Payment Schedules   **266**

Appendix C: Sample Function Sheets   **277**

Index   **303**

PREFACE

Two of the tips in this book alone would have saved a recent gala fund-raiser several thousands of dollars in unexpected costs, and could apply to *any* event held at a hotel, convention centre, private venue or even your own home.

What you do not know or do not know to ask can have a major impact on the success of your event and on your budget. In *Event Planning* I take you behind the scenes—from conception to on-site operations—to show you how to make your event as memorable as it can be, with as few surprises as possible at the end of the day. The magic begins in the detail, which through this book, I will attempt to bring to you.

For the past several years, I have been very involved in fund-raisers and other events—both as a volunteer and as a consultant. It was here that I first saw a need for a step-by-step guide for event planning. I believe that the expertise I have gained from 15 years of working events world-wide will be of tremendous benefit to you.

Here is your first tip: *write everything down*. I can't stress enough the importance of writing the information down—including the date and time, the supplier, who you spoke to and what was said. Refer back to your correspondence and always be specific. The more detailed you are, the less the margin for error. Whenever and wherever possible get everything in writing—all your requests and confirmations—the person you spoke to today may not be there tomorrow.

I wanted to design a book that would be used as a working tool, one that would contribute to successful event planning—whether it be a premiere, tribute, meeting, corporate event, fund-raising gala, conference, convention, incentive, wedding or any other special event. Whatever your event may be, there is something in this book that will contribute to making it special. Creating memorable events without unexpected surprises and expenses is what I am most passionate about. This is what I want to bring to you.

To further help your event planning needs visit our companion website. There you can access the sample forms in the Appendices, as well as additional samples not included in the book. The web site address is www.wiley.ca/go/event_planning.

Judy

ACKNOWLEDGEMENTS

This book owes a lot to Oprah Winfrey in a roundabout sort of way. I have never met Oprah, but I did listen when she said, "Take what you can do and use it for the highest good to benefit others." That is what I have set out to do with this book. I am also indebted to Vicki Spina, author of *Success 2000: Moving into the Millennium with Purpose, Power and Prosperity* (New York, Wiley, 1997) who I saw first on the *Oprah* show. Through her book and her personal encouragement she me the final push I needed to sit down and share what I know. Teaching others and sharing knowledge is to me taking what you can do and using it for the highest good to benefit others.

I would also like to thank all the wonderful people at John Wiley & Sons. Editor, Karen Milner, who taught me all of what goes into making a book. Elizabeth McCurdy for believing this book would be of value and taking it to the next step. Literary Agent, Daphne Hart, at the Helen Heller Agency, for all her much-needed and appreciated advice. Ron Edwards, my copy editor on this book (I will never look at a yellow "sticky" note in quite the same way again.), who took the manuscript, literally turned it inside out, and presented it in a way that will work best for both the experienced and first-time event planner. Also, I'd like to thank the many people behind the scenes at John Wiley and Sons who worked on my book. This book, like event planning, is a team effort and I thank you all.

I would also like to thank my family and friends for their continued encouragement and support. My mom and dad, my sister, Marilyn, my nieces Natasha and Jasmine and my friends—Angela, Barb D., Barb S., Brenda, Fran, Honey, Louise, Jayne, Jill and Roger, Liane, Marguerite, Nanci, Roneet and Sue, Barbara and Joe, Doreen, Lisa, Lynn and Bob, Lynn S., Marianne and Dave, Shelley, and Susie V. Thank you all for being a part of my life.

1

THE FIRST STEPS: INITIAL PLANNING & BUDGETING

Designing and producing an event—whether it be a meeting, corporate event, fund-raising gala, conference, convention, incentive or other special event—has been compared to directing a movie but is actually more like a live stage production. It is a high-wire act without the safety nets. Once your event starts there are *no* second chances. It's done in one take and there are no dress rehearsals. You can't yell "cut" and reshoot the scene. You are simply not able to predict—as you can with a movie script—how your guests and suppliers will interact and react. But you can plan, prepare and then be prepared for the unexpected. Never forget Murphy's Law: what can go wrong, will go wrong.

At one wedding, the waitress tripped and the wedding cake landed upside down. Luckily, it had been covered with a cloth as it was being carried out and only the top layer was damaged. Back in the kitchen, with some new icing, flowers, and tulle from the bridal bouquet, the cake was soon ready for the traditional photographs.

Although you are not creating an Oscar-winning movie, you are creating something that may be a lifetime memory for someone. Any event, whether it's for 50 or more than 2,000, needs to be as detailed and as scripted as any film production, and so does the budget. Budgets for meetings, corporate events, product launches, conferences, conventions, incentives and special events can go from tens of thousands to hundreds of thousands of dollars and even exceed half a million dollars. The aim is the same as the old Holiday Inn slogan about no surprises.

Before you begin planning, you should decide whether or not to have an event in the first place. If it is a go, the next decision is the scope of the event. Two criteria will determine this: money and objectives.

HOW MUCH CAN YOU SPEND?

The first thing you need to do is to establish how much money you can set aside for the event. Even the smallest event requires a serious financial commitment. You may decide that you cannot afford to do one at this time. Remember, it's better to wait than to stage a shoddy event on a shoestring budget. If money is not an obstacle, you must determine ahead of time how much you can spend, and plan the event to fit the budget. It is a good idea to do a rough estimate of costs before anything else, because, very often, budget approvals from the higher-ups are required before an event is given the green light. Below is a sample of a preliminary budget that allows you to arrive at a very rough estimate of the main expenses for your event. More detailed budgets will be covered in Chapter 3.

PRELIMINARY COST ESTIMATES

Generally, you can get written estimates from suppliers for the various items you are considering. These will be firmed up later after the preliminary budget is approved.

Sample preliminary budgets should include main costs such as:

• Invitations

• Accommodation

- Transportation
- Venue rentals
- Rehearsal costs
- Food
- Beverage
- Floral arrangements
- Decor
- Music
- Entertainment
- Speakers
- Staging
- Audio-visual
- Lighting
- Special effects
- Photographer
- Place cards
- Menus
- Gifts
- Insurance
- Security
- Labour charges
- Power charges
- Promotional material
- Communication costs
- Translation
- Shipping and handling
- Customs
- Staffing
- Miscellaneous

   Make a detailed wish list that includes everything possible regardless of cost. Then, with a coloured marker, highlight the items that absolutely must be included in your program. The remaining items are optional and can be factored in once you have established your preliminary budget. If your preliminary cost estimates, including only the non-negotiable items, exceed your proposed budget, you will need to give serious consideration as to whether or not you should proceed with your planned event. If your preliminary cost estimates are well under your proposed budget figures you can then begin to factor in your optional items.

THE PURPOSE OF THE EVENT

The next thing to consider is the purpose of the event. Why are you holding it? What are your goals and intentions? What do you hope to achieve? Be clear about your objective. It should be significant, such as launching a major product, say a new car, or rewarding top sales performance, to justify the cost of the event. Don't use an event as an excuse to cover up internal strategies. For example, staging a costly event to "launch" a minor product that has not sold well because of some defects will not only fail to solve your problems but also will add to them by wasting your money and tarnishing your company's reputation. Make sure the event is worth it. Below are some examples of different objectives for various types of events.

Some Objectives for Different Types of Events

Meetings

- Provide new information about your product or company
- Bring people together outside the office setting
- Exchange ideas
- Find solutions to existing problems
- Launch a new product
- Provide training

Corporate Events

- Employee appreciation
- Client appreciation
- Supplier appreciation
- Award dinners
- Bringing suppliers and staff together
- Product launches
- Support a fund-raising endeavour that the corporation advocates
- Public awareness
- Brand-name recognition
- Milestones (50th anniversary, millionth customer or widget sold)

Fund-Raisers

- Raise funds for research
- Media attention
- Public awareness
- Attract new sponsors
- Solicit new supporters and donations
- Increase number of volunteers
- Develop a mailing list for future events or sponsorship and donation requests

Conferences

- Bring a wide range of people together to exchange information and ideas
- Launch new products
- Sales recognition
- Opportunity to bring staff, sales, suppliers, clients and dealers together

---

Incentives

- Create one-of-a-kind events to recognize increase in sales
- Bring top sales force together to discuss future strategy
- Get top sales force and senior management together outside the work environment
- Enlist the support of family and partners

Special Events

- Media attention
- Public awareness
- Attracting new clients
- Product launches
- Award presentations
- Tributes

Your objectives will affect how you plan and set up your event. If you are planning a client appreciation event where attendees at a conference may have several choices on the same evening, your objective would be to create something that will pique their interest, get them to your event, keep them there and have them interacting with your people.

For example, stockbrokers attending a conference flocked to an evening of fun, food and adventure at a brand-new entertainment complex. Motor coaches were waiting at their hotel to take them to the site and to bring them back. As guests boarded they were presented with a sealed package and told not to open it until they arrived at the private cocktail reception. Inside the kits were logoed golf towels that served a dual purpose: team designation and take-away gifts.

The first purpose of the golf towels was to divide the guests into six teams identified by different-coloured golf towels. Each team was led by a senior member of the hosting company, allowing them to spend quality time getting to know the team members. The golf towels easily clipped onto waistbands or purses and made each team member easily identifiable. At the cocktail reception guests were given instructions and then they set out on a two-hour adventure, taking part in something unique—a virtual-reality Olympics. Afterwards, they met for a "clock-in" dinner and an opportunity to share experiences. Scores were quickly calculated and prizes awarded. Then guests were free to stay and enjoy the facilities at their leisure, with the private area remaining if they wanted to relax and enjoy beverages, coffee and dessert. Shuttles left every half hour to take them back to the hotel if they chose to leave. Guests had such a great time that at the end of the evening most had not left. They had had an entertaining experience and the company's objectives had been met; they had spent quality time interacting and getting to know their guests.

The second purpose of the golf towels was as take-away gifts. Too often, such gifts are ill-considered, useless trinkets, but since most stockbrokers play golf, the towel was something they could actually use, and it would serve as a visual reminder of the event. Had the event been planned as just a cocktail reception and dinner at the facility, people might still have had a good time, but the company's objectives would not have been met. Without the structure of the competing teams, there would not have been the same quality interaction. If the guests had been left to explore the facility on their own, they would have been too spread out and with little to keep their interest they might have simply dropped in for a cocktail and a quick game before heading off to another event.

If your objective was to capture media attention (for example, in launching a new venue) you would want to look for ways to capture the imagination of the journalists. Teaser e-mails could be sent out reminding them of the date of your event by giving a behind-the-scenes look at the preparations for the event. A live chat room could be set up to discuss the facilities. An exclusive reception could be held for the media, their guests and celebrities, ensuring photo opportunities and time for quality interviews. Photographs of reporters with celebrity guests could be taken, developed and placed in discreetly logoed frames to be handed out at the end of the evening with their press kits. Remember that it is not enough to simply invite the media to your event and leave them on their own. You have to know what they need and make special provisions for them. Assign someone to greet them, show them around and to introduce them to key individuals.

First Steps Questions

1. Should I hold an event?
2. Do I have sufficient funds to stage an event?
3. How much money can I set aside for the event?
4. What is the purpose of the event?
5. Does it justify the financial outlay?

INITIAL PLANNING

You decided to hold an event. After preparing a preliminary cost estimate, you have concluded that you have sufficient funds and have allocated a set amount for the event. You have defined the purpose of the event and decided that it would justify the financial outlay. You are now ready to begin the initial planning for the event. During this stage, you will decide whether you need outside professional help, set up an internal event team, establish the type of event to have and the timing and visualize the whole thing from top to bottom.

When planning major events too many people think in terms of dollars and cents, not sense. You need to know when and where to bring in professional assistance, including an expert in public relations, a creative director or a producer to handle the logistical management of your event. Do not think of consultants as an added expense and a luxury. They can actually save money in the end, especially if they are brought in at the appropriate time. For example, a good public relations company can assist with your guest list and ensure that the *right* people are invited to your event; they can also help create press releases and press kits to get you national and international media exposure. A creative director works to provide you with a strategic conceptional overview of the event design including planning, organizational, logistical and negotiating elements and the tiny details that make the magic. A producer ensures that all that is visualized becomes reality and is responsible for ensuring that fire and safety regulations are met, all appropriate permits are obtained and that the proper insurance is in place.

Imagine the fire marshall standing at the front door about to close your event down because you don't have the proper permits, have too many guests for the size of the room or you haven't met all safety regulations. How costly is that? Or what is the cost if you do a fabulous event and you need the momentum from positive press but nothing is done about it? How costly is it if you are not on top of what is new, fresh and exciting and the media report that people bolted for the doors before dessert was served? You need to know where and when to bring in the professionals. Will it be dollars and cents, or sense? Know where. Know when.

EVENT COMMITTEE OR TEAM

When setting up an event committee or team seek to match skills and areas of interest with areas of responsibility. You want to avoid having anyone feel as though they are a deer caught in an oncoming car's headlights. A useful introduction to project management and bringing people together to work as a team is Mackenzie Kyle, *Making it Happen*.[1] Remember when dealing with suppliers to have one person assigned to handle all communication with them. This ensures that suppliers are not receiving conflicting sets of instructions from a number of sources and that approval for expenditures is not given to them by someone not in a position to authorize them.

TYPE OF EVENT

When determining the type of event look at your targeted audience. Busy professionals may not take time out from their schedules to attend a symposium that will cut into their designated family time but may attend if the event is designed to

---

[1] Mackenzie Kyle, *Making it Happen: A Non-Technical Guide to Project Management* (Toronto: John Wiley & Sons Canada, 1998).

include their family members, such as a private showing in a theatre or an exclusive booking of an entertainment centre. The symposium could be held in the morning while their families are at play. They would then meet for a catered luncheon with the balance of the day for them to enjoy the facility with their family members.

A company seeking to introduce its new venue to a targeted area may choose to partner with another company to create an event that will generate media exposure in addition to bringing the clients to their doorstep. For example, an entertainment complex opening in the downtown core might join with a car manufacturer that is looking to introduce its new product to the public. Together, they could approach a local charity and create an event that would draw media attention and promote goodwill. The new vehicle could be on display at the site and charity volunteers could raise funds by selling chances or "keys" to win the vehicle. These could be sold in advance of the event. If the prize is large enough, it will attract people—they will come to see if the key they purchased will unlock the door of a brand-new car, not just for a free drink coupon or some such. They will use the free coupon but only if they were already planning to go there. A radio station could do a remote from the site and help to create excitement and coverage around the event. Always keep both your objective and your targeted audience in mind as you begin to plan your event.

TIME REQUIREMENTS

Bear in mind that many details will not yet be determined but in an ideal world you would be able to plan your event at least a year in advance. Yes, it is possible to put together major high-profile events for 1,000 + in under six weeks, but there is always a cost. You run the risk of not being able to get the most sought-after locations and entertainment. Why settle for second-best if you can plan ahead?

In deciding the amount of planning time required, list everything that you will need and assign a time frame to each item. Begin with the end in mind. What needs to done for your event to be a success? Work backwards with your calendar and start to pencil in the proposed schedule of events. Remember to build in some buffer. Take the time to research in order to determine realistic time lines.

Allow yourself sufficient time to achieve maximum results. Are there any factors that could contribute to not meeting targeted deadlines such as your suppliers being closed for holidays or a conflicting deadline? For example, printing companies traditionally close for vacation the last two weeks in July. Be sure to check with your suppliers and to factor this into your time lines. Summer is a bad time in general—even the media are away.

Will any key people be difficult to reach or out of the office over prime planning and operations deadlines? Will year-end affect timing in any way?

One gala fund-raiser had a three-month time line to secure a venue, obtain sponsors, arrange entertainment and printing and sell 5,000 tickets at $500 apiece. A flurry of meetings followed and the event was postponed after they concluded that it would not be a success if they went ahead with their plans with just three months lead time. They would not be able to secure a quality venue and an entertainer that was a draw. The timing just could not be worked out, including obstacles such as the start of a new school year and the Jewish holidays. In the end the plans were revised to allow for sufficient time to properly plan, secure sponsorship and contract name entertainment.

VISUALIZATION

Visualization is an important factor in ensuring a successful event. It is a step-by-step process that walks you through your event and allows you to see areas that could pose potential problems in advance. It allows you to address these areas in the planning stages and not be surprised on the day of the actual event. For example, if your guests will be arriving all at once and there is both an up and a down escalator leading to the ballroom, you may want to have both escalators set to go up to alleviate congestion and speed entry. (At the conclusion of the event the reverse is true.) This could allow you to set up two separate registration desks at the foot of the escalators and help to lessen the waiting time in line-ups. In addition, you may find that you could also use two separate coat check areas.

Visualizing such things in advance will help you decide the staffing you will need to greet and direct guests, sit at the registration desk and have both coat checks adequately staffed. Visualization allows you to consider all your options and to see how they affect your budget before you finalize your plans.

Try to envision your event from beginning to end. You need to be able to do a complete preliminary visual walk through in your mind. The following are just some of the questions you will have to ask (and answer):

- What is the purpose of your event?
- What time of year are you considering holding it?
- What day of the week?
- What time of the day?
- Who will be attending?
- What type of venue will be the best fit, the best setting, the best backdrop?
- Are you planning far enough in advance that the best sites will be available to you?

Remember, your event is a reflection of your company image. Keep in mind that what you do today sets the tone for tomorrow and can work both for and against you in building momentum for your next event. Of key importance will be the ambience you create, the rhythm, the flow and the schedule of events from beginning to end.

This is just your starting point—we will cover detailed specifics in another section. Create a visual image of your event. List every element that you want to include. What are your priorities—must haves—to make your event a success? Have you included one major "Wow" factor in your event? What atmosphere are you looking to create? What take-away memories? What perception of your company or cause?

One guest on a four-night incentive program in San Antonio said, "Each day was like Christmas. Each event was like opening up one exciting gift one after another." Events included a private golf course booked exclusively for the company's golfers. The golfers teed off in the morning and did not return until 6 p.m. Had any guests preferred basketball to golf, going one-on-one with a celebrity player could have been arranged.

Complete make-overs were provided for those who chose to be pampered instead. The salon was entirely theirs for the day. Appointments were scheduled and limousines shuttled guests from the hotel to the salon and back. Lunch was provided and most guests did not leave but chose instead to oversee the other make-overs. The transformations were amazing. Professional photographs were taken and mailed to the guests. There were many requests for additional copies.

When the winning sales executives returned to work on Monday, their motivation was high, their enthusiasm contagious. The carefully designed and orchestrated incentive program had boosted the exact feelings the client was hoping to achieve—they had reached their objective. The San Antonio winners clearly felt taken care of from beginning to end, and their spouses were delighted as well. Every detail had been looked after and all their needs had been thought of in advance and attended to. And that all reflected directly back on to the company and its image as one that took excellent care of its staff. The staff who had not met the targeted sales goals this time were motivated by the positive energy of the returning winners and were looking forward to the possibility of attending the next incentive program, which was announced at the farewell award dinner in San Antonio.

An important factor in such incentive programs is that company sales targets are not excessive; they must be obtainable by all, and the number of participants who could attend the event must not be limited.

From the initial invitation to on-site operations, your event must be a true reflection of your company image and will mirror how your business is run and your personal style.

BUDGET BREAKDOWN

Cost Sheets

As you begin to plan your event, laying out your proposed budget on a cost sheet will allow you to clearly see what items can be included and still keep you within your budget. It will also show you how you are choosing to spend your money, enable you to look at alternate choices and see how they would work within your cost parameters. For example, once you have laid out your cost sheet and taken a look at where you stand in meeting your targeted budget you may decide to use simple candles supplied by the hotel as opposed to a more elaborate floral arrangement and put the money saved towards the cocktail reception. Your goal is to create a memorable event while staying in budget. You want to ensure that you have taken all possible steps to do so. Don't wait to find out at the end of your event that you have greatly exceeded your budget projections.

Since each event will include different things there is no set formula or format for a cost sheet. As you start to build your cost sheet, walk through your event from beginning to end and start to build the outline. Then go back and fill in the costs. Remember to get all your estimates in writing. Never accept verbal quotes. Today, staff changes are the rule rather than the exception—people are here today and gone tomorrow. You need written confirmation of what is and what is not included. Make sure that your suppliers spell it out. Have them be specific when it comes to items as seemingly unimportant as tipping—are gratuities calculated as a straight percentage of the total bill, or are there other considerations that need to be factored into your cost sheet such as tipping being taxed? That amount can add up, especially if it affects both food and beverage. Similarly, taxes on food and liquor can be different—sometimes liquor can be taxed at, for example, 10 per cent while the tax on food could be at 8 per cent. Don't assume.

Find out what additional costs may be added to the final bill and make sure you include them in your budget. Some venues will bill you for your actual usage of electricity. In those cases, for your costing purposes, ask for the figures from a recent similar event that can provide you with an estimate for your budget. With entertainment, royalties must be paid to the artist (ASCAP or BMI in the United States and SOCAN in Canada). Make sure that the company that is handling your entertainment needs has included it in your written proposal. Computer spreadsheet programs, such as LOTUS 1-2-3 or Excel, allow you the flexibility to quickly see how your overall costs are affected if you have 750 or 1,000 guests. You can also easily add and remove items and see how that affects the bottom line.

Keep updating your budget as items are added and subtracted and save these on separate files. Date and number them (i.e., Revision 1, Revision 2). You need to stay on top of your budget so that you can make informed decisions on what to include. As bills come in, make sure nothing is paid out until it has been reviewed. Make sure that what is submitted is what had been agreed on, with no hidden surprises. Adjust your cost sheet accordingly. As each bill is received, record the actual amount on your cost sheet and compare it to your projected figures. Are they accurate? Are there any costs on the final billing that you had not included in your original estimate? Be on the lookout particularly for items that were verbally approved and charged for, but not recorded. How do they impact your bottom line? Do you need to make any budget adjustments in other areas to compensate for them?

As you move from the creative planning stages of your event into the actual operation, the items you originally decided to include may change. For example, you may decide to welcome your guests with a specialty drink that will require the rental of specific glassware as opposed to your original plan for a standard open bar. This would have an impact on your budget projections. Little by little, the cents add up to dollars, and the dollars can quickly escalate. If you are not keeping your cost sheet updated, you could find that you have blown your budget. By constantly updating your cost sheets, your budget will be close to being reconciled as you go into your event. It will also allow you to make those last-minute additions that often come up, and knowing where you are financially allows you to make a responsible decision, such as whether you can afford to host the bar after dinner or set it up as a cash bar. Perhaps you now have sufficient funds left in the budget to include a farewell gift for your guests. See Appendix A for sample cost sheets. You can also visit our companion web site at www.wiley.ca/go/event_planning to access these forms, as well as additional ones not included in the book.

Payment Schedule

Before you sign a contract you need to prepare a payment schedule to see if the due dates need to be adjusted. Hotels and other venues will work with you if payments need to be changed to match cheque runs or cash flows. Your cost sheet is the base from which to create your payment schedule. Your payment schedule will need to be revised should the items you plan to include or number of expected guests change. Adjust amounts accordingly before sending the next payment off. See Appendix B for a sample cost sheet and the payment schedule that has been created from it. Again, for access to these samples, as well as others not included in Appendix B, please visit our companion web site at www.wiley.ca/go/event_planning.

2 ORGANIZATION AND TIMING

CRITICAL PATH

Being organized and paying close attention to detail are two of the most important elements of running a successful event. Checking constantly that things are on track and moving forward as scheduled is essential. An event committee needs to adhere to the guidelines set out and agreed upon. Taking two months to approve an item could result in poor event project management. You could spend hours on a creative invitation design, but if it doesn't arrive at the printers in sufficient time to make your mailing deadlines, it can have a disastrous effect. Creating a critical path should be one of your first steps after you have decided to go ahead with the event.

To create your critical path take out your calendar and start working backwards from the date of your event, looking at what has to be done when. There are numerous horror stories of things nearly going wrong. At one fund-raising event, the programs and signage had to have last-minute changes and barely arrived on time. At another event inserts arrived *after* the programs had been distributed and, at a third, the logoed T-shirts arrived literally hot off the press—the boxes were steaming as they were opened! Each of these things sends a subtle signal of disorganization to those attending your event. Such missteps and near-disasters show that the event was poorly planned and coordinated. There have to be cut-off times that need to be *strictly* adhered to, otherwise you will suddenly discover what the domino effect is all about. It is surprising how an apparently small thing can have a major impact. At one fund-raising event they were changing the seating plans up until the very last minute and left themselves no time for a final review. This resulted in some embarrassing errors; one table had been assigned to two companies, which resulted in an additional table having to be set up at the final moment as the guests stood and waited. There were no extra tablecoverings and centrepieces so that the table could not be set up to match the others. By taking last-minute requests for table seating they had not left themselves time to properly check the revisions that they had made to the seating plan. Your goal is to have everything finalized the day before set-up begins so that everyone involved can take that time to look after last-minute details. You want everyone to arrive the day of your event refreshed and at their best.

Take all of your contracts and make sure that all key cut-off dates become a part of your critical path. Pay close attention to attrition and cancellation dates. These are the final dates when you are allowed to alter your attendance figures (attrition) or scrub the whole event (cancellation) without penalties. Often, you can lower the guaranteed guest count on food and beverage or the number of guest rooms booked at a hotel without incurring charges if the numbers are reduced by a certain date. Include the deadline and also a date to review it. Allow yourself time to make informed decisions. If you miss an attrition date and a chance to reduce your guest numbers it could be a costly mistake as you would then be charged based on the original numbers of guests or guest rooms contracted.

As your event develops, continue to update your critical path along with your cost sheet and payment schedule. Make sure you have included all areas. Give a description of each item, who is responsible and what the deadline is. Take the time to prepare your critical path.

You will find a sample critical path below for an event scheduled to take place on November 1. This example takes you through some suggested time lines for the preparation of guest lists and invitations. In this example, a professional mailhouse was contracted to address the invitations, insert them into the envelopes and mail them out. This could also be done in-house, as long as you allow for additional time and staff to do this. If staff are handling the mailing in addition to their regular work you could experience delays in meeting time lines. This outline includes key dates in the critical path. Of course, times will vary depending on your specific requirements, your suppliers' deadlines and the time of year.

> **T**
> **I**
> **P**
>
> Whenever you are doing a mailing be sure to address one piece to yourself. This way you will know if there are any unexpected delays in delivery, and if you check the date stamp on the envelope you will know if the invitation actually went out on the scheduled date.

Critical Path: Guest List and Invitations

Task	Person Responsible	Completion Date
Guest List Development	Michelle	May 01
Invitation Design	Judy	May 01
Details to Designer	Judy	July 12
Mailhouse Booked	Michelle	July 12
First Review of Invitation Design	Judy	July 26
Second Review of Invitation Design (if required)	Judy	August 03
Invitations to Printer	Judy	August 09
Envelopes Sent to Mailhouse	Michelle	August 23
Invitations Mailed to Guest List A	Michelle	September 13*
VIP Passes Mailed to Guest List A (if applicable)	Judy	September 27*
RSVP Cut-Off to Guest List A		September 27
Invitations Mailed to Guest List B	Michelle	September 27*
RSVP Cut-Off for Guest List B		October 12

| VIP Passes Mailed to Guest List B (if applicable) | Judy | October 12* |

* Depending on delivery schedule

FUNCTION SHEETS

Screenwriters have their scripts, songwriters their music sheets and event planners their function sheets. Each fulfils the same function. Like a good story, there is a beginning, a middle and an end. Each step of the way is scripted, each note is laid out exactly as it is meant to be played. Everyone is operating off the same page. Everything is clearly detailed. It lessens the room for error and eliminates the "but I thought...." It reduces the grey areas and things that could slip through the cracks. From the detail comes the magic, whether it's Glenn Gould's brilliance with practicing scales or Doug Henning with card tricks.

The function sheets become living and breathing things, and you are their creative director. They are the heart of your event, encompassing it from beginning to end. One person needs to be in charge of preparing them, to control all the information coming in, and that person must be the *only* one dealing with the suppliers and finalizing the plans. The creative director needs to know the event—every moment, every step, every detail—inside out, just like a conductor leading a symphony or a director making a movie. Each player needs to know what their part is and when to come in, but one person is in charge of the overall event. The leader can't be someone whose role it will be to host the event or to socialize. Make sure everyone knows their particular role. Don't have half a dozen people calling a supplier; that's a certain recipe for disaster, and it reflects badly on your professionalism and that of your organization.

As an event approaches you will probably no longer need to refer to your function sheets because you know them by heart. You know—as a conductor does—when the wrong note has been played. One wedding planner booked a private estate for a celebrity wedding months in advance, and found out 10 days before the event that a large pond and hot tub had been constructed on the lawn where the couple had planned to say their vows. He was quoted as saying that the couple couldn't get married there unless they arranged to walk on water. For such a calamity to happen is unthinkable—especially not knowing about it until 10 days before! That is the purpose of the function sheets—to make sure that everything is in place with no surprises. A solution was found, but at what cost to make the new layout work? Who needs to have that kind of stress and all the additional expenses?

The function sheets are the information guide that tell your suppliers how *you* want your event to be handled. They set out exactly what has been contracted, what is included, the costs agreed upon and how you want the details arranged. For example, say a hotel usually has a dessert and coffee station with the cups and saucers stacked separately. You may want the cup and saucer stacked together for a more polished presentation that allows guests to pick up their cup and saucer in one fluid motion. The hotel needs to know this in advance so that they can direct their staff to change the set-up. This is just one tiny aspect of the overall event—multiply that by, oh, maybe a million, and you see why event planners must be well prepared.

Hotels and venues appreciate the detail. They may refer to your function sheets as a "book" at times—they can exceed 100 pages—but it is a book that they will read because come the day of the event they know everything must be in place. They can't say "I didn't know" because it will have been presented to them in great detail. If the wiring on the twinkle lights is to be a specific colour to better blend in with the colouring of the leaves, state this in your function sheets. Make it clear that on the day of the event what you have requested is what you expect to see. Anything else is simply unacceptable. If there is a problem with your request or your proposed layout, you need to know in advance and not on the day of your actual event. Let suppliers know that you will be having a staff member assigned to advance or oversee each aspect of your event. Make note of who will be supervising each specific area and when they will be arriving to oversee set-up to ensure that everything is according to plan. What is important is the total visual effect. What will the camera see? What will the guests see? What is the impact? The ambiance created? Your function sheets are a step-by-step guide to creating the setting you want.

The function sheets are the working script. Every supplier and key player receives an initial copy in time to review it and make any necessary changes. Suppliers have often remarked that it is helpful for them to see the event laid out in its entirety. For example, it will help a tent rental company to know what the caterer is proposing to bring into the cooking tent and at what time they will be setting up so they can schedule their staff accordingly and have their people out of the way by the time the caterer is scheduled to arrive. This way the caterer is not off-loading their supplies and trying to work around the tenting staff. Ideally, you will have brought the tent supplier and the caterer together at the initial walk through of the site and the function sheet will be a review of what was discussed as well as the finalized plans.

Once your suppliers have had a chance to review your initial set of function sheets, and together you have fine-tuned any areas of concern, a revised copy is sent out to all. A precon meeting is set up to take place a few days before your actual event. This is a meeting where all suppliers and key staff members review the final set of function sheets to make sure that there is a clear understanding of what is expected, and a final walk through is done at this time. (These meetings were originally named to take place before (pre) a convention, but "precon" now refers to any advance planning meeting.) On the day of the event each and every aspect is advanced by a member of the event planning staff, who will be on hand to supervise the setup and ensure that all is laid out exactly as outlined in the function sheets. They report any areas of concern back to the creative director, who will handle any problems.

Function sheets should begin with "contact sheets" that include all names, titles, company names, addresses, telephone, fax and cell numbers, e-mail and, at times, home numbers. This serves two purposes. The first being that the creative director has all numbers in one central area. For example, if the creative director needs to reach a limousine driver who is transferring a VIP guest, he or she has that cell number immediately accessible to them. The second purpose is that with that list you have everything you need to be able to sit down after the event and write your thank-you letters; those contact sheets have all the information and serve as a checklist.

For those doing events for the first time, hotels and venues can supply a list of their preferred suppliers. In some cases, you are restricted to using only the suppliers they have recommended. Be sure to ask if you are permitted to bring in a supplier of your own choosing.

The information in your function sheets is confidential. Make sure your suppliers and all others receiving a copy are aware of that. Key staff will have their function sheets with them at the event—a binder works best—and must make sure that these are never left unattended. Each staff member is personally responsible for his or her copy. The sheets are also a good place to write down any notes to be discussed later when you do the review of the event.

The function sheets are used to identify who will be doing what. And as you begin to complete the sheets, they will clearly show you how many people you will need to have on hand, their responsibilities, duties, where they will need to be positioned and when. See Appendix C for sample function sheets. These samples can also be viewed on our companion web site at www.wiley.ca/go/event_planning along with others not included in Appendix C.

If you have assigned specific duties in your function sheets to volunteers at a fund-raiser, make sure they know the importance of being there on time on the day of the event.

At two separate fund-raisers there was a noticeable lack of volunteers—over half had not shown up, and it impacted the success of the event because the remaining volunteers were not able to handle things smoothly. They had needed the extra hands. The problem is not the committee members, who are generally strongly committed to supporting their causes, giving endless time and energy, but "day of" volunteers. It is extremely important that you tell them how much you appreciate and need their support and how essential they are to the success of your event. Take the time to fill them in on the schedule of events and the part they will play. Let them know what will be expected from them (dress code, protocol, hours). Don't have them show up on the day of the event uninformed; make sure that you have assigned a member of the event planning committee to review their responsibilities with them and oversee the volunteers during your event. They will need to have someone they can report to exclusively.

TIMING IS EVERYTHING

Deciding on an appropriate date is a major factor in the success of your event. Along with ensuring that the most people will attend there are other factors to consider when selecting a date. For example, what else will be going on around the time of your event? If you are thinking of inviting families with children, a school night would not be a good idea. Guests would not stay late because both parents and children would need to get up early the next day for work and school. Moving the event to the weekend would be more appealing and would reduce the possibility of having to take two cars per family to get there if one or both parents are coming from work. If you still decide to go ahead with a week night, do you know if it is before or during exams? This could have an impact on your event. One company was considering having their gala opening, one that would involve children and teens, on a school night immediately following Halloween. It was suggested that this would be a mistake because with two consecutive busy nights, both filled with excitement, young children could be overtired and fretful at the second event.

Imagine arriving at a hotel one Saturday night in June for your black-tie gala reception and dinner to find police stationed in the halls and a school prom going on in the next ballroom. There is commotion and confusion. The fire department and an ambulance arrives. Someone attending the prom has passed out and needs medical attention. It could happen—it has!

Holding your event next door to a school prom is something you wish to avoid. Make sure you ask what else is scheduled to take place at your venue during your event.

Consider the seasons before you finalize your plans. May and June are peak months for weddings and proms and November and December for holiday festivities. Are there any possible areas of concern that you need to be made aware of? One hotel had two major competitors at the same time. Is it the time of year when the destination you are considering travelling to is known to have major electrical storms and flash floods? Is it hurricane season? Have the roads consistently been made unpassable due to major snowstorms at a certain time of year? This could affect meetings being held in ski resorts.

If yours is a corporate event, such as a car launch and you are locked into specific dates and times, you may be considering holding your farewell event at a hotel for a variety of reasons. These could include the hotel having been promised the dollar revenue on food and beverage for the farewell night in exchange for financial considerations on the hotel room rates and meeting space. Or the corporate guests are all from out of town and have been staying at the hotel, and they are scheduled to leave early the next day. Holding the farewell event at the hotel allows guests to retire early from the farewell function, pack and get ready for their departure instead of having to stay to the end and wait for transportation back to the hotel from another venue.

TIME OF YEAR

Give careful thought to the time of year you are planning to hold your event. Are there any holidays that might interfere? If your event is being held in another country you need to consider local as well as international holidays that could have an impact on your event. For example, in Malaysia, there is a festival called Eid Festival—Hari Raya Puasa, which is a celebration of the conclusion of a month of fasting and abstinence, and it is a very special occasion for Muslims. It involves two days, which are considered public holidays, and most businesses are closed for the duration. If your event is in Kuala Lampur you need to know this and factor it into your program. Consider how it could affect your activities and plan them accordingly. It can be a memorable part of their stay for your participants to see local celebrations such as the candlelight parade through the streets that occurs in Mexico on the Anniversary of the Virgin of Guadalupe (December 12), but make sure that you know in advance how and where it could affect your events. In our secular culture we often forget the enormous impact religion has in other parts of the world.

> When I was in Morocco doing a location inspection travelling the country by limousine, I saw firsthand how religion can have a bearing on your planned itinerary of events. Our limousine driver was Islamic and answered the call to prayer five times a day. We were able to schedule our appointments around these halts and respect the beliefs of not only our driver but our suppliers.

Make sure that your event does not overlap any long holiday or celebrations such as Mother's Day or Father's Day, which are typically times when families get together. March Break can be a problem (times vary), and in summer it often seems that virtually everyone you have to talk to is out of town.

WHAT TIME OF YEAR WORKS BEST?

Look at the reasons why the time of year you are considering would work best to help you succeed in meeting your objectives. Is this the right time to be planning your event, or is there another time that could be a better fit?

Meetings, Conferences, Conventions

Traditionally new car launches take place in the fall. This is a time when car dealers expect to get together with manufacturers to see the new product line. What you want to make sure of is that the time between launching the new car—where you build anticipation and excitement—and it arriving in the dealerships is not too long. You want to keep the momentum high. Keeping up the momentum applies to any product, as well as policies or procedures. Don't introduce new company policies or procedures and not be prepared to implement them in the near future.

Fund-Raising Galas

Is this a time of year when the people and support you are trying to attract will be in town? If your event is a society event remember that they could be out of the country for an extended period of time over the winter months.

Will your event be overshadowed by another major ongoing event such as a film or music festival? What will you be competing with? Check local newspapers, magazines, tourist and convention offices to see what's going on when. There are also companies that specialize in providing information on upcoming events to their membership. Ask your tourist and visitors office to see if one exists in your area.

Incentives

Will the time that you have chosen work well for the company as well as the intended guests? Are you taking everyone away from traditional family time such as the summer holidays or over long holiday weekends?

Will the destination hold maximum appeal at the time of year you are considering travel? Sunny Barbados as an incentive during cold winter months has major appeal but less so in summer. Are there any weather concerns at the time of year you are planning to go? Hurricane season? Monsoon rains? Check with local tourist boards to obtain past weather history.

Are there any price advantages to moving the date? For example, for foreigners, times such as Memorial Day, Thanksgiving and election week in the United States have proven to provide excellent rates and availability at top US hotels. The savings on the hotel accommodation can then be applied towards expanding the program.

When looking at dates where hotels have high vacancy rate some areas that can be successfully negotiated are:

- Complimentary welcome check-in reception
- Complimentary room amenities or gifts
- Complimentary spa/health club admission
- Early check-in
- Late check-out

- Foreign currency accepted at par (i.e., Canadian dollars accepted on par for US dollars)

- Complimentary breakfasts

- Upgraded rooms. Some hotels offer conceige floors where complimentary continental breakfast is served each morning and hors d'oeuvres each evening. The participants not only enjoy better rooms but the complimentary breakfast also allows you to spend those food dollars elsewhere.

- Complimentary welcome cocktail reception

- Additional VIP suites

- Special rates can be extended to participants arriving in advance of the group or staying after.

THE TIME OF THE DAY AND THE DAY OF THE WEEK

The day of the week you are considering holding your event can have an impact on meeting your objective as can the time of day. You need to take into consideration where your participants will be coming from. It may be better to have an early morning start to your meeting and serve light refreshments than to schedule your meeting to begin later and risk your participants being tied up in rush hour traffic. If you have planned your event to take place on a Friday during the day, by mid-afternoon your participants' thoughts will be turning to how can they can best beat the weekend traffic, to their personal plans and how fast can they make their escape. They will not be tempted to linger and discuss the events of the day.

MEETINGS, CORPORATE EVENTS, CONFERENCES, CONVENTIONS, INCENTIVES

Anyone who has attended a meeting, conference, convention or incentive has seen the long lines at the telephone booths, people talking quietly into their cell phones during break or slipping out quietly to take care of pending business never to return . Are you scheduling your event over a particularly busy time period where your participants' minds are going to be elsewhere? For example, at the close of a sales period your sales force needs to be out signing contracts instead of being in a ballroom. Would midweek work better than scheduling your event on a Monday, or are you traditionally more quiet over Thursdays and Fridays? If your event is taking place far away, you need to take into consideration travel time, costs (airfares are lower if you are staying over a Saturday night), overnight stays enroute to the final destination and how the company will be handing requests for extensions. Do you need staff back and ready to work in the office Monday, or is there any flexibility?

CORPORATE EVENTS, FUND-RAISERS, SPECIAL EVENTS

For corporate events, fund-raisers and special events either midweek or a Saturday night is the most successful for achieving maximum attendance. Scheduling an event on a Friday night could limit attendance for those for whom it is a religious day and for those who want to get away for the weekend. Many things come into play in selecting the perfect date for your event. Consideration should be given to:

- Whether it should be a daytime or evening event

- What time would it start? What time would it end?

- Will it be formal or informal dress?

- Will guests have time to change clothes if coming to/from work?

- Will volunteers have sufficient time to leave work and have everything ready well before your guests arrive?

For most of these events, your guests may be invited to bring their partners. If the event is planned to take place during the day mid-week, it could be difficult for the one of the partners to attend, and an evening event may be a better choice. Or you could look at moving it to the weekend when both may have more flexibility.

Where will your guests be coming from? Take this into consideration as you plan your start time. Will they be coming directly from work? When does their work day typically end? If they are bringing a guest will this work for them as well? Could they be caught in traffic? Are you bringing them from uptown to downtown? Both scenarios could apply depending on where each of the partners work or live. How late will your event go? Is the next day a business day where both partners may need to get up early? Partners may arrive independently, in separate cars. Is there enough parking?

If the event is black tie, will your guests have time to go home to change, or will they need to bring a change of clothes to work? Will they be in a position to leave work early?

Have you left sufficient time for your set-up crew or volunteers to travel to the event, park, have everything ready, change, eat and be ready to go at least a good half hour before the first guest is scheduled to arrive?

Several years ago, a private gala dinner celebration was planned in Los Angeles. It was deliberately timed to coincide with the Academy Awards and included a themed Oscar night party. Guests were all from out of town, and this was their farewell event. The magic of Hollywood was in full swing and star sightings were everywhere. For their L.A. arrival party a film set was taken over, and the guests had the opportunity to film their own "movie" complete with scripts, make-up artists and costumes. Their Oscar party was going to be taking place away from their hotel, and they would require transportation. Twenty-five stretch limousines were reserved well in advance, contracted and deposited long before others began to think Oscar night. As you can imagine, limousines are at an absolute premium during this time and it had been planned that the guests were to have them at their disposal for the evening. After the party ended the guests headed out to their waiting limousines to experience Los Angeles on a night that is like no other. It was a memorable event and still talked about to this day.

Will limousines be a factor in your event? Will weddings and school proms be in full swing at the same time? What could have an impact on the success of your event?

DATE SELECTION

Although we touched on it briefly in the last chapter, before finalizing your date, take out your calendar and fully investigate the following seven areas and look at the impact they could have on your event:

1. Major holidays
2. Religious observations
3. School breaks
4. Long weekends
5. Sports events
6. Other special events
7. Other considerations

1. MAJOR HOLIDAYS

Check to see if there are any major holidays around your event when guests may have their own personal plans and attendance could be limited at outside functions.

There are some areas where holidays can work in your favour with proper planning. For example, silent auction fund-raisers held before the holiday season can be extremely successful when guests use the occasion to purchase gifts and donate to charity at the same time. One Saturday afternoon fund-raiser had all that potential and wasted it. They had a silent auction right before the holiday season, but sales were disappointing because the invitation failed to mention the auction. Guests were delighted with the quality of merchandise, but most had already completed their holiday shopping and others had not brought cash, credit cards or cheques. The idea was excellent, the guest list impressive and the timing could have worked in their favour. Where the event fell down was in the advance notice on the invitation. It should have announced that a silent auction was to be one of the main attractions and possibly included a list of some of the items available.

2. Religious Observations

Is the date in conflict with any religious observations, such as Friday night for Orthodox Jews or Sunday for practicing Christians? Holding a gala fund-raising on such a day would limit attendance by excluding religious individuals.

Black-tie galas (corporate or fund-raising) work well on a Saturday night especially if the event has been geared to couples. Saturday is generally considered the middle of the traditional weekend and allows couples to leisurely dress and prepare for the occasion. They can avoid taking two cars to an event, which is not always the case if both parties are coming directly from work. Guests can enjoy themselves more fully as they are not concerned with having to get up early for work the next day.

If you are scheduling an out-of-town event and feel that some of your guests may wish to attend local church or synagogue services, the hotel conceige desk can assist them with location and times. If you feel this could apply to a majority of your participants, consider the group activities you are planning for this time period so that these guests are not excluded from events of major importance.

3. School Breaks

Is the date in conflict with any of the major school breaks? Guests could conceivably be out of country, and attendance could be low. School breaks vary from country to country and even region to region. If your event is scheduled to take place over one of the school breaks (times and schedules may vary from originating destination and final destination) you may want to give special consideration to your choice of location. If the break is taking place at home, you may get a poor turnout, and if it is scheduled at your destination you may have problems booking accommodations and activities. For example, don't try to go anywhere in Latin America around Easter or on the fifth of May. Travelling to certain locations at less-peak times often makes good sense. For example, Orlando is more enjoyable when lineups are shorter. We have all heard the stories about Daytona and other beach destinations popular with college and university students over spring break and how the town is transformed for the duration of their stay. You may prefer to chose to travel at a time that may be more appropriate for your needs and requirements.

4. LONG WEEKENDS

Are you considering scheduling your event on a Monday or Tuesday or a Thursday night around a long weekend? Guests may have chosen to extend their time off and this could also affect attendance at your event.

Long weekends are eagerly anticipated, and often plans are made well in advance. The Thursday night before a long weekend is frequently used to get an early start on a drive to the cottage or for final preparations—shopping, food preparation, cleaning—for the weekend ahead. Similarly, the evenings immediately following a long weekend can be used for personal catch-up after being away.

> **T**
> **I**
> **P**
> The days before, during or following a long weekend are not considered the most favourable for achieving maximum attendance at your event. People's energies and focus will be elsewhere.

5. SPORTS EVENTS

Are there any major sports events going on at the same time as your event?

There was one corporate client who had chosen to hold an out-of-country special event in Tucson on the same dates as the World Series. The company was fully prepared to hire a private plane to bring their guests back home for the day to see the final game if their local team made it all the way. Do not underestimate the importance of sporting events—particularly play-offs—when considering the date of your event. Check all possibilities and record your findings.

Another gala corporate sit-down dinner is a cautionary tale. The company had planned their client appreciation banquet, selected a beautiful menu and taken great care with their presentations. The company had taken pains with most of the details—all except one. Obviously none of the event planners was a sports fan, and they had not done their homework. The dinner was scheduled for the same evening as a major baseball play-off game. The planners had received RSVPs and had signed guarantees to the hotel for cocktails and dinner. Of the 150 guests invited only 45 showed up, but the company was on the hook for all 150 dinners. Even if guests called on the day of the event to cancel, it still would have been too late to adjust the numbers. The attendees looked lost in the room set for 150. Some invited guests were at the game, others at home watching it on TV and some choose not to venture downtown because the dinner was being held close to where the big game and other major events were going on, and they just did not want to get tied up in traffic. Game time and the start of the reception overlapped.

Had the event planners realized the conflict in dates before finalizing things, they might have still salvaged things even if they had no flexibility in dates. They could have moved the event out of the hotel in the centre core and to a place that had a little more appeal, which would have enhanced their objective of promoting their destination as a possible incentive site. The host company had the choice of many beautiful and exclusive restaurants and private clubs. Any of which could be taken over in whole or in part for a private dinner and presentation. That may have pulled more people in, especially if they were away from the downtown congestion with ample parking nearby.

Another possibility had they realized the conflict in time would have been to set up a private sports bar theme event with large screen TV's. An even better idea might have been to take private boxes at the stadium and hold the event there. If it is something exclusive, fun and out of the ordinary, people will battle traffic without a second thought.

6. OTHER SPECIAL EVENTS

Is there anything else scheduled for the same day as your event? Take the time to do a blitz of the city. Are there any theatre openings or movie premieres scheduled for that day? Are any new performances coming into town? Are there any conflicting events such as jazz festivals, fireworks displays or major special events such as the Academy Awards? Pay attention to other fund-raisers, galas and special events similar to your own.

Again, as with sports, other special events can have an impact on attendance. This can affect corporate events, fund-raisers and other special events. As mentioned previously, there are companies you can subscribe to that track events in the city. They will register your event and let you know what could be in conflict. Check with your local tourist/convention board to see if there is such a company is in your area. Look at your targeted audience—who will make up your guest list? Will your event be competing with any others that will be inviting the same people?

7. OTHER CONSIDERATIONS

What else could be taking place over your selected dates that could impact your event? What could be at a premium? If your event is over the peak period for weddings and proms, would limousines need to be reserved well in advance?

Limited availability often leads to surcharges and other increases in costs at peak times. In the Los Angeles example, not only were limousines at a premium, weekend hotel accommodation was significantly higher during the Oscars compared to alternate dates in March and April. As well, reservations at top restaurants could be difficult to get and the waits longer.

3 LOCATION, LOCATION, LOCATION

SITE SELECTION

As they say in real estate, location is everything. The selection of the site (location) where you will be holding your event is of primary importance; it can make or break your event. Consider a seniors exhibition that was being held in a large convention centre that has two separate areas—a north wing and a south wing. The north wing is older but has good access to the ballroom. Parking is convenient and close by. The south wing is newer but it is over a 20-minute walk from the parking area. In this particular case, the south wing was chosen as the site of the exhibition, but considering the targeted audience—seniors—the north wing would have been better. This south wing was also the site for a large garden show, where guests could purchase plants of all sizes. Again, the distance from the parking area to the ballroom and back again carrying heavy purchases may not have made it the most convenient choice for the guests. Make sure that you match your site to the type of event. Look for ways to make it as accessible as possible for your guests.

There is one large specialty show that comes to Toronto twice a year. It is extremely well attended. The location of the show offers underground parking—those attending can leave their coats in the car, take the escalator up and be right at the site. The show organizers provide carts to make shopping easier. Aisles are wide and there is room to manoeuvre between them. Purchases can be dropped off at a parcel pick-up area located by the main doors if your cart or your hands become too full. Assistance is provided if you require help getting your purchases to the car. There is plenty of scattered seating. There are also several refreshment areas catering to different budgets. The venue also offers excellent washroom facilities, and the building is handicapped accessible. It has everything for a comfortable experience.

You are not limited to hotels, convention centres or restaurants when it comes to site selection. Chic boutiques will allow you to take over their facilities for a private cocktail reception and dinner, followed by a fashion show introducing their new line-up of clothes. Some even have cooking facilities attached to the store making it easy for caterers to set up and serve. You can take over yachts, roller-skating rinks or do a gala in an armoury. You can tent a parking lot or do a catered affair on a covered tennis course. Private clubs, restaurants, or empty warehouse space can be taken over and completely transformed. You are limited only by your imagination and your budget. You may have to pay a premium or surcharge to have the venue closed to the public, and you must take that into account when you are considering your site options. You may decide that it is cost prohibitive and look for a venue that has a private room that will accommodate your guests as opposed to taking over a facility exclusively. What is most important is finding the right fit.

Spectacular 30-foot ceilings and four massive fireplaces are the perfect site for a winter wedding, where the service can be conducted in the mezzanine overlooking the dining area. You can "see it," "feel it," "visualize it." It is the perfect fit—it feels as Goldilocks once said, "just right." She didn't settle for second best; she wanted what was just right for her. And that is what you must look for when you plan your special events.

Whenever and wherever possible try to get out of the ballroom. When it was decided to hold Disney's opening gala for Beauty & the Beast at Movenpick, one of Toronto's most popular restaurants, the Marche had never closed to the public before. It is one thing to feed 1,000 customers over the course of the day and another to feed 1,000 guests arriving en masse, but Movenpick Marche felt "just right" for this event. So many elements from the stage production were already there, such as the market village scene, where the food stations were renamed after the various characters from the play: Lumiere's Flaming Grill, Mrs. Pott's Tea & Coffee Bar, Le Fou's Tossed Salads, the Silly Girl's Sushi Bar, Gaston's Bar, Cogworth's Seafood Buffet, Marie's Baguettes, Babette's Desserts, Madame De La Grande Bouche's Rosti & Pasta, the fountain and the enchanted forest, which was enhanced for the evening. It was a perfect fit. Of course, it could have been recreated in a ballroom, but why go to that considerable expense when something wonderful already exists and can be enhanced. Having the event at Movenpick Marche was a much more exclusive feel added to the fact that holding it there was doing something that had not been done before—another first.

In many parts of the world it is common practice for top restaurants to close for private events, but some restaurants are still not open to the idea, and you could run into resistance. The restaurants' greatest fears are that guests once turned away will no longer return. The following are suggestions that could help overcome any concerns. These are areas of negotiation with the restaurant as there are costs involved. The restaurant may pick up some of the charges and you may be responsible for others. You need to find out in advance what will be covered, have it listed in the contract and add the costs for which you will be responsible to your cost sheet:

• Post signs announcing the closing well in advance.

• Have reminder table toppers during the week of the event.

• Post "Private Party" signs on the day of the event.

- Advise the concierges at local hotels that the restaurant will be closed for the day.

- Hand out coupons for complimentary beverages or appetizers to any walk-in customers as a thank you for their understanding.

- Advise neighbouring restaurants so that they can be prepared to handle additional walk-in customers.

- Set up a transportation shuttle to another restaurant.

- Have staff positioned at underground parking to advise guests that the restaurant is closed before they park.

Aside from these courtesies and goodwill gestures, there are many other things that have to be taken care of in planning an event in a restaurant:

- If the restaurant is in a mall, make sure that you obtain permission from mall management and find out what restrictions could apply regarding your event. A number of malls operate on a percentage rent basis where they receive a percentage of what the store takes in, and an event could provide them with extra revenue if you are holding your event on a night that is traditionally quiet. If your event will have a high profile in the media it could bring the mall added publicity. If you can, invite top mall officials to the party.

- Inform the mall tenants that a special event will be taking place so that they can plan accordingly. You will find most quite understanding as this is an opportunity for them to bask in the reflected glow of the publicity. Also, the location is being introduced to clientele who may not have visited it before.

- If the restaurant is free-standing check with local fire and police authorities to see what concerns they may have and areas you need to be aware of. If the location is in a mall check with the management of both the mall and the restaurant so that you are not violating any lease agreements or fire and safety rules and regulations.

- If you have negotiated for the restaurant to close after breakfast or lunch, have staff ready well before this to make sure that this is carried out. Don't allow late arrivals to be seated and have their service rushed as you begin set-up. They will be unhappy, and so will you. This also applies when you are closing down just a section for your guests. Always be ready well in advance, and be very clear with management about what time you will require the room or section closed. Guests are usually understanding and amenable to being reseated when offered an explanation and a complimentary beverage.

Always know specifically what is taking place before your event. Make sure that the contracted access time for set-up and décor is clear and that you have it in writing. For example, there is a fabulous venue that is often used for special events. It is also very popular for weddings. You need to know what is scheduled to go on before your move-in and make sure that there is an adequate time buffer built in. Here, you could run into a wedding rehearsal scheduled to take place just before your move-in. Wedding rehearsals are notorious for not beginning on time as well as running late, resulting in time delays. You want to be aware of this in advance and you want to ensure that the wedding party is well aware of the time of move-in so that there are no misunderstandings. They must know well in advance the importance of keeping to a schedule so that they can do their rehearsal without being rushed at the end.

I can remember going up and down the coast of a Caribbean island in torrential rains one October (even the cows were huddled under the bus shelters) looking for the perfect venue for a farewell gala that would take place in January. I found myself knee deep in water and mud at times. One word of caution: be wary of dropping by restaurants before they are opened—I was met at one by two very efficient and effective guarddogs. Local agents had suggested many places, but none of them felt "just right." I had a very clear picture of what I was trying to achieve that night. This particular island is very dear to my heart as a destination; it feels like a second home. I have very happy memories of being there both on vacations and for work. I wanted to make sure that the participants came away experiencing the full beauty of the island.

> The restaurant selected was just right for that event. It was a magical evening—row after row of all-white limousines took guests from their hotel to the site, which was exclusively theirs for the evening. Here they enjoyed cocktails as the sun slipped into the sea scattering brilliant bands of gold, red and orange across shimmering waters. Tables were set with white on white, soft candlelight glowed, a private performance was put on by one of the island's premiere performers, and guests danced under a canopy of twinkling stars. It was absolutely picturesque. It was pleasing to the eye. It was a perfect farewell event.

It is always worth the effort to take the time to find what would be just right for your event and to do everything possible to make sure the evening is flawless. If you are doing an outdoor event, investigate and know when the sun will be setting, and time the cocktails appropriately. There is no additional charge for a spectacular sunset. Look at weather history—are you in the middle of the rainy season and considering holding an outdoor event?

When planning open-air events weather back-up is a must, particularly in cooler climates. Another consideration for outdoor evening events is heaters. A number of outdoor gala events are held on the cliffs overlooking the ocean in southern California, and free-standing heaters make guests extremely comfortable. The setting here is so dramatic—imagine listening to the strains of a classical guitarist as silver moonbeams dance on the gentle waves below. That kind of magical setting can't be recreated in a ballroom but, as magical as it is, that setting would not be just right for a gala fund-raiser that included a silent auction where items would be on display, or if you were looking to include audio-visual, staging or speeches. What is essential is that the site be a match for your event and for your guests.

If you are doing an out-of-country event some key considerations are:

• Will overnight airport accommodation need to be included in your budget?

• Are there direct non-stop flights to your destination?

- If your guests will be required to change aircraft will they have a long wait in the connecting city?

- Does the total travel time justify the length of stay? For example, North American companies considering holding a meeting in Hawaii or the Orient should look at a seven- rather than a three-night stay, unless all guests will be departing from the west coast, because you are looking at two full days of travel and jet lag.

- How long a trip is it from the airport to the hotel?

- Does the hotel and the destination meet all of your needs?

- What concessions will you need to factor into your program to allow for time change and jet lag? For example, upon arrival your guests may enjoy a light repast in their rooms and time to settle in and adjust to the time change, with the welcome festivities taking place the next night rather than when guests first arrive.

LOCATION REQUIREMENTS

When you start to plan, begin with an overview of your event and start to map your requirements out on a grid similar to the one on page 44. This will enable you to establish in your mind the initial flow of events and an overall picture of what needs to be included. Your grid can then be sent to the different venues you are considering using to see if they can accommodate all of your needs.

Do a visual walk through of the event to determine the appropriate space requirements (including set-up and tear-down time needed). Start to investigate availability and begin to prepare your cost sheet. Be very specific. If you need to have a 20-foot ceiling to accommodate your audio-visual and staging, you need to make note of it on your grid. Include advance set-up and rehearsal space as well. If you need to have a ballroom on a 24-hour hold, so that your set-up remains in place until the day of your event, list this as well. If you will require dressing rooms for entertainers, offices for your staff or an area to prepare or set up displays, make sure that you advise the venue

Program Outline	Day 1	Day 2	Day 3	Day 4	Day 5	Special Notes
Breakfast						
Morning Activities						
Lunch						
Afternoon Activities						
Cocktail Reception						
Evening Activities						

management of all your possible needs. It is easier to release space and scale down than to try and work with inadequate space once you have signed the contract.

In order to prepare an accurate budget you need to look at all aspects of your event to make sure that you include as many costs as possible. As you work through this section you will find mention of different areas that need to be included in your costs such as street permits, off-duty police officers and so on, where to include them and why. Keep updating the costing as you go along, adding and subtracting items as changes are made. It is important to know where you are at all times in your proposed spending so that you can make adjustments as you go along. You may decide to keep in the one major item that provides the "WOW" factor to your event, and serve chicken instead of lobster at dinner. It all depends on what your final objective is. It could be that fine dining, tantalizing wines, the best seats in the house at a theatre opening, private limousine transfers, decadent desserts, fine brandies and cigars are what the objective is and that taped background music and simple floral arrangements are the perfect fit as opposed to spending additional dollars on live entertainment and lavish floral displays.

Your objective could be to do something extravagant, an event that will be talked about in the years to come, such as a symphony under the stars in the desert with a well-known performer to entertain your guests exclusively. You could have your guests arriving at sunset by hot air balloon with champagne served when they land. Along with the creative aspects of your events you also need to factor in the practical realities such as back-up transportation in case weather conditions or the winds are not right for the hot air balloons to take off, return transportation—hot air balloons do not travel after dark—a clear plastic tent (for visibility) as weather back-up, a cooking tent, porta potties, the cost to have everything transferred to the desert, medical assistance on standby, security, lighting, heaters and someone to handle any curious critters that may decide your event requires closer inspection. Once all of these costs have been added to your budget, you may decide that holding that particular event in the middle of the desert is cost prohibitive and that you need to consider a different idea.

> If you are holding a fund-raiser you need to have a firm budget before you can determine the cost of the tickets and the amount of dollars required for sponsorship to underwrite the event. This can't be stressed enough. You have to look at the worst-case scenario: what if all the tickets don't sell, what if corporate sponsorship doesn't come through or it does but not in the amounts hoped for?

With the cutbacks in government funding, corporations are being pursued vigorously by more and more organizations for sponsorship dollars. There must be a "perfect match" and more than simple name branding at the event—where their name appears on all print material. And whenever and wherever you can, support your sponsors or the celebrities backing your event by including them in all media coverage and in all your promotional literature so that they receive maximum exposure.

More than one fund-raiser has announced the cost of the tickets and had them printed and sold before a final costing was done. It is hardly surprising that these events ran at a loss. If the objective was simply visibility for future sponsorship dollars, they should have done promotion as opposed to a fund-raiser. But if the objective was to raise dollars, why put all the energy, time and work into doing an event that is going to end up losing money? Know all your costs ahead of time so that you can make responsible decisions. Sometimes what looks like an opportunity isn't, and it is best to walk away. Ask yourself whether everyone involved will benefit by what is being offered, or is someone going to get the short end of the stick. If so, you lose nothing by stepping away from it.

HOTELS AND CONVENTION CENTRES

The differences between hotels and convention centres will affect your budget. Both facilities can be wonderful, but make sure that you know where they differ and what needs to be included in your cost breakdown.

If you will require guest rooms as well as function space, holding your event at a hotel may be a more cost-effective way to go. Because the hotel will be receiving revenue on the guest rooms, in addition to the food and beverage, there could be concessions made for such things as room rental charges for set-up and rehearsal time. Generally, hotels do not charge a room rental fee for the time the event is actually scheduled to take place if they are receiving food and beverage revenue. This, of course, will depend on the total dollars being spent at the hotel.

Holding your event at a hotel will mean that your guests will be able to easily walk to the meeting rooms, eliminating costs for additional transportation needed if they were staying at a hotel and attending a meeting at a convention centre that is not within walking distance.

Not all convention centres have agreements with nearby hotels for special guest room rates, and you will probably be negotiating with the hotel and the convention centre separately. You may want to do a cost comparison to see how they differ in price. In addition to room rental charges, there are other cost factors to consider as well.

Most hotels will allow your set-up people to pull up and offload their vehicles, and there will be staff on hand to assist with transporting the items. (Remember to include dollars for tipping in your budget.) Hotels usually do not charge for tables and chairs for registration or display, and they can often provide most specialty glasses, such as martini glasses for a special martini bar as part of your event, at no additional cost, depending on numbers. Day rooms or change rooms can be negotiated for set-up staff and VIPs. Hotel ballrooms are usually carpeted so there is no additional expense to bring carpeting in, and there is usually no additional charge for room clean-up. Hotels can generally provide you with locked storage areas and are frequently willing to replace lost keys at no additional charge.

With convention centres none of this necessarily applies. There can be labour charges for offloading of goods, and in some instances you could be looking at three- or four-hour minimums or overtime costs. There can be charges for tables, draping and skirting. Convention centres may not have specialty glasses on hand, and it will cost you extra to bring them in. Exhibit space is not necessarily carpeted, and rental carpet is another additional cost. There can be extra costs to cut keys and for vacuuming being done at a trade show exhibit. Find out in detail what is or is not included and where you can negotiate.

If you have done your cost comparisons, you will know exactly where you differ in price and can address specific issues with the hotel and the convention centre. The convention centre may be able to waive certain rental charges as can the hotel, but before they can do that they need to know exactly how much will be spent at their facility in terms of guest rooms, food and beverage. Be prepared to have rental charges increase should your numbers decrease. This will be laid out in their contract. Pay special attention to this area as it can have a major impact on your budget.

You need to find out before signing any contract what additional charges could apply:

- Are there any charges for tables and chairs?

- Does anything need to be brought in for reception or dinner?

- Are there charges for clean-up?

- What overtime charges could apply?

- Are there specific firms you must work with?

- What are the charges for electrical power?

Have the venue management list all additional charges, and include these in your budget. You cannot afford surprises at the end of the day, especially if you are working with limited funds. With any facility you also need to ask:

- Are staff union or non-union?

- How will this affect your labour and other costs?

- When are contracts and wage negotiations coming due?

- Are renovations being planned and, if so, what impact will they have on your event?

You don't want to have your event taking place in the middle of labour negotiations or under the threat of a possible strike. You need to know in advance what renovations are planned. How major will they be, and what impact will they have on service, on the state of the facility and on what your guests will see and experience during their stay.

Hotels and convention centres each have their strengths and weaknesses. What matters most is finding the facility that best meets the needs of your particular event and making sure that you are fully aware of all possible charges that need to be included in your budget.

RESTAURANTS, PRIVATE VENUES, CATERING

You may decide to take your event out of a traditional ballroom setting and find something just a little different. A better fit might be: museums, art galleries, theatres of the performing arts, private estate homes, heritage buildings, exclusive restaurants, airport hangers, yacht clubs, race tracks, local attractions (Universal Studios, Disney's Pleasure Island, Sea World), exclusive nightclubs, skating rinks, enclosed tennis courts, indoor volleyball facilities, golf clubs, retail stores, aquariums, converted warehouses, armouries, film studios, boat charters—the list is limited only by your imagination and your budget.

LOCATION: Q&A

What time would you have access to the facility?

Be very clear about exclusive access time to the facility and make sure that it is noted in the contract so that there is no room for misunderstandings at a later date. Keep in mind that the person you are working with now may not be there at a later date, so get everything in writing.

Is that enough time to set up?

If you require more time for set-up than the venue is prepared to give in exchange for the realized dollars from your event for food and beverage, you may need to negotiate a flat rate with them for additional set-up time. Remember, although they are receiving revenue for your event, asking them to close for an extensive amount of time will cost them additional dollars in lost food and beverage sales. They may agree to a longer set up in exchange for additional compensation.

Q & A

Will any furniture need to be removed?

When looking at space do not be limited by the furniture that is in it. Most facilities will agree to moving furniture out and having it stored elsewhere in order to accommodate more guests.

Q & A

What extra costs could be related to that?

You could be looking at additional cost to bring staff in to move the furniture out. If the facility does not have accessible storage space it may be necessary to utilize moving vans and store the unwanted furniture overnight. You may also need to factor in the cost for staff to move in and set up the furniture before the start of business the next day. Make sure that you have proper insurance for the furniture in case of damage or loss. Another area you may need to look at is street parking permits for the time supply trucks need to load and offload.

Q & A

Will you need to provide a cleaning crew before, during and after the event?

Do not assume that this will be provided at no additional cost. It is an item that can often be negotiated but you need to know this before signing the contract.

Q & A

What is the legal room capacity?

The importance of knowing the room capacity and adhering to it cannot be stressed enough. Sometimes the solution to maximizing the number of guests is to issue invitations with two or more specific times such as separate morning, afternoon and evening functions. In these cases it is essential that there is an official beginning and end to each event, and all guests are gone before the second event begins. This can be tricky because there is no way you can control when guests leave if there are not two very specific and separate events. One invitation may read 6:00 p.m.–10:00 p.m. for

Group A and the second invitation 8:00 p.m.–12:00 a.m. for Group B. When the party is in full swing and guests are having a good time, how are you going to force Group A to leave at 10:00 p.m? Even if you use "visible" ID so you know who is in each group, do you really want to put yourself in a position of asking your invited guests to leave if they have extended their stay? You are best to honour the legal capacity of the room or hold two separate events.

There are many creative ways to increase capacity, which can sometimes be governed by the number of washroom facilities available to guests. If the venue is attached to an office tower, for example, it may be possible to open up additional facilities by using additional security staff. Upscale portable bathroom facilities are also available for rent. Check out your creative options with local authorities. It is much better to work hand in hand with them than to have them show up at your event and close it down because you violated regulations. Your guests' comfort should also be of concern. They will not be comfortable if they are packed in like sardines or if they have to line up forever to use the bathroom facilities. They will simply leave your event in frustration.

One fund-raiser was held at a private venue where there were hundreds of invited guests and just one bathroom! The size of the room was fine, but there was no way it would have passed inspection with only one bathroom. Had inspectors dropped by—as they can and do without notice—the event would have been closed down on the spot. And as could be anticipated, the bathroom was out of commission well before the end of the event.

What is the zoning? Are there any restrictions or regulations that should concern you?

Find out what can and what cannot be done. You need to check with local authorities—fire, health, police and city officials. If your event involves search lights or tethered hot air balloons, for example, you need to check with nearby air-ports to obtain written clearance from them, as these could be potential flight hazards. One company wanted to do a team-building event on the water and needed approval from the harbour police. The cost of rescue boats and staff and standby medical care needed to be built into the program.

Q & A

Are there any noise restrictions?

If the facility is in the middle of a residential area there may be noise restrictions, which could affect how late your event can be open and how loudly and where music can be played.

Q & A

What insurance do you need to protect you, your guests and the facility?

Make sure that you have investigated this and that every-thing is covered. In the case of team-building corporate events it is necessary to obtain a signed waiver from guests. Remember, if guests are taking part in any physical activi-ties, serve alcohol *after* the event, not before. For example, a fun team-building event can be a car rally with various refreshment checkpoints along the route. One of these stops could be lunch, but it should be a non-alcoholic one. Drinking and driving don't mix. You can serve alcohol back at the hotel at the end of the rally at a check-in party, where guests gather and discuss their day over a drink. Or if you want to have the check-in party at the luncheon location and want to include alcohol, have motor coaches waiting to transfer your guests back to their hotel and arrange for the cars to be ferried back to the rental agency.

Safety must go beyond insurance concerns; a partici-pant was killed at one of these road rally events in Europe. If you are considering a road rally in a country such as Bar-bados, where the driving is on the opposite side, there are ways around the problem rather than to risk guests becom-ing confused. For example, you could turn the rally into a scavenger hunt and have guests driven around in limos, mini mokes or mini vans. Clues could be given in the local dialect and with a contest to create a limerick using the new words they have learned. An added twist in Mexico could be that guide drivers are instructed to speak only Spanish.

Whatever event you undertake, consider guest safety and find out how much insurance you will need to make sure everyone is covered should anything ever happen.

Q & A

What restrictions would you need to work around?

Historical buildings, museums, art galleries and other locations have some very specific guidelines about what can and cannot take place there. Ask to see a copy of their rental agreement. It will outline what specifically applies to each venue—there is no standard form. The restrictions that could apply are as varied as the venues.

You may not be able to smoke in a historical building. You may not be able to attach anything to the walls. You need to know what you can and can't do. In museums you may need to pay for additional security. Guests may not be permitted to enter certain restricted areas. At an art gallery guests may be able to look but not touch, and areas might be roped off. You may not be able to serve food or beverages in certain rooms. If you have rented a private estate, are you renting just the grounds, or will guests have full access to the house? Find out all restrictions that could apply before you sign the contract. If there are additional charges, such as security, they must be included in your cost sheet so that you can calculate the effect they will have on your budget.

In one car museum you are not allowed to serve certain beverages because they might damage the paint finish if splashed on a vintage car.

Q & A

What needs to be brought in?

Some venues can be perfect with just a few additions; others need to be virtually transformed. One of the first things to look at is lighting. Lighting adds interest and adds ambiance. It can be dramatic. It can be romantic. It helps to create a mood. You may want to bring in additional greenery or rented furniture to enhance what is already there. Prop houses are an excellent source of a large variety of items to rent. Meet with local decor companies, and do a walk through of their inventory to see what ideas they may trigger for your event.

Q & A

How are the sight lines?

If you are considering having speeches or audio-visual presentations you need to pay particular attention to the sight lines. Are there any pillars or anything hanging from the ceiling that will block the view? Can the room be completely darkened? In many restaurants you cannot do this, and you would need to look at bringing in pipe and draping—free-standing fixtures on which material is hung—to cover the windows or to divide up the room.

Q & A

Where are the kitchens?

How will the food get to your guests? What other areas does the kitchen service? Is the same kitchen used to prepare food for restaurant guests in addition to private functions? How many functions will be going on at the same time? How many can the kitchen comfortably serve at one time?

One particular restaurant has one kitchen servicing two entirely different areas physically separated by a walkway. But in order to service the other side, it is necessary for the waiters to take the food orders through the main section of the restaurant. They can do this discreetly, but you should know this in advance and decide if it is appropriate. You do not want to be surprised on the night of the event.

Q & A

How large are the kitchens?

Find out the capacity. If you are having your event catered at an private venue, plan to meet at the site with the caterers so that you are aware of all of their needs and any areas of concern. It is essential that caterers do a site inspection—they need to be familiar with the layout, capacity, and any potential problem areas from the standpoint of food preparation and service. This includes such seemingly minor points as will the caterer's cooking pans fit into the venue's oven, fridge or freezer? How many electrical outlets will they require? What will they need with regard to parking and offloading of equipment and food? Do they have any special requirements such as a separate cooking tent? Ask where food will be prepared—off-site and finished at your venue or fully prepared on-site?

T I P

Accept quotes from caterers only in writing. Make sure your quotes include menu selection, quantity, price, taxes, delivery, and the number of experienced staff they will be providing. Have them detail the number of hours they have been contracted for—including preparation, arrival time and clean-up. Make sure that they lay out what their staff will be responsible for. Will they taking and serving drink orders? Will their staff be replenishing and clearing the tables? Will they be taking care of clean-up and dishwashing?

Q & A

Are there enough utensils and enough staff to replenish them?

The last thing you need at an event is your guests standing around waiting for glasses, dinnerware and cutlery to be replenished. At one restaurant food tasting fund-raiser with just under 1,000 guests this is exactly what happened. Over 25 top restaurants were offering assorted food tastings to the invited guests. What had not been anticipated was that some of the restaurants were using

the facility's wineglasses for their desserts, which caused a
shortage. In addition, guests were going to each station
and picking up clean plates and cutlery. Once finished,
they would lay them down wherever they could find space
and proceed to the next food station, and begin the procedure all over again. Needless to say, 1,000 guests went
through an enormous number of plates, knives and forks
in minutes. The dirty dishes were everywhere in unsightly, dangerous precariously towering piles. Clearing staff
had not been provided in sufficient numbers to handle the
situation, and there were only three people in the kitchen
to handle the onslaught of incoming dirty dishes. It was
not enough. The number of staff required to clear the
dishes, clean and stack them in the dishwasher, unload it
and bring the clean utensils back out needs to be reviewed
in great detail when you are planning your event. You also
need to know how fast the dishwasher turnaround is.

Another gala fund-raiser faced the same situation as
above but handled it differently and successfully limited
the number of utensils used. As you arrived, you were presented with the wineglass and plate that were yours "for
the evening." The hostess made it very clear that you were
meant to keep them for the whole food tasting. The wineglass was attached to the plate with a clip making it very
easy for guests to keep track of their glasses.

Q & A

*Have you considered hiring professional help and included
the cost in your budget?*

At any event, be it a corporate gala or fund-raiser, you can
look to save dollars on professional help by using in-house
staff or volunteers for additional support. But what happens—and it does happen—if some of the volunteers are no-
shows? Or what happens if volunteers are pulled away to
mingle with the guests? Considering that the additional costs
for professional help amount to only pennies per guest, do
you really want to have your event appear unprofessional or
unpolished to save a few dollars? What is key is the perception of the event and how well it reflected the company's
image. Guests will be looking for polish and finesse.

> **TIP**
>
> If you are planning a gourmet food tasting where your guests will use a number of different plates, glasses and cutlery, make sure that you have sufficient quantities. Also, find out whether there are any specific requirements such as speciality glassware. Include the cost of professional, experienced help in your budget, and use your in-house staff or volunteers in other ways.

Give thought to how you want your event to be handled. Plan for it, right down to the number of staff clearing the plates and in the kitchen. Make it as polished and as professional as you can.

Q & A

What are the dishes at the venue like? The glassware? The cutlery?

Make sure that you actually see the utensils that will be used. Well before the event, do a walk through to make sure that all is in readiness and up to standard. A walk through at a location before a client's breakfast meeting revealed that the glasses that had been put out for breakfast were cloudy, spotted and still had old pulp clinging to them. They were disgraceful, but because of doing the advance well before the scheduled meeting, there was time to replace them.

At an event on a quality property in the Caribbean, the walk through showed a number of the dishes that had been put out for dinner were chipped and totally unacceptable.

At an afternoon social event, which was held in a private venue, the dishes they used were completely wrong for the event. They were chunky, heavy, standard diner restaurantware, and this was meant to be a light and elegant social affair with fine china and silverware. Proper planning and a site inspection before signing the contract might have avoided this problem. Better-quality utensils would have added to the event and raised the level of the experience.

How many bathrooms are there?

How many of them are there and what state are they in? Do they require any touch-ups? How will they be refreshed on the night of your event? Will bathroom attendants be provided?

One restaurant holding an event seemed to do an outstanding job—everything was gleaming. The only thing that was not up to snuff was that in one of the bathrooms a piece of wallpaper was missing. It was a small thing, but it took away from the total effect. It had not been missing during the site inspection or the precon meeting—it had been damaged just recently and they had not had the opportunity to have it fixed. Knowing how important this was to us, they immediately contacted the designer who brought over a piece of the wallpaper and put up a temporary bandage.

Some upscale restaurants have bathroom attendants in place who expect a tip for providing you with a hand towel. At a special event, guests may sometimes have to pay for their own parking and coat check (a sign is usually posted), but it is tacky to expect them to have to tip for any other service. And if the bathroom attendants, luggage porters, coat check and other services have been prepaid in lieu of tips, make sure that the staff do not accept any additional tips from the guests. Discuss this with the facility management, and make it clear how you will handle tips and such. You can provide for them in your budget and have this added to your bill, or you can distribute tip envelopes at the end of the evening as you are personally thanking those involved in making your event a success. It is perfectly acceptable to let both guests and staff know that their tips have been taken care of. Make sure that a tip plate is never left out, and if a tip is offered instruct staff to say that the service is being provided by their host for the evening. If perfume is offered, it must be complimentary. Make sure that you have someone review these policies with the staff on the night of the event.

Q & A

Is there a separate area away from the event where the staff can take their breaks?

Think about where the staff will take their breaks. If you don't want them gathered around a front entrance smoking, where do you want them to be? It is important to take good care of the staff and for more than just humanitarian reasons. If they are exhausted, hungry or thirsty the level of service and your whole event could be affected. Make sure that refreshments are made available to them—food, juice and soft drinks. Find out if separate washrooms for the staff can be arranged. This is important to know for the comfort of both guests and staff. If you are hosting a gala event you want to be sure that your guests are not kept waiting in the bathroom line longer than need be, and their conversations are kept private. The staff should be comfortable and looked after as well, not delayed unnecessarily from their tasks. Your guests do not want to be subject to the personal conversations of the staff.

Q & A

How experienced are the staff?

You want to make sure that you have the best, most-experienced and professional staff. Take time to go to the facility and observe it—see if there are any areas of concern. Will it be acceptable if the waiters have earrings, lip rings, colourful hair? What is the host's company image? Is this in keeping with their profile? Discuss all areas of protocol with senior management. Be clear on the tone you want to set. Do you want the staff to be friendly and upbeat or more reserved? Management can then pass the word to their staff. Ensure that you make note of it in your function sheets. If you can't guarantee that the staff's appearance will be in keeping with the clients image, you may have to book another venue. On the night of the event, prior to final set-up, have the management address their staff for one final review of the evening's expectations, and have them introduce their staff to the main contact person, usually the event planner. This would be the perfect opportunity to thank them as a group for their efforts and for all they have done and are about to do in making this event a success.

Q & A

Have they handled events of this nature before? How large?

Ask for references and also speak to suppliers who have worked at the facility before. Ask what went well and what could have been better? What is the maximum number of people they have handled at one time, not over the course of a day, but at a private event. What level of experience do they bring to you? Ask for proof. Have them be specific. Who have they worked with, and what have they done in the past? Get names and phone number from both past clients and suppliers.

Q & A

Have you, the special events planner, handled events of this nature before?

What personal experience do you or your company bring? If you have handled only smaller events in the past, look at who you may need to bring in to handle a large event of, say, over 2,000. Don't put your event at risk by trying to bluff your way through. It is better to work and learn from someone who has done it successfully before than to get in over your head. Creative directors can be brought in on a project basis and provide you with creative design and logistics, work with your event planning team and share their knowledge with you.

A restaurant that normally did not do private catering handled a fund-raising event at another location. Their service at the restaurant was absolutely five-star, but at the event it was not up to par. Catering staff are trained to look for different things than regular restaurant staff. They are used to circulating looking for empty glasses and plates wherever they may be laid down. This can be especially important if the event logistics were not properly planned. If insufficient thought is given to where used items are to be placed at a stand-up reception, left to their own devices, people can be very creative. Catering staff know instinctively when to remove a glass or offer a napkin, and such finesse and proper protocol are essential elements to the success of your event.

> **TIP**
> A restaurant that has a separate catering company works extremely well for stand-up receptions with food stations. You may want to bring in catering staff to handle the VIP areas.

Q & A

Are there any things that should to be put away?

If there are items normally offered for sale at the venue that you are taking over exclusively, have them removed and put out of sight, or you may find yourself charged for items guests may have "assumed" were part of the evening's events. At one fund-raiser shelves were stripped bare of merchandise guests thought was being offered as free samples.

Q & A

What are the fire and safety regulations? What permits do you need, and what permits would the facility need to obtain?

It is imperative to know the regulations and who is responsible for obtaining which permit. Do not assume that the facilities will provide all that you will require. You may need to obtain a special liquor license, a permit to extend bar closing time, which can be obtained for special occasions, or a tent permit. Ask for copies of every permit for your files.

You will also need to know the maximum capacity the fire marshal will allow in the venue and how it could be affected if you removed some of the furnishing or brought in additional washroom facilities. Remember, it is your responsibility, not the facility's, to make sure you do not exceed capacity. Which doors have to remain clear and unlocked for fire safety? Will you have to clearly post exit signs?

Discovering new venues and creating one-of-a-kind events is how you make memorable occasions. You want everyone to go away feeling as though they have attended the event of the year each and every time. Don't be afraid to try something new, but be prepared to do your homework, to plan and prepare and bring in the experts where you need to. You can take events out of the ballroom and make magical memories, but be prepared to be involved in all aspects of planning and operations. Remember, no detail is too small. Will the rugs in the venue need to be sent out to be cleaned for your event.? Is the bathroom up to par? How is the paint? the wallpaper? Give all areas your full attention. It is worth it. Create events that guests could not duplicate on their own. Look for ways to make them special.

The following farewell event was held at a private villa. The look, the feel and the energy of that very special night could not have been duplicated inside the ballroom.

Imagine holding a private dinner poolside in the villa where they filmed the movie *10*. The white cabanas you see in the movie were carried up to the villa and scrubbed spotless, providing a dramatic backdrop, serving as the bar stations. The back garden wall was freshly whitewashed, the grass was cut and sprayed, the pool was cleaned. The villa was immaculate. Everything was white on white in keeping with the mood of the resort. There was fine dining under the stars. Candlelight glowed softly, beautiful fragrant florals, soft music and a sky filled with fireworks at the end of the evening. That evening—a perfect 10. The mood—magical and memorable.

THEATRES

There are many ways theatres can be utilized for special events. Some of the newer theatres have space you can rent for your function, and you might decide to hold your entire event under one roof, or you may want to do the opening event at the theatre followed by a reception at another site. Alternatively, you could start with dinner at another location, provide transportation to the theatre and return to the original site for cigars, coffee, liqueurs and desserts.

When you are considering holding your event at a theatre make sure you do a complete walk through. Find out the true capacity—how many seats are obstructed, broken or otherwise unusable? Go behind the scenes. Make sure the fire exits are completely cleared. You might be surprised to find they aren't. although you would be even more surprised when the fire marshal closes down your event because you forgot to check.

Find out when the theatre is accessible for you to set up. What costs are involved in theatre rental, staffing and bringing in a clean-up crew? If you are previewing a film, do a run through before the event to make sure all is in working order. Find out what the costs are to bring in a projectionist the day before the event to screen it, and make sure that is included in your budget. When one film was previewed it was found to have 10 minutes of dead air time in the middle that was originally meant as an intermission, but this film was to run without a break. The film had to be cut and spliced. Other reasons to preview are to check the film quality and to screen it for dirt and tears. If a film is arriving from out of country make sure that you allow sufficient time for it to clear customs. It is better to have it in your hands well in advance than to risk it being tied up in customs the day of your event. Check with the individual film companies regarding their film rights and applicable charges. Some companies have local representation, and they can assist you with bringing the film in. Theatre management can also provide you with contact names and phone numbers.

Other ways to help ensure a successful film event include changing the marquee, rolling out the red carpet, having existing carpets cleaned and floors washed. Have beverage cups and popcorn bags with custom logos. Think about the arrival. Are people coming with tickets and invitations or not? Set up two line-ups to avoid congestion and unnecessary waiting. What signage will you need? Do you need to bring in registration tables, draping and skirting or tables for the beverages?

Everyone will arrive at once. Do you know how long it will take to pop popcorn for 700 people, package it, place those bags in miniature shopping bags with other handouts, and place all that on each theatre seat? Don't wait until the day of the event to find out. Discuss the beverage set-up and distribution. Do you need to remove candy displays or have them filled with a specific product? Do you need ropes and stanchions? Do you have a "private party" sign? How will you handle movie regulars? If you are putting the name of the movie up on the marquee, do you have someone to field the phone calls that will come in? Will you require crowd control? Search lights? Are there any special theme or entertainment give-aways?

Are you providing transportation to have guests shuttled between locations? Do you need to add in traffic control if all guests are arriving, departing and going on to a secondary location at one time? Give thought to congestion and line-ups and how to avoid both in all areas. Will the theatre be open to the public for a later movie seating, or will it be yours all night? If they are doing a late seating you need to discuss where the people that are purchasing tickets for the late show will be able to wait. You want the lobby area and bathrooms held clear until all your guests have departed. Make sure that it is included in the contract prior to signing that no others will be allowed in until your event has ended, and the theatre has been cleared. And, last but certainly not least, make sure all costs are factored into your budget.

TENTS

If you are considering holding your special event in a tent you should watch *Betsy's Wedding* so that you can fully appreciate the importance of including certain elements in your budget. In the film, the tent they rented had patches in the roof, and small tears quickly became large tears when rain poured heavily. The roof on their tent was unable to support the weight of the water and partly collapsed. The grass floor became a sea of mud.

Tents can be used to create a main venue or provide additional space and serve as a second area. For example, if you were considering doing a wedding or a special event you could use the main area to greet guests and hold a reception, and then move guests into the tent for a sit-down dinner. Or, you could do your entire event in a tent from beginning to end. A tent can provide shade—important for sporting events—as well as being a back-up space in case of inclement weather. If you are doing an event where smoking is not permitted inside the building, such as a historical home, you could even set up a smoking tent adjacent to the main area.

 Allow 20 square feet of floor space per person when calculating the size of tent you need. This will give everyone breathing room especially if bad weather forces all of the guests indoors.

You need to give consideration to the type of tent that will best suit your requirements. Pole tents have the higher peaked ceilings like those found in a circus, while framed tents generally have higher installation costs but provide more structure. Contract your local tent rental companies and make sure that you see actual samples of the quality of tents they supply. All have catalogues, but ask to see first-hand what the company has to offer. A clear sidewall may look great in the catalogue picture but turn out to be cloudy and full of cracks in real life. Take the time to do a site inspection at their place of business so you can determine the quality as well as the options offered. Do you want a solid colour or a striped tent? What type of sides do you want? To ensure that the tent they install does not have scratches, cracks, tears, or visible repairs and is installed in pristine condition, note these items on your contract. Be specific. A tent with dirty sidewalls is not acceptable and must scrubbed and clean. State it on your contract, and note it on your contract. Be specific about when this must be completed. At one event, tent installers were seen cleaning the tent walls as guests were arriving.

Have them do a site inspection with you at the venue to determine the tent that will best fit your needs. It doesn't matter how pretty a tent looks in a picture; what is important is that the tent design works with your location and your specific needs. The tent rental company will need to decide if the tent can be set in the ground or if it will need to be anchored, and what additional costs could be incurred. For example, if you were covering a parking lot you could not set the tent into the ground without damaging the surface of the lot; in this case the tent would need to be firmly anchored. If you were setting the tent in a field, then you could look at a design that could be set in the ground. If the tent is covering an area where there are permanent trees, you will need to ensure that the ceiling on the tent will still be high enough. And the reverse applies if there are any low-hanging wires. Are you considering setting up the tent in an area that could be a potential wind tunnel?

You need to know what type of tent will best suit the site and not what simply looks good. Never sign a contract without having done a site inspection with all involved. Have the tent rental company, the caterers, and the people who are supplying the tables and chairs all present at your site inspection. Don't assume anything. Accurate measurements will need to be taken. The proposed site must be measured off to see if it is workable. The caterers will need to advise of their needs. If they will be cooking inside the tent, it will need to be well ventilated. What are their lighting and electrical needs? Is the site covered in uneven patches of land? A floor may not be an option but a necessity. You also need to check the fire regulations regarding how close the tent can be to existing buildings.

Who owns the land where you are planning to set up your tent? Whose permission and what permits will be required? Will you need a tent permit? A building permit? Will you need a land permit? What other permits could come into play? You could be setting up a tent on restaurant grounds, and the restaurant has the land permit and owns the right to your putting your tent on their property. Or if your event is being held in a park, you will have to obtain permission and the land permit from the parks and recreation department. Will you need a hydro permit? Are you planning to be hooked up to electricity and have access to running water, or will you be bringing in generators? What you decide to include in your event will affect the permits you will require. Who will obtain them? Each case is different, there is no standard rule of thumb. Check, check and double-check. Spell it out in the contract who is responsible for obtaining each specific permit, and insist on receiving a copy of each well in advance of your event. And on the day of the event make sure that you have all permits in hand in case inspectors drop by, and have an additional copy in your files.

Know all potential costs up front. Are there any site rental charges? Will you need a separate cooking tent where the caterers can set-up and prepare the meal out of sight?

> **Always anchor your tent. They can and have blown away. The day before one gala event in LA the tent actually did blow away and another one had to be flown in—there were none large enough left in LA.**

How many days will set-up and installation involve? A car dealership was planning to tent their display area for a private event until they found out that it was going to take two days to set up the tent prior to the event, which meant moving their cars off the lot for a total of three business days. As this would drastically affect their business sales, an alternate venue was found. They had originally anticipated having the cars off the lot for only one day.

What steps do you need to take to obtain a liquor license? What will you need to do to conform to it? In some areas, alcoholic beverages may be served only in an enclosed area. How will your tent need to be set up to conform to the regulations? Does the tent rental company have fire exit signs or will you need to provide them? Will you need to set up portable bathrooms? Check regulations on how many are acceptable. (Your event could be closed down should you not comply with regulations.)

> **A good rule of thumb is to have approximately one bathroom for every 75 guests.**

Budget permitting, provide separate facilities for the men and the women. Upscale bathroom trailers, complete with a sink and running water, are available for rent for gala events; you are no longer limited to those portapotties that you find on construction sites. Staffing must be assigned to make sure that the facilities are kept refreshed.

When you are holding a tent event, build into your budget the extra cost of security for the tent overnight between set-up and the actual event. This will ensure three things: that the tables and chairs that have been set up are secured overnight; that unexpected guests do not "camp out" under your tent; and that the tent is still standing the day of the event. Other items to factor into your budget will be the rental of tables, chairs, china, silverware, linens, napkins, decor, caterers and other related items such as the caterer's cooking tent and electrical needs. And remember, inclement weather could delay installation of the tent. Make sure that this is taken into account when you are scheduling deliveries and calculating total preparation and set-up time. Be sure to find out what clean-up charges apply before and after the event to the site the tent is being set up on. Will you need to have the area cleaned? The grass cut? The area sprayed?

These are all items that need to be factored into your budget, as well as flooring, lighting, generators, air-conditioning or heaters. Many consider tent flooring optional, but unless you are working with an absolute bare-bones budget, consider it essential if you are setting your tent up in a grassy area. Tents can take up to two days to install. If the ground is wet and doesn't have time to dry out, without flooring you will find tables and chairs sinking into the ground at odd angles. As guests struggle to get out of their sinking chairs, they will grab onto the tables, which then are driven even further into the ground. That could spell diaster for the centrepieces, the place settings and the whole food and beverage service. And, what if it's black tie and women are in heels? Or it's night and the air has cooled and the grass is damp under your feet? Flooring will ensure your guests' comfort.

If you are looking at early spring or late fall be sure to include heat in your budget in addition to flooring and lighting (for evening events). In cooler seasons, heaters ensure your guests' comfort. Remember, heat rises, so use ceiling fans to push warm air back down from the roof of the tent. Heaters will also equalize temperatures. For example, if you are looking at having cocktails served in a main venue—such as a house—and using a tent to serve the main meal, you want your guests to remain comfortable when they move into the tent.

There are also many different sidewalls you can consider. You can have sidewalls installed that can be rolled up if the day is warm, with a lining of mesh to keep insects out. The sidewalls can be lowered if the weather turns inclement. And if you are having any special effects such as indoor fireworks you may need to cost in an exhaust system as well.

If you were doing an event that offers both indoor and outdoor facilities, you should look at tenting as both as weather back-up in case of rain or shade from the hot sun and as a separate venue. And if total capacity and the number of invited guests has been based on using both the outdoor and indoor area in entirety, tenting becomes much more than an area to handle the overflow comfortably; it becomes a critical part of your event. You need to make sure that guests will move out into this area and spend time there so that the indoor area does not get too crowded. One way to do this is to serve the main meal in the tent to draw the guests to the outside area. Make sure that the tent has adequate seating, a buffet dinner set-up and music or other entertainment, otherwise there will be nothing to keep guests there. Rather than a full buffet, finger foods and hot and cold hors d'oeuvres could be passed, which allows more room for additional tables and chairs. Tables can then be smaller in size, making the area less like a banquet and more like a nightclub. You have then created two areas of high energy and atmosphere as opposed to one main room with the tent being merely the overflow area, devoid of any atmosphere. If guests encounter dead air (no music or entertainment), a lack of ambiance and just some food stations and a few seats, your tent will appear bleak and uninviting, especially if you have created an atmosphere of high energy in the other area. Providing these things in the tent will draw guests out and keep them there. When you are spending major dollars on any type of special event, it makes no sense to skimp on the arrangements for your tent. With a high-energy band in the tent, with specialty lighting or laser show, you create another area of excitement and fun.

CONTRACTS

In addition to having copies of all permits with you on site always make sure to bring with you a copy of all signed original contracts and key correspondence in case there are any areas of dispute. Having your paperwork with you allows you do deal with any concerns immediately.

On an incentive program in Mexico the client was very explicit about which guest rooms she was requesting and did a walk through of each and every one—beachfront rooms, the best on the property. During the precon it was discovered that the hotel was trying to put the client into other less-desirable rooms. After we had signed the contract the hotel had changed the names of all the room types and categories. The function sheets had always referred to the rooms by name and type in addition to the specific room numbers that had been contracted. They showed me their new map. I showed them my old map with the signed contract. They said others had now signed contracts for the beachfront rooms and that nothing could be done. I disagreed. One of the first rules of event planning is not to accept "no" for an answer. We ended up calling the vice-president of the hotel chain who quickly resolved the matter, and the client received every room originally contracted. It was of utmost importance that I had the original contract and map with me. Because of that I was able to act quickly and have everything resolved before the client and guests arrived.

When you are doing an event, particularly one out of country, arrive well in advance of the group to ensure that everything is ready. Always make sure that you do a final review of contracts and function sheets with the hotel and all suppliers involved in any aspect of your event. A precon can involve anywhere from three people to a cast of thousands depending on how intricate the program is. Everyone's actions must be in sync. They must be orchestrated to come together perfectly layer after layer. It is like a relay team, each person passing the baton to the next at precisely the right moment. If someone drops the baton, someone else must be ready to pick it up and run with it without missing a beat. By reviewing your contracts and function sheets with all those involved, you are ensuring that nothing that has been contracted for has dropped through the cracks or been overlooked. Your goal is to ensure that all involved are operating from the same page and that all that has been agreed upon is in place.

In another instance an incentive group was on a Caribbean cruise. I was flying to each port of call in advance of the group to set up special events in preparation for their arrival. In the final port of call we had planned to hold the farewell gala away from the ship. When I arrived late Friday night I noticed a number of large unsightly construction trucks in the parking lot outside of the main entrance to the venue where we were holding our farewell. Visually the trucks greatly detracted from the impact of the site. In all contracts and correspondence it had been noted that this area was to remain clear. The owners of the trucks had left them to be parked over the weekend. Because it had been specified in the contract, and I had copies with me, I was able to get them to trace down the company that owned the trucks and have them moved.

GALA OPENINGS IN NEW VENUES

Doing event planning for venues that are just opening to the public brings new elements to be aware of, which can play a major part in determining whether the opening can proceed as planned. Below are two very different examples what to look out for:

A gala opening event with over 2,000 guests was almost placed in jeopardy because building contractors had not been paid, and there were still items in dispute. The contractors were on hand on opening night and were preparing to remove fixtures or even close down the event. Make sure that you are familiar with the terms and conditions of any contracting work and that any disputes have been resolved prior to opening night. You need to know in advance if there are any outstanding issues that could affect your opening.

One major gala restaurant opening almost did not occur. They had neglected to obtain final clearance from the fire marshall and building officials to open to the public. One hour before guests were due to arrive they were told to stop food preparations and to begin to take down fixtures from the wall. Make sure that you know what needs to be done before opening to the public. Find out from city officials what permits are required and what needs to be done to meet all safety and fire regulations.

In both cases planners were fortunately able to scramble around and work out an agreeable last-minute solution, but you can't count on that kind of luck. So plan ahead and try to consider every eventuality.

4 TRANSPORTATION

LIMOUSINES

If limousines are to be a part of your event you have to know how many you will need to supply and which VIP guests will be coming with their own limousines. You will need to know all this so that you can arrange parking spaces for them. If it is simply an informal gala and guests are arriving in their own limousines, drivers may simply park on nearby side streets and wait until the guests call for the car to be brought round. But if it is a formal event where you have major celebrities and VIPs, you may be required to secure reserved parking for them. You will need to know if the limousines they will be arriving in are regular sedans, stretchs or super-stretch limos. The capacity of the limousines does not determine the number of arriving guests, since a super-stretch limo may have just one or two in it while you can have half a dozen in a regular sedan. It depends on the effect the individuals are personally trying to achieve. If limousines will be a major consideration at your event, you need to take this into account during your site inspections before you finalize the venue. Where can they park? Will street permits will be required? How many limousines can be accommodated?

The calibre of limousines and drivers varies from company to company. Ask for referrals. Where possible, go and look at the company's operations, and compare the quality and condition of the cars. See how the drivers are dressed and how attentive they are. If you find a particularly good limousine driver find out his or her name and ask for them each time you book. As you begin to develop a long-term working relationship you know what to expect, and how your clients will be looked after.

The limousine should arrive spotless, fully gassed and 15 minutes early. If the driver has a cell phone make a note of the number and keep it handy on the night of your event. Make sure the limousine fits the occasion and the client. Some people are uncomfortable stepping into a limousine that seems as long as a city block; others revel in it. Know your client and their needs.

If you are hiring a number of limousines think about visual presentation. Do you want a row of gleaming white stretch limos pulling up one after another, or does it matter? It may be more important to have all of them similar in style rather than colour.

Think protocol. In some countries it is essential that the president's limousine reflect his exalted status. The same is often true in companies. It may not be acceptable to have two limousines of similar quality. Handle this matter discreetly by checking with the president's personal assistant. Do not put your client in an awkward position by asking him or her directly. He or she may not be comfortable telling you that they would prefer a super-stretch limousine with all the amenities just for themselves. Others may prefer a less-showy arrival and something a little more subdued. You can offer gentle guidance. It would not be appropriate at a fund-raiser for the committee members to arrive in extravagant rented limousines unless they are personally paying for them or the limousines have been donated, which should be displayed prominently in the program. Limousines could lead guests to wonder how the money being raised is spent. The same would apply if a company has recently undergone major downsizing.

What extras should be included in the limo? Should you include favourite beverages, snacks, magazines or newspapers?

Be attentive to detail. Although the beverages can be alcoholic, they do not necessarily have to be. Having fresh Florida orange juice on ice when in that state is always a nice touch; in fact, including local specialities is always a good idea. Look for what is produced in the area. Are there any items they are known for or consider to be regional favourites? New Zealand has a wonderful bottled water, the Caribbean offers an array of tropical fruit beverages and in Hawaii fresh pineapple juice would be a natural choice. The same applies to snacks as well as beverages. Do something that has a little flair.

Find out the configuration of the limousine. How many will it comfortably hold? How are the seats positioned? Some limousines have seats that pull down to provide additional seating and while this may be acceptable for a short distance, it will not be desirable for long drives. Is there another layout that will work better? Depending on your numbers and your budget, you may want to look at the cost of renting two smaller limos rather than one large one and making sure that everyone enjoys a comfortable ride. If the limousine is rented for a gala event will the seating allow for a graceful exit from the car? This is especially important if media will be present.

What happens if the limousine breaks down? Does the company have back-up? Always book with an operation that has more than one car, and find out how quickly they can respond to an emergency situation.

How tight is the limousine schedule? Is it booked to be somewhere else just before your pick-up time? What happens if delays such as air or ground traffic throw off your scheduled arrival time? Does it have to be somewhere else immediately after your event? Is there a possibility your event could go on longer than planned? Do you need to budget for buffer time at the beginning or the end? Will the limousine be at your disposal for the entire evening, or are you booking it strictly for pick-up and drop-off with the limousine going on to other calls? If you do not have the driver and car booked for the entire evening, you will not be able to leave anything behind in the car. On the return trip will you be picked up by the same driver and car? If not, the new driver will probably not be familiar with the exact location where you were dropped off, and neither of you will know what the other looks like. In a large gala event with a number of guests exiting at the same time to waiting limos, having the same driver and for both drop-off and pick-up is recommended.

If you are having guests met at the airport, provide the limousine driver with appropriate signs. When meeting celebrities make sure that their names are not being held up on display. Have them instead look for a sign with the name of the event. You want their arrival to be handled quietly, quickly and with finesse. If they prefer publicity, that is a different matter—make sure that you respect their preferences.

Limousines are only one transportation option; you can do a number of fun things for transportation. Classic cars can be arranged for special events with their owners as designated drivers, or you can use convertibles or exotic luxury cars. Contact local speciality automobile clubs to see what can be arranged. Horse-drawn carriages, sleighs, rickshaws, gondolas, barges, helicopters, horses, camels, outrigger canoes, hot air balloons, jeeps, all terrain vehicles and even bicycles have all been used successfully around the world. Look at how you can incorporate what is special to the region. On an incentive trip to Holland, one company was transferring their guests to an afternoon event by motor coach, which "broke down" right by a bicycle rental company so guests could bike to their final destination. Of course, the motor coach was "repaired" for those who chose not to ride the bicycles. The guests got to experience the typical mode of transportation in the region. Make sure you have proper insurance and waivers signed for any less-conventional transportation such as horseback or hot air ballooning.

MOTOR COACHES

Motor coaches come in many shapes and sizes. You can rent anything from a standard bus to a motor coach with a custom interior complete with sofas, entertainment centres and no company logo painted on the sides—these are often used at weddings. The first step is to decide what your needs are. On a long transfer you may want to make sure that the motor coach is equipped with a TV and VCR. The transfer time can then be used to view a corporate message, to watch a motivational speaker or to simply enjoy a movie to help the time pass more quickly. Companies doing a team event may want to keep the preassigned teams together on the transfer, allowing them to spend quality time with one another, the purpose of the teams in the first place. This could mean having to hire additional motor coaches since keeping the teams intact may mean that each vehicle is not filled to capacity.

[handwritten margin note: Purpose of the event determines type of motor coache require.]

Figure out the total number of people you will be transferring. Will some guests be making their own way to the site rather than taking the motor coach? Will that be an option? Double-decker buses, school buses, streetcars and trolley cars can all be privately rented should you be looking for a less-traditional means of transportation. Consider the length of time your guests will be in transit. A classic motor coach would provide more comfort than a school bus for long transfers, whereas a double-decker bus or school bus could be a fun way to shuttle guests from the parking area to the venue.

Always check to see where motor coach parking is located, how many can be accommodated, how much it costs and be sure to include that in your budget. Check to see if there are any obstacles such as ceiling height to contend with. Can the bus drop guests directly at the front door or will they need to use the side entrance because the bus cannot fit under the front overhang? Motor coaches should arrive at your event spotlessly clean and fully gassed at least a half hour before the event to allow one of your staff to do a walk through to make sure everything is in order.

When renting vehicles find out what is included in the cost. In some areas a "barn to barn" cost needs to be factored into your budget. Barn-to-barn charges mean that you are billed for the motor coaches from the moment they leave their garages, not from when they arrive at your pick-up point, until they return to the garages. You also need to be very clear if you want the buses to remain at your disposal for a certain number of hours or if you simply want two one-way transfers. As with the limousines, find out where the buses will be before and after your event. If you are concerned about tight schedules or time buffers, you will need to add in additional hours especially if there is the possibility that your event could extend past the expected departure time.

Motor coaches do break down. How quickly can the company send a replacement if this happens? Always have a back-up plan. Once, during a conference on an airport return shuttle, the last returning bus broke down. It was faster to send the remaining guests on to the airport by taxi than to chance missed connections waiting for a replacement to arrive. In such situations it is best to have either plenty of cash, a credit card or taxi vouchers. For unexpected emergencies it is a good idea to have an agreement with the hotel or facility to have taxi charges billed to the master account. Get the bus dispatchers' phone number or the bus drivers' cell phone numbers, and make sure they know how to reach you in case of an emergency or delays.

> Where are the motor coaches coming from? On an incentive program to Ochos Rios, Jamaica, the return airport transfers were scheduled for very early in the morning. Since the buses were coming from Montego Bay which was two and a half hours away depending on traffic conditions, it was decided to bring the buses in the night before. The drivers were given a room for the night and breakfast the next morning at the hotel. The additional cost was minimal, but the peace of mind was invaluable. No one had to worry that the motor coaches might be delayed by early-morning rush-hour traffic. It allowed time to leisurely load up the luggage and stock the motor coaches with refreshments.

PARKING

The last thing you want is your guests arriving at (or departing from) your event frazzled and frustrated, and parking—both its accessibility and its availability—play a part in the success of your event, which, when you think of it, actually begins and ends in the parking lot. Who doesn't have a parking horror story to tell? Don't let your guests arrive to find a parking lot full because of construction or a major sporting event. Don't leave them circulating the lot getting more and more frustrated. With research and planning this can be avoided.

What time does the parking lot close, and why is this important to know? Say a parking lot closes just after midnight. There is a sign to that effect, but it is so small that most people miss it. Nevertheless, the gate is closed, and cars are locked in. To add insult to injury, guests have to pay overnight parking charges in addition to the normal parking charges. Add to this the expense and inconvenience of finding alternative transportation home and then back the next morning, and you can expect some unhappy campers. That is not how you want your guests' evening to end. But there is a solution. You can arrange to have the lot's hours extended for an additional cost, which would need to be factored into your budget.

Always look for ways to make the experience as pleasant as possible. Events that involve moving guests from one location to another can be a challenge. Often the first part of the evening takes place in a theatre for, say, a product launch or a private film screening with the reception following elsewhere. If transportation is not being provided, and guests are to make their own way to the reception, you need to keep in mind that they will all be departing the theatre and arriving at the second location at the same time, which can lead to a congestion problem. Remember that hotels reserve the majority of the parking for their own overnight guests, which could limit the space available for your guests. Find out what other options are available. For example, one hotel that is often used for special events has limited parking and, although there is additional parking nearby, the hotel does not have a sign out front announcing that its parking is full and directing patrons to the other lot. This leads to massive confusion and frustration, which is complicated by local traffic patterns such as one-way streets and left-hand turns. By having an off-duty police officer directing traffic and uniformed hotel staff guiding guests to the alternate parking, the wrinkles are all smoothed out, and everyone is happy.

If it is at all possible, leave the cars parked in the original parking lot, and set up a shuttle between the theatre and the second venue. That way guests are inconvenienced as little as possible—they don't have to park and pay twice. Remember the extra costs to factor in, such as the police officer to direct traffic as well as obtaining street parking permits for the motor coaches or limousines.

> **Always have your street permits with you on the day of the event, and keep a copy in your files.**

Your transfer can even become a part of your event. At an event in Singapore, guests were transported from one location to another in a unique manner; they were greeted by a line of rickshaws waiting outside. Themed T-shirts on the runners designated the rickshaws that had been provided for each guest. The return trip was made by more prosaic motor coaches.

There are times when you may need to be inventive with parking and transportation. Where else can you park in the area? Are there nearby shopping malls or other places with larger parking facilities that you can rent? Shuttles to ferry your guests to and fro will solve all parking problems. You can make them fun—double-decker buses, school buses or, in some places, chartered ferry or yachts. In Key West, you can use open-air "conch" trains to transport guests from one place to another during "progressive" dinners, where you have cocktails at one location, dinner at another, and end up at a lively night spot. But always let your guests know what to expect in advance. Make sure that they receive detailed instructions with their invitations.

TRANSPORTATION: Q&A

Where will most of your guests be coming from?

Where are they coming from and what could affect their arrival? Will they be coming from work and fighting rush-hour traffic for an evening function? Have you factored that into the start time of your event? Will your participants be making their own way to the facility? What is the cost of parking? Compare that to the cost of renting vehicles. Does it make more sense to have your guests leave their cars and be transported as a group? Remember, many motor coaches have facilities that allow you to show a company message or entertainment video. Transferring guests as a group works well for employee appreciation events as well.

No matter what type of event you are holding, you will have to consider where the motor coaches will park, whether you will need street permits and what other charges will apply. For example, if you were looking at taking your employees to a sporting event such as a car race, will your buses need any parking passes or permits to obtain a designated parking spot at the facility?

Q & A

Does your event need to be located in the downtown core?

Where does it makes the most logistical sense to hold your event? If you are hosting a client appreciation event and your clients are located in the suburbs, does your choice of venue warrant bringing them downtown? Will all of your guests be arriving by car? When considering a location, in addition to parking, you also need to look at ways your participants will get there. Is public transportation available? How accessible is it, and how late does it run? You may need to change your schedule of events to coincide with transportation schedules. For example, if one of your objectives is to address your guests after dinner, and the last commuter train departs at 9 p.m., how many guests will leave immediately after dinner to catch that train?

Q & A

What is the estimated number of cars? Will guests arrive as couples or individuals?

If your event is for couples anticipate two separate arrival times and twice as many cars to park. If you are including vouchers for complimentary parking take this into consideration when you are arranging the printing of the vouchers. This will also affect the number of staff required if you are including valet parking. Base your budget costs on the maximum number of cars.

Q & A

Will factors other than rush-hour traffic have an impact when considering start time?

In addition to standard rush-hour traffic, another factor that can hold people up is other major events that are taking place at the same time. This can include a variety of things such as concerts, sporting events, road repairs, street festivals, movies being filmed, local parades and weather. Remember to take all these into consideration.

Q & A

Where is the closest parking?

Physically check out the available parking. How far is it from the venue where you considering holding your event? Is there an attendant? Will your guests be required to bring change for parking? How many parking spots are available? Are there any under construction?

A trade show at a local convention centre ran into problems when it was discovered that most of the parking spaces were under construction and that there wasn't access from all floors. Exhibitors with bulky items had a particularly difficult time getting through. They had not been advised about the problem with parking and the difficulty in getting to the elevators. Had they known in advance they could have arranged to have the material delivered directly to their booths.

Q & A

Who does the parking lot belong to? Is it owned by the venue or is it public parking? How secure is it?

Find out who owns the parking lot and how safe it is. Have they had any problems with break-ins or thefts? Is it well lit? Do they have security, or is the lot left unattended? Are there any special concerns with regard to parking and security? For example, if you are doing a car launch it is sometimes necessary to store the cars in a designated area where they can be prepped and detailed before bringing them into the display area. It is important that the cars be secure and that they be away from public view. You can make arrangements for special security for the cars while they are in most hotel parking lots, but it is essential to know if the facility has had any problems such as theft or vandalism. In extreme temperatures in Las Vegas, cars have been known to explode due to intense heat building up inside. The secret is to dissipate the heat by leaving a window open a crack, something that would be rather important to know in advance.

Q & A

What time does the parking lot open and close?

You need to know this in advance. If you have access to the venue at 5:00 a.m. to start setting decor, staging and lighting, you need to know that the parking lot will be open to accommodate your suppliers. You may need to make special arrangements to have it opened early. You need to speak directly with the owners of the parking lot and make any necessary arrangements directly with them. The same applies to closing time. It usually costs only a minimal amount to extend parking hours. A main objective of any event is to bring people together, and you want to make sure that they can relax, mingle and engage in conversation without worrying about their car being locked in overnight. Even worse would be guests not realizing that the parking lot closes early and ending up carless at the end of their evening. If you are not extending the parking hours at the very least make sure that parking attendants inform arriving guests about the early closing.

One high-powered event was filled with *very* influential guests. There was an abundance of food and drink, budget was not a concern, but one detail had been overlooked—extending the parking lot hours because it was scheduled to close early. The company's presentation had started quite late, leaving only a limited amount of time to enjoy the lavish display and have conversations with other guests. People dashing off to rescue their cars put quite a damper on the whole evening.

Q & A

What is the capacity of the parking lot?

When you speak with the parking authorities be specific regarding the day and the time of your event. Find out the capacity, the general availability at that day and time and how many spaces are reserved for monthly pass holders. If you are holding your event at a hotel you need to take into consideration that a majority of space could be utilized by hotel guests.

Q & A

Who uses the parking lot? For example, if it is the prime parking area for major sporting events, that could limit access for your guests. Have you checked if there is anything that may affect parking scheduled for that day?

This is key as well. Your guests can be left circling the block looking for parking, which will not only delay their arrival at your event but also leave them in a less than festive mood. For one client appreciation evening where timing was critical—the client had chosen to do a reception and sit-down dinner before the opening of a new theatrical show in the downtown core—guests who were driving into the city were advised in advance and then reminded personally the day before the event that a ball game would be going on as well and that traffic could be heavier than usual and parking limited.

Q & A

What is the cost for parking?

Keep in mind that if you are competing with a special event, in addition to parking being limited, parking costs are usually increased for the night. If you are picking up the cost of parking for your guests, you need to factor those increases into your budget.

Q & A

Can a block of space be sectioned off for the attending guests?

Check to see if this can be made available for your guests. You will probably be required to pre-pay or, in the case of hotel parking, have it billed to the master account, for the number of designated spots that you wish reserved. You may need to add in the cost of additional parking staff to monitor this and direct your guests to the designated parking area.

Q & A

Can parking be pre-paid?

If you are doing a special event at a hotel generally the cost for parking can be added to the total bill if you are picking up the cost of parking for your guests. The hotel may also have agreements with nearby parking facilities. Most other parking facilities are also open to pre-paid parking or having their lots taken over exclusively for the evening.

You can also look to pre-paying parking spaces in order to set up prominent display area in the parking area. For example, a company launching a new product might wish to set up a dazzling display in the parking lot to greet its guests and to introduce the product to the public.

Q & A

How will pre-paid parking be designated?

Custom parking vouchers can be included with the invitations. This way the vouchers can be handed in, providing you with an accurate count for payment. These can be professionally printed with theme logos or simply done up by computer.

Q & A

Are there special rates that can be negotiated for attending guests if the parking is not pre-paid?

This is another area that you can negotiate prior to contracting your event. Arrangements can be made to have special rates for your guests. Guests showing their invitation could receive a flat rate as opposed to the standard hourly charge. This could be one area that you negotiate with a hotel or at a public venue, but the amount of concession you get will depend on how much you are spending at the facility.

Q & A

Does the facility have any complimentary parking passes for key guests or staff?

This can be negotiated in advance as well. Check to see if the facility can provide parking passes for staff and key VIPs. These should be negotiated up front especially if you need a substantial number.

Q & A

Is the parking lot fully wheelchair accessible and if not how many accessible spaces are available? Are there fully automatic doors or buttons to activate them? Doors that open only manually could present difficulties to disabled guests arriving on their own.

Many parking facilities claim to be wheelchair accessible but are not. There may be ramps to the elevators, but these are not much good if they do not also have doors that open automatically or at the push of a button.

What is also important is the location and the size of the parking spaces. Many converted vans require extra-wide spaces to allow wheelchairs to be lowered.

Also make sure that there are no lips or other obstacles on entrance doorways and that the doors are wide enough to allow for wheelchair access.

Q & A

How many parking lot attendants will be on duty for both arrival and departure?

Let the parking lot management know what will be happening. What could be a typically slow night for the parking lot with only minimum staffing could be the cause of major delays and lengthy line-ups when 400 cars show up at the same time for your event. Inform lot managers well in advance how many are coming and when so that they can arrange to have adequate staff. If your guests are arriving for their evening out as people are leaving from work, make sure that there are extra people on duty to handle everyone with maximum efficiency.

Q & A

When are shift changes and breaks scheduled?

Let the parking people know your timing so that they can schedule shift changes and breaks.

If you're planning a split program where guests will be driving their own cars to a second location make sure they have been advised. You don't want 800 guests arriving back in the parking lot at 9:00 p.m. to find that everyone has gone on break!

Q & A

Is there a "lot-full sign?" Where is it positioned?

The location of the sign is key. You want guests to see it before they turn in, and thereby avoid any unnecessary delays. If the parking lot does not have a sign, have one made up. Consider hiring professional staff to direct the parking and to advise you when the lot is full.

T I P

Make sure that the sign has been made with aircuts—cuts in the signboard or banner that allow wind to blow through it instead of knocking it over or tearing it. Have the sign frame built so that it can be weighed down with sandbags to ensure that it won't be knocked over. Make sure the sign is large enough to be seen clearly by someone sitting inside a car. You want guests to know when the lot is full so that they do not waste time turning in or circling the parking lot.

Q & A

Do you need shuttles to transfer guests from the parking lots to the venue?

Is parking within walking distance, or will you need transportation? Give thought to things such as weather and what people will be wearing. If it is a dressy affair, is the distance from the parking lot easily walkable in heels? Do your parking attendants need to advise guests that they may wish to drop off their passengers for their convenience and comfort?

One event was just beginning when a sudden, heavy rainstorm struck. Disaster loomed, but good planning prevailed. Attendants with huge umbrellas waited in central locations in the parking lots to escort guests indoors, and others waited street side for passengers being dropped off. A lone saxophonist played in the outside covered stairwell greeting guests. The planners had taken great care with their event, and you could tell that before you even got in the door. They had thought of their guests' comfort, and it showed. The heavy rain and the music merely ended up adding to the atmosphere.

You can make parking shuttles fun. Use horse-drawn carriages in Montreal, Niagara-on-the-Lake, Nassau, Bermuda, New York or New Orleans; mini mokes in Barbados; rickshaws in Singapore; outrigger canoes in Hawaii; or covered stagecoaches with drivers in western garb in Arizona. In winter use horse-drawn covered sleighs with carollers to greet guests at the entrance (depending on weather temperatures—performing in the cold is difficult for singers). As they disembark provide hot roasted chestnuts and hot chocolate to warm them.

Q & A

Is there an area for VIP limousines and cars to park? How many will it accommodate?

You may wish to make arrangements with the hotel for the president and other top VIPs to have their cars valet parked or parked immediately out front so that they are not kept waiting when it is time to leave. It is a good idea to know the license plate numbers of VIP vehicles to ensure they are positioned right in front. Most hotels are able to come to terms with this request.

For black-tie galas, where you know you will have a number of limousine arrivals, you can make special arrangements to ensure that there is parking available for your VIPs and celebrities. Obtain street parking permits and hire an off-duty police officer to oversee this. The officer must have a list of key guests and their license plate numbers so that they can secure the spaces reserved for those guests.

Q & A

Who is responsible for obtaining permits?

Will you be arranging the street permits, or will the facility will be getting them on your behalf? Keep several copies of the permits with you, and make sure that all key staff members, including those designated to oversee the parking, have copies.

Q & A

Where do you get these permits and what do they cost?

Check with the police in the area where the event is taking place. Procedures can vary from area to area, even within the same city, so never assume that what applies to one region applies to another. Most police divisions have someone handling special events and assigning off-duty officers. They can advise you where to go and who to contact. The cost of permits varies from location to location. Make sure that you include that cost in your budget. Street permits may be required for a variety of reasons. For instance, you will need to obtain one for any display areas or if you were including search lights and the like.

Q & A

How much time do they take to process? Will a site inspection be required?

Check to find out how much time will be required for them to process your permit. Often it is necessary to meet with officials and do a walk through of your event with them before your permit can be processed. They will want to see exactly what you have planned—where guests will be arriving and where the transportation will be stationed. They will look at how your event could obstruct traffic; they may permit this, but usually with the provision that an off-duty police officer be responsible for directing traffic and ensuring the safety of guests. They will also advise you of which street vendors have a license to be there, as well as designated taxi areas and bus stops that may need to be re-routed.

Q & A

Will parking meters need to be bagged?

If there is metered parking right out in front of the venue where preferred space for limousines would be, the meters need to be bagged to reserve them. Ask police what time works best. These spots have to be reserved before the end of rush hour even though your event may not start until much later. For example, if no parking at meters is allowed during evening rush hour from 4:00 p.m. to 6:00 p.m., you would need to have the meters bagged by 5:00 p.m. with a police officer on duty to oversee and enforce. To try to bag these meters after 6 p.m. would be impossible.

Q & A

Will any orange cones be required to designate the area?

Orange cones are recommended because they clearly mark your designated area and are quite visible. They are very effective in keeping drivers away from your designated areas and can be set out and removed just before your guests are due to arrive. Your local police department can provide names of suppliers and, although the cones are available at minimal cost, that should be included in your budget.

Q & A

Do any licenced street vendors need to be informed? Will they cause any congestion? Can they be temporarily relocated? Is there a cost for doing so?

This will be one of the areas you will cover when you do your site inspection of the area. You need to know who the licensed vendors are and where they are located so that you can avoid these areas of congestion. You would need to speak with them and the authorities about the possibility of relocating them for the evening. Generally, street vendors are very helpful and cooperative particularly if you are willing to compensate them for lost revenue.

Q & A

Are there any authorized taxi stands stationed right out front that could hinder the arrival of your guests? Can these be temporarily relocated? Is there a cost involved?

Again, this is another area that should be covered on your site inspection. You will need to speak to both the authorities and the head of the taxi association to see what can be negotiated for the benefit of all.

Q & A

If the media are attending is there a location where their trucks and cables can be situated?

This is important and needs to be factored in if you want media coverage of your event. Find out their needs. What equipment will they be bringing? What time will they be setting up? How will this impact your event? You don't want your guests tripping over an assortment of cables at the entrance.

Q & A

Are additional off-duty paid police required for crowd control, traffic direction and security?

Look to see where you might need assistance. Paid off-duty police can be in uniform, which is advisable for traffic control, or dressed in suits when more subtle security is called for, such as at gala, black-tie events. You may wish to have some on horseback or in full dress uniform for added effect. Police are usually wonderful to work with and excellent on site.

Q & A

Does the area that will be blocked off interfere with any public transportation such as bus stops and subway entrances? Can they be temporarily re-routed?

Look at where the bus stops are located. Are there any areas of congestion? Review this during your walk through, and discuss options with the proper authorities. At one area where motor coach shuttles were in competition with public transportation, an off-duty police officer was all that was required to see to the safety of both the guests and those using public transportation. Visit the location at the day and time you are planning to hold your event to see exactly what you will be dealing with, but remember that what you see by day could change at night. Will cars and limousines be contending with extra public buses put on to handle the rush-hour crowds or for local events? How busy is the street? Be familiar with how the traffic moves at that time of day.

Are there any concerns with traffic flow? What else is going on in the area at the same time—sporting events, theatre, major concerts that could cause delays? What time would they begin and end?

Know what other events are going on around you, and know what is going on during the same time period. Know the times they start and finish and what effect this usually has on the traffic in the surrounding area.

At one venue the entrance to the subway is located inside the building. During the day this area was quite congested with a steady stream of commuters that would present a barrier to guests arriving for an event in the restaurant. At night after rush hour the place is nearly deserted unless there was another special event at the same time.

Are there any movies being filmed in the area during your event where traffic and accessibility could be obstructed?

Depending on the season and the number of movies being filmed, this is another area that can affect your event. Find out if there is any filming going on in your area. Again, check with the local police division. They are generally on hand overseeing this area as well. Find out if any streets have been blocked off. Will there be any trailers obstructing traffic flow? What you can do to work around this? Ask if they will be filming in your facility either directly before or directly after your event. If they run into any delays in filming, your start time for your set-up could be affected.

Q & A

Can private valet parking be arranged?

Valet parking is a wonderful touch—budget permitting—for any special occasion. It adds a touch of elegance and finesse to your event and takes looking after the comfort of your guests to the next level. It can be arranged at specific hotels and convention centres as well as private venues. Check with your facility to see if this is something that could be offered for consideration. You want to make sure that the company handling the valet parking is familiar with the site. Check to see who has worked on their premises before. Get references, and talk to someone who has worked with them. Were they pleased? Was service efficient? Was it professional? Check with both the event planner and the facility where the event was held. Something that could have looked fine on the surface could have had some areas that you need to be made aware of behind the scenes.

Q & A

What does valet parking cost? Is tipping included?

Find out what needs to be factored into your budget. Consider how you will handle tipping. Do you want it leave it to the guest's discretion, or have the tipping picked up by the host? If the tipping is being included, make sure that the attendants are told and that they inform the guest that the host has taken care of all gratuities.

Q & A

What ratio of attendants to cars will you need?

The number of attendants to handle a specific number of cars will vary from location to location depending on loading area, drop-off lanes, separate access, distance to parking area, length of time and other factors. You will need to schedule a site inspection and do a walk through of your requirements in order to obtain an accurate cost.

Q & A

How will the attendants be dressed?

Generally, valet attendants will be dressed in black pants and white shirts, but for something fun and casual you could have them dressed in custom-themed shirts, if it is appropriate and in your budget. How they are dressed must be in keeping with the tone of the event.

Q & A

What insurance does the private valet parking company have?

Have the valet company outline in writing their insurance coverage, both automotive and general. Check with your insurance agent to see if you need additional coverage. This is extremely important. You must know what insurance the parking company has. How is their record? Do they have any claims?

Q & A

Does the valet company have an upcoming event where you can see them at work?

If you can see the valet company at work that is always advisable. But keep your distance. Be respectful of the event that is in progress. You would not want uninvited guests at your event, and you need to be mindful of that for others. Check to see how efficiently the valets are managing the cars, how they greet the guests and how long guests are kept waiting.

T I P

It is possible to take over parking lots exclusively to use them as part of test drive programs for launches of new cars, motorcycles or bicycles. Parking lots can also be transformed into party venues with tents, carpeting, decor, staging and lighting. Be creative when it comes to utilizing existing space. Hollywood premiere parties have been held in parking lots, and a hotel in Mexico uses theirs regularly to hold their Mexican fiesta. Budget permitting, parking lots can be totally transformed.

Q & A

What arrangements can be made for parking your shuttle buses at airport pick-ups and drop-offs?

For out-of-country meetings where you are having your guests met at the airport and transferred to the hotel, check with local ground handlers to see if anything can be done to ensure that your buses can be positioned as close to the airport entrance as possible for your guests' convenience.

At an airport two major competitors were arriving at the same time. The buses for the one group were lined up all in a row right outside the front doors and bore their company logo. This group felt well looked after. The second group was grumbling as they walked past the long row of their competitors' motor coaches to finally reach theirs.

Q & A

Where will staff be parking?

Is there a separate area for staff parking? Can your own staff and suppliers park there as well? If not, where can they park? While you obviously want to make sure that primary parking is reserved for your guests, you also need to give consideration to where designated staff parking will be. Remember, they will be arriving earlier and leaving much later than your guests and not necessarily as a group. Make sure that they are parked in a safe, well-lit area. Once the guests have left, your staff may want to move their cars closer to the entrance before clean-up begins. This will also make it easier if you are transporting any materials back to the cars.

5 GUEST ARRIVAL

WEATHER CONSIDERATIONS

Each season brings with it its own set of considerations and items that should be factored in when considering both your choice of location and your budget. The one thing we know for sure is that we can not predict the weather, but we can be prepared. What is crucial is your guests' comfort and first impressions.

With meetings in other countries, some of the best values can be in off-season. Before you book, consider the impact the weather will have on your program if it is less than ideal. You don't want to be in the Caribbean or Florida during the hurricane season or in Arizona when there are flash floods and electrical storms. Check with local tourist boards to find out past weather history—temperature, precipitation and humidity—before you make your final decision. Ask to receive the official weather history statistics—they are available—do not simply accept a verbal report. And even if it has never rained or snowed before during the time period when you are planning to hold your event, secure weather back-up for outdoor events—it snowed in June in

Banff recently—and be prepared. Make sure that you have somewhere to fall back on should the unexpected happen. On the day
of the event, if the weather looks uncertain, there will be a time
when you will have to make a call on where to commence set-
up. Find out at what specific time you or your client will have to
make a final decision on where to hold your event.

With some destinations high temperatures are not a problem. In Las Vegas temperatures can soar to well over 100 degrees
Fahrenheit and not affect the program. Guests are picked up in
air-conditioned motor coaches or limousines and whisked to
their air-conditioned hotels. During the day they are comfortable
in their meetings or out by the pool and in the evening the temperature drops, and they can enjoy a very pleasant walk along
the strip. The hotels and casinos are all very close together and
have been designed to make you want to stay inside anyway.
Any excursions are usually just a matter of going from air-conditioned hotel to air-conditioned bus to air-conditioned venue and
back again. The heat is not a major factor.

In a hot climate, it is helpful to have ice-cold water, fresh
lemonade and iced tea waiting when guests first arrive. In the
Caribbean many hotels hand out ice-cold cloths along with
refreshments to arriving guests. The hotel staff can dip clean
facecloths in lemon water, wring them out thoroughly, and slip
them into individual plastic bags to freeze before transporting
them to the airport in coolers.

> **TIP**
> When guests are flying in winter weather and they need
> to make connecting flights, try to fly them as far south
> as possible. For example, if a group is flying out of
> Toronto in winter and have a choice of connecting flights
> through Chicago or Dallas, choose Dallas, be-cause the
> chances of weather delays there would not be as great
> as in Chicago.

Winter weather can cause more than flight delays. Roads can
be closed during severe storms in certain destinations, and this
can affect transfers to and from the airport. Find out in advance
what can be done should this occur. Are there airport hotels?

Depending on the length of the transfer are there other hotels en route should the roads become impassable? Are you prepared to be able to pick up the cost for each member of the party?

Weather also affects water temperatures and what can be found swimming in it. For those planning a program down south during the summer months, in certain areas you may find more jellyfish than during the winter season when the waters are a little cooler. For those planning a meeting aboard a cruise ship, find out how weather will affect your sailing—is there a time when the seas will be calmer? For day and evening cruises on private yacht charters find out how much shade and how much shelter the boat provides for guests. Can everyone be comfortably accommodated inside should a sudden rainstorm occur, and is there sufficient protection from the sun?

Remember that weather can have an impact on your event almost anywhere. Be prepared.

ARRIVAL & WEATHER CONSIDERATIONS: Q&A

What is the arrival area like?

What will be your guests' first impression as they arrive at the venue? If you are doing an evening charter cruise, don't just think about the appearance of the ship—which of course is important—but take a look at the area surrounding the pier as well. Is it clean? Is there a clear path to the boat? Do guests have to step over piles of freight and other unpleasant things? Are there any unsightly messes that must be cleared away so as not to spoil your guests' first impressions? Is the area covered?

At the launching of a new ship guests were put off even before they got on board. The cleanliness of the area where the boat was docked left much to be desired and, to top it all, the crew forgot the gangplank. Arriving guests had to jump from the pier to the ship, which was a little daunting for those in heels. Apprehension increased after the evening's cruise and drinks. Despite the fact that they sailed around all evening there was still no gangplank by the time they docked—and this evening was supposed to showcase their newest yacht to potential clients!

Remember, the ship you inspect may not be moored at the pier from which is usually sails. Find out where it will be sailing from and check out the condition of the surrounding area. This would also apply if you were to arrange for an alternate pick-up location (you would need to budget for the cost to transfer the vessel from one location to another). Take the time to check out the area and make arrangements to have it cleared of any debris before the day of your charter. Find out what, if any, restrictions could apply and what needs to be put in place in case of inclement weather.

Q & A

How do you arrive at your venue? Is there a unique or picturesque way to approach it?

Sometimes it's not just the entrance but how you arrive there that can set the tone of your event. If you were staying on the west coast of Barbados, there are two ways to get to your hotel. You can take the fast route through the centre of the island, or you can take the East Coast Road, which follows the coastline and offers guests wonderful views of the beautiful blue Caribbean waters, although it does take a little longer to drive. Depending on the time your flight arrives—such as an evening arrival when the ocean is not as visible—you may choose to take the faster route to the hotel, and use the picturesque East Coast Road route when returning to the airport, allowing your guests one last look at the island before they depart. If you are arriving early in the day, do the reverse. Or take the East Coast Road both ways if you are not in a hurry.

In some areas of the world, such as Holland, you can even choose to arrive at your hotel by boat instead of by bus. You may need to use buses to take the guests to the canals or a central spot first, but this will provide them with a relaxing introduction to the city. International flights arriving at an overseas destination may arrive too early for the standard hotel check-in time of 3:00 p.m. Including a canal tour as part of their transfer allows guests to adjust to the time difference, enjoy local specialities—coffee and pastries—and have their first view of their destination at a leisurely pace. Make every step of your event as enjoyable and as visually memorable as possible. You could do something similar in London and Windsor as well. Of course, budget permitting, you could have paid for an additional night at the hotel and thereby have the rooms available for immediate occupancy or negotiate early check-in for your guests depending on the season. It is not a good idea to put guests on a bus tour as soon as they step off the plane. They will be tired from the trip and due to the time difference they will not fully take everything in. Also coming directly off the plane, they may not be dressed for a tour. But being on the water is always soothing and relaxing.

Q & A

Is there a convenient drop-off point at the venue?

What main doors will you, your guests or your suppliers be using to enter your venue? Whether it's suppliers dropping off materials, guests choosing to drop off their passengers at the front door for a gala event or motor coaches or limousines offloading guests and luggage, the convenience of the drop-off point is important. You want to make sure that access into the area where you are holding your event is easy and suitable for everyone's particular needs.

If your guests are dropping their passengers off at the front door because of inclement weather, and they are exiting into busy rush-hour traffic, they are going to need to proceed with caution as they open their doors. You may want to consider having someone to control traffic.

If is it volunteers dropping items off for a silent auction at a convention centre where there are no doormen, bellboys, or staff on hand to assist with the offloading and transfer of items to the display area, you need to make sure that there are enough hands on deck to assist them.

If you are transferring a group by bus you need to know whether or not the vehicle can come right up to the main doors or if its height prevents it from doing so. There is one hotel in Arizona where the motor coach will not fit under the roof and the passengers and luggage are generally offloaded at the side door. That is a bit of a disappointment especially given the impressive panorama of the hotel lobby when they enter through the main doors. One solution is to have the guests disembark and walk through the spectacular main doors. The bus then pulls around to the side door and offloads the luggage. On the return trip to the airport guests can board the motor coaches at the side door so they can identify their luggage. After all, they've already been wowed by the entrance on arrival.

Q & A

Is the entrance covered?

Is the entrance covered, or do you need to have umbrellas ready in bad weather for those guests who are being picked up or dropped off? No matter what the location, you have to figure out how to get your guests from A to B without getting wet.

> In the middle of an unexpected torrential tropical downpour, arriving guests were met at the airport with souvenir umbrellas, theirs to keep. They were going on a luxury cruise, and the walkway between the bus and the gangplank was not covered. The cost of the umbrellas was minimal, but it demonstrated the event planner's commitment to the comfort and care of each participant. Everyone arrived on board ship happy and dry—a thoughtful beginning to their week.

There is one resort in the Caribbean that had wonderful huge logoed umbrellas that were part of the gifts for arriving guests. The umbrellas were tastefully done, well-made and useful and they served as great promotional items long after the vacation as guests took them home afterwards. The walkways from the villas to the main restaurants were not covered, and umbrellas were the perfect solution in case of rain.

If you are doing a program in the Caribbean make sure that the hotel or your program directors have access to several of the larger varieties of umbrellas in case they are needed to help escort guests from one uncovered area to another. Don't wait until it starts to rain to go in search of them. Downpours in the Caribbean can be very sudden and very heavy at times. The rainy season traditionally takes place in, but is not limited to, the summer months.

At Disney World, they have great bright-yellow rain ponchos in all the stores. Whenever it rains the park is quickly transformed in a sea of bright yellow with thousands upon thousands of Mickeys staring at you from the backs of the ponchos. They keep you absolutely dry and your hands are left free to hold onto little hands, cameras or bags. They fold up to nothing. If you were doing an event at a destination where your guests will be out and about walking and exploring, consider doing something similar with a custom company logo in place of Mickey. The ponchos are inexpensive, easy to pack and because of this utility are great advertising pieces.

Q & A

Who will be available to ensure walkways are kept clear of snow, ice and slush in winter or of slippery rain puddles and mud in summer throughout the event?

You want to make sure that the walkway and the entranceway are kept clear of hazards. If you are doing an event in winter, one of the areas you need to review is who will be responsible for shovelling the walkways, keeping them salted and cleaning up snow brought in on people's boots at the front entrance. Does the venue have all necessary supplies on hand? Make sure that they don't wait for the day of the event to be out searching for bags of salt or additional snow shovels. Also, find out who maintains the parking area and when you can expect it to be cleared.

A front entrance of pure marble or other tile can be extremely slippery when wet. If non-slip carpeting needs to be laid down in front, make sure that it is anchored firmly in place. Depending on weather conditions you could require more than one carpet; you may need to have it replaced if it becomes to wet. Do you have insurance coverage if anyone should slip, fall and injure themselves?

Don't depend on the venue to have sufficient coverage—get your own insurance. Remember Murphy's Law? At one fund-raising social, not only were there both ice and snow to deal with but also a broken water pipe next door that flooded the street with water which quickly turned icy.

Not all events are black-tie galas with ball gowns and tuxedos. What if your meeting takes place somewhere more rural—for example, a visit to a plantation in the Caribbean where guests are taken out into fields to see something that is relevant to the work they do?

One particular incentive program included an agricultural farm conference that was taking place in the actual fields. Guests had been advised to bring tall rubber boots with them. What do you do with a busload of delegates wearing muddy knee-high boots back at the hotel? One solution is to greet them at the hotel entrance with inexpensive slip-on terry slippers, and have staff on hand to handle, remove, clean and return the boots to the guest rooms. That way delegates did not have to worry about trekking mud through the hotel and into their rooms and figuring out how to repack the boots.

Which services are supplied and which cost extra?

Find out what is available and what needs to be brought in. In some five-star hotels shoe cleaning is part of the service they offer. Ask what is provided at no addition charge and what needs to be factored into your budget. In a case such as the one above there could be extra dollars involved to bring in additional staff to handle that number of muddy boots. Remember, when negotiating costs for something of this nature that it is in the hotel's best interest to not have to clean up behind the guests' muddy boots.

Hotels provide many services: stocking minibars with personal requests, dry cleaning, laundry, faxing, typing, photocopying, providing extension cords through their in-house audio-visual suppliers, cell phone rentals, walkie-talkies, telephone hook-up at your registration desk, the installation of banners (this one can be surprisingly expensive) and allowing the use of their computers for the middle-of-the-night changes to speeches that always seem to occur the night before a presentation. But beware, there can be a charge for each of the above-mentioned services. Always find out in advance, and ensure that you authorize all expenses posted to the master account. Make sure you note clearly on your copy exactly what the charge was for so that you can include it on your reconciliations. While it may be less expensive to go to the local copy centre to make copies or send a fax, is it worth your time to do so when you are in the middle of running an event? That's dollars and sense. Hotels will provide you with a list of the services they provide along with applicable costs. Include these costs in your budget wherever you can. For example, if you know you will want telephones at your hospitality desk, you need to include the costs for hook-ups and the charges for local calls. (It varies from hotel to hotel; at some hotels there is no charge and at others it could be over $1.00 per call.) You will need to estimate this number, and include it in your costs, because the dollars can quickly add up.

Q & A

Is the entrance fully wheelchair accessible?

Find out if the main entrance is fully wheelchair accessible and, if it is not, find one that is. The next question is which public rooms and facilities are wheelchair accessible? Be familiar with their location. Make sure there is sufficient room to easily manoeuvre in. Some hotels have whole rooms adapted for guests in wheelchairs. Be sure to request this when making your booking.

At one hotel, the front entrance is not wheelchair accessible, but there is one entrance nearby that is, and it is located right next to the elevators. Knowing that in advance prevents the added inconvenience of going to one area only to be redirected to another.

An important consideration is the width of the door. Can the wheelchair be easily accommodated? Find out the required width in advance—not all wheelchairs are the same width. Some models have wheels that can be popped off in cases of extreme necessity.

In addition to accessible rooms, guests in wheelchairs may want someone nearby in a connecting room if they require assistance. Ask in advance if this is possible.

Q & A

Are there doormen provided?

Whenever and wherever possible have the venue's professional security staff or, if they are not available, paid off-duty police staffing your doors. Do not rely on corporate volunteers. Their job is to mix, mingle, make your guests comfortable and help with introductions. As guests are arriving it is too easy for the corporate volunteers to be called away, and you really need to have someone stationed permanently at the entrance with specific people designated to relieve them during breaks. Professional staff are trained to handle difficult situations and, if at all possible, it is always good to have them equipped with walkie-talkies in case of an emergency.

> At one event, the singer engaged for the evening had invited some local couples, who were considering hiring her to sing at their wedding, to drop in and to see her perform. Unfortunately, it was a private event, they were not on the guest list and they were inappropriately dressed. The couples were very unhappy and very vocal about it. The situation was handled swiftly and with discretion. Assistance was called for and the couples were escorted away from the main doors.

In the downtown core, it is not unusual to see, at the front doors of a restaurant—even very upscale ones—homeless people appear to act as doormen in the hopes of tips. And as soon as one is asked to leave, another appears, unless someone official staffs the doors for the duration of the event. This is another good reason to have the doors staffed by professionals.

Q & A

What does a front entrance attendant cost? Has tipping been included, or do you need to budget for it?

This is an area you may be able to negotiate in your contract. They may be able to provide a doorman at no additional cost to you, but you will probably have to budget for gratuities. Always remember, you may be using a facility more than once, and you want to make sure that all staff have been looked after adequately. Find out the appropriate amount to tip the doorman, and add it into your budgets. Tipping procedures and amounts vary around the world and are ever changing. If you are doing an out-of-country event, your hotel and most other venues will advise you what amount will be posted to the master account for doormen and others. You can use these rates as guidelines at other venues.

Q & A

How are the doormen dressed?

Find out how the doormen will be dressed. At an informal event you may want them to be wearing theme T-shirts or dress shirts for the evening, but for a more formal affair, you might wish to consider renting a traditional doorman uniform complete with top hat to add a little more splash.

Q & A

Is there a sign announcing that the event is a private party?

It is always a good idea to have a "private party" sign at the entrance, and on your initial walk through examine the entrance and consider where and how the sign will be displayed. Does the venue have its own easels or frames, and, if so, are they suitable? Do they need to be polished, or are there any missing or broken parts? You may decide to bring your own frames. Restaurants often have menu displays under glass outside, and your private party can have your sign made to size.

Where is the coat check in relationship to the entrance? Are there any problems that could cause congestion?

Always keep traffic flow patterns in mind when laying out the room.

At one event the venue had a very small coat check area, but the room beyond was open concept. The planners positioned a food station extremely close to the coat check area, and the two line-ups intersected and caused noticeable problems and delays. The food station could easily have been moved to the other side of the room, where it would have provided better flow and have had the added advantage of drawing people into the room. You also need to keep traffic flow in mind when considering the position of your registration tables.

What is the capacity of the coat check? Does it have enough racks and hangers?

How many coats can it handle and how quickly? How many staff will be required to staff the coat check to provide optimum speed and efficiently? Is it effectively laid out? How much more would it cost for more racks or hangers? It is always better to have too many than not enough.

At one fund-raiser the volunteers staffing the coat check were inexperienced, there were not enough coat racks and hangers and it was in the dead of winter—everyone wore a coat. Coats—many of them very expensive—ended up being piled one on top of the other, and the resulting confusion was horrific. Guests were kept waiting, some well over half an hour, to retrieve their coats. It projected an image of total disorganization and rank amateurism.

What type of hangers are there? Will flimsy wire hangers handle the weight of heavy winter coats? At gala fund-raisers you often have a number of fur coats, and using wire hangers is asking for trouble; expensive fur coats do not belong on the floor.

Q & A

What provision is there for umbrellas, boots, briefcases and other items? For example, in Bermuda coat checks have room for motorbike helmets.

At many special event evenings, guests arrive after work with their briefcases. Since these evenings often involve having a private dinner, being transferred to the theatre and returning to the dinner site for dessert, coffee, liqueurs and cigars, guests need a safe and secure area in which to leave their briefcases.

Q & A

How many people are staffing the coat check at arrival and at departure?

Find out how many staff will be on duty at arrival and at departure. How far in advance of opening will they be arriving? If the evening is extended—which can sometimes happen—will staff be able to stay on later than originally planned?

Q & A

Who are your most experienced staff? How experienced are they? Can they be scheduled to work during your event?

The arrival is absolutely crucial, because first impressions are lasting. How professionally guests' needs are looked after sets the tone for your event. Find out about the staff. Make sure the most experienced staff are assigned to your event.

Q & A

Are there any additional costs for staffing, coat check, tipping, or are they included?

Is the cost of the coat check included in your overall bill, or will there be a separate charge? Will you be hosting—paying them on behalf of the guests—the coat check, or will it be at the guests' own expense? Will you be picking up the cost for gratuities? Be very clear about how you want to handle the issue of tipping. If you are hosting the coat check, you do not want to see any tip plates left out for tipping. Make sure the staff knows this.

Q & A

How secure are the coats?

Are the coats kept in a safe place, or are they left at guests' own risk? If the latter, are there signs to that effect? If not, make your own sign and have it clearly posted advising guests that items are left are at their own risk. In the long run, it is better to budget for additional staff and make sure that the coat check area is secure and adequately staffed at all times. In the event of a mishap, are the coats insured?

Q & A

What is the staff break schedule during the event?

Review your schedule of the event with them so that they are aware of timing. Make sure that breaks are scheduled after all guests have arrived and are finished before guests begin to leave. Remember that there could be a staggered departure with the majority most likely leaving as a group.

Q & A

Should the inside walkway by the coat check become wet or slushy, who will be on duty throughout the event to attend to it? Is this included, or is there an additional cost?

Make sure that you know how this will be handled in advance. You do not want to have it left to the actual day of the event to find out that there are no provisions on hand. At one event at a venue that is not used frequently they had to go out to buy mops and a bucket while the event was in progress.

Who do you call in an emergency? Find out who is responsible in case of an emergency, and make certain that you have a phone number where they can be reached throughout the event and during set-up and tear-down. At one gala event held in a convention centre the main bathroom flooded and water was everywhere. You want to make sure that you can reach the proper people quickly and that any areas of concern are dealt with quickly, efficiently and as discreetly as possible.

FANFARE

Simply stated, fanfare is more than the blare of trumpets; it is anything that plays a part in the arrival atmosphere. The red carpet has been rolled out, search lights sweep the sky, excitement fills the air. Everything is in place and you are ready to go...or are you? Have you covered all your bases? Have you informed proper channels that the search lights were being used? Have you received clearance in writing? Local airports will need to know about anything that could affect their flight patterns and the safety of their arrivals and departures. The same applies to events involving hot air balloons, the release of helium balloons into the sky and even kites.

A festive summer event taking place on Toronto Island planned to give custom logoed kites as their take-away gifts. But there is an airport on the island. The event planners reviewed the proposal with airport authorities and received clearance for the kites to be flown on the island with the provision that the kite strings not exceed 30 feet. The lesson is to plan ahead and act early. The last thing you should ever be doing is dealing with the authorities as your event is about to start. Never assume anything. Dot your i's and cross your t's.

And what about that red carpet? Did you receive clearance from the city to have it there? Is it securely in place? Have you met all safety regulations? What happens if someone trips and breaks a leg on the carpeting—who is responsible? Are you insured? Ask the questions. Avoid the surprises. Do you know what a dent it can put in your budget to have a union team remove helium balloons from the ceiling with a cherry picker? You probably don't want to know, but you have to.

One fund-raiser was using helium balloons for a "balloon burst," a type of silent auction where the name of a donated prize is inserted into the balloons. Guests purchase a balloon, are given a pin with which to pop it and can then pick up their gift at a designated table. The proceeds from the sale of the balloon goes to the charity. But helium is tricky stuff, and a lot of the balloons escaped. In addition to the added expense of rescuing fugitive balloons, planners were unable to auction off all of the prizes as there was no way of knowing which prize was in the balloon that had escaped. They needed a numbering system so that they could track the balloons. If one then escaped it could easily be replaced. Another consideration in such situations is knowing the ceiling height you are working with and making sure that the strings attached to the balloons are long enough so that they can be retrieved.

FANFARE: Q&A

Q & A

Will you be planning any special arrival activities?

Give some thought to creating energy in the arrival area. How do you want it to look and feel? You want to create a build-up of anticipation, not a dull, flat and listless entrance. You want your guests to feel they have arrived somewhere special, that there is excitement in the air.

When you hold special events in other countries or regions take particular effort in greeting the guests as they step off the plane. Check with local tourist boards to see what can be done for minimal cost or possibly as part of the board's own promotional budget. Often they can supply a local band to greet guests as they are waiting to check through immigration. A welcome banner can be displayed and a local beverage provided.

But greeting arriving guests is *not* the first step—that takes place at the originating airport where guests are departing and includes such things as arranging for a private group check-in, having someone to provide luggage carts for your guests' convenience and perhaps a private room with refreshments reserved for your group. It is also a good idea to arrange pre-boarding and group seating so that your guests can all sit together. This is actually a plus for the other passengers as they are not being disturbed throughout the flight by people talking across one another.

On board the aircraft there are other things that can be done. These include welcome aboard announcements, custom-printed headrest covers, upgraded menus, complimentary drink coupons and movie and headset vouchers. And, depending on the numbers and availability, groups can sometimes be upgraded as well. If the whole group cannot be upgraded you may choose to decline the offer. One incentive group did a random draw to see who would be upgraded to first-class as there were only a limited number of seats available. Keep in mind that guests will need to be dressed appropriately. Many VIPs do not like to sit in first class themselves when the balance of the group is in coach. VIPs who favour first-class travel will often book on a separate airline and arrive in the destination in advance of their guests. Some items can be negotiated with the airlines prior to signing the contract or made available at minimal cost. Perhaps it is a birthday cake presented on board to celebrate a very special sixteenth birthday or visits to the cockpit for younger children.

When guests arrive at the destination they are offered a touch of local culture. It is a nice beginning to be welcomed to Hawaii with a lei, Jamaica or Barbados with fruit punch (with or without rum) or local beers such as Red Stripe or Banks, and listen to the sounds of the steel drums. On the shuttle there are refreshments and cool towels, and at the hotel a private group check-in set up exclusively for them. Here packets containing keys to their rooms and the minibars, as well as general hotel information and express checkout forms will be waiting for them. Credit card imprints to cover incidentals can be taken at this time. This arrangement ensures that they do not have to wait in line with other arriving guests.

Hotels around the world swear that they cannot do private group check-ins, but they can and do. Be persistent. It is simply not acceptable to have travel-weary guests standing in huge line-ups to check in, when they could just as

simply wait in a private room with refreshments and a private check-in. If the flight has arrived too early for their
rooms to be ready (other guests have not checked out as
yet) it is a simple matter to arrange for day rooms so that
clients can change, leave their carry-on luggage in a safe,
secure area and go out to enjoy the hotel's facilities. (Their
checked luggage will be handled separately by the bellstaff
and be sent directly to their rooms once they have been
assigned.) Make sure that you assign a staff member to
oversee the guest day room and their possessions. A hospitality desk can be set up in this room. The event planner
must do everything to make sure that the guest rooms are
available as quickly as possible—request extra maid service
in advance, provide the hotel with an arrival schedule well
ahead of time so that the rooms can be assigned in order of
flight arrival and request early check-in wherever possible.
If the budget allows, you can book the rooms for the
evening before your group arrives so that they are available
for immediate check-in. If that is not possible, sit down
with the rooms manager the night before the group arrives
to see how many rooms are vacant and how many you can
start to pre-assign. Don't wait to begin the next day.

> **T**
> **I**
> **P**
>
> Special note: In Las Vegas always make sure to note in
> your contract that the rooms are to be cleaned before
> being assigned. Some hotels have been known to assign
> "dirty" rooms, allowing the guest to go up and drop off
> their luggage and usually head down to the casino to
> wait and perhaps play, which was the hotel's intent.

Once guests arrive in their rooms it is always a nice
touch to have a welcoming phone message and a small gift
waiting. In Hawaii, it can be something as simple as tropical juices on ice and fresh baked pineapple bread. In the
Orient, a hot pot of tea with an assortment of local fruit. (Be
careful in choosing the fruit—in Singapore there is one
fruit that at first glance looks like a large spider in your fruit

bowl.) In Morocco, exotic juices and a plate of local delicacies or a huge bowl of fresh Moroccan oranges are always tempting and visually pleasing. And the local long-stem roses are unusual in colour, exquisite and relatively inexpensive. Now is not the time to bring in the snake charmers, the animal acts and the local artisans. Save those for later in the program. Guests will be tired from travelling and will want to be looked after and pampered. Look for ways to make something ordinary anything but.

Q & A

At your special events will there be searchlights, displays, red carpets, crowd control, staging, special effects, lighting, audio-visuals, lasers, fireworks?

Before you begin to plan do a walk through of the area. This is called a site inspection and may reveal whether or not your fabulous idea will work logistically. Before you spend your time and energy (and that of your suppliers), take the time to do an initial inspection on your own to get a feel of the facility. The next step would be to return at a later date to do a planning site inspection with the suppliers you are considering working with. It is always a good idea to have your key suppliers meet at the site at the same time beforehand, so that on the day of the event you will all be coming together and operating as a team. That way your caterers can talk directly to the person who is installing the cooking tent to ensure all of their needs will be met and that you are not losing time continually going back and forth over issues that could have been resolved with one joint meeting. All the key players have to be operating off the same page. The more they know about the event in advance, the better they can meet your needs and offer recommendations based on their past experiences. Once you have decided what you want to do, the next step is making sure that all of your plans fall under the proper rules and regulations, that you are fully aware of all that will need to be done, and that includes all permits and requirements such as safety and fire regulations.

Q
&
A

How much set-up time is required?

You will need to find out from each supplier how much set-up time they will require, and begin to plan the order of each sequence. For example, the stage and the band equipment would need to be set up before moving in the banquet tables. They will need the area clear to bring in their equipment—as will lighting, audio-visual and decor—rather than trying to manoeuvre between the tables. Then the tables can be moved into place. If you are providing special lighting, such as pin-spotting that highlights each table, the lighting crew will need to know when the tables have been moved into their final position so they can make any necessary adjustments. Look at the total time each area requires. Does it all fall within the time parameters you are working within? Do you need to request earlier access to the room? All these items are key because each could affect both your budget and whether the site is feasible or not. If you do need earlier access to the room, you will probably have to pay additional rental charges if that means the facility is losing revenue.

In addition to finding out from the facility what time you can move in, you also need to know what else is happening just before you set up. Could there be any delays? Find out if it is a simple breakfast or luncheon set-up that will take place just before you move in, or is it something much more complex? Try to anticipate anything that means the preceding event might not be out of the room on time. If it is going to be touch and go to pull everything off and you cannot get earlier access to the room this might not be the right venue for you unless you are willing to change your set-up. Find out how much time you will need *before* you sign the contract.

> One venue being considered for a car launch proved to be unacceptable because although it had sufficient space to hold the event and the access time was good, the only way to move the cars from the loading docks to where they were to be displayed was through another ballroom, and that space was booked for another event. Look at all areas that could affect your move-in and set-up.

At one fashion fund-raiser they were tearing down and carrying out the runway, and guests were arriving at the main doors. Guests had to repeatedly step aside for the workers. The planners had not taken into consideration what else was going on in the room and, once the food and food stations were set-up, they found that there was no adequate room left for the guests! Obviously the planners had not thought this through.

Q & A

Is there any special equipment that needs to be brought in? What will this cost? Have you factored in labour costs such as overtime? Is the facility union or non-union?

Find out in advance what equipment is needed. For example, will you be doing ceiling decor or special lighting and require the use of cherry pickers? Have all of your suppliers factored in what they will need? What does the facility have, and what needs to be brought in? Will the facility charge you for the use of their equipment? Make sure that you build these costs into your budget. It is also very important to find out if the venue is union or non-union because this can have an enormous impact on costs. If the facility is union, ask them to provide you—in writing—with a list of everything that could affect your costs. For example, you could budget installing a banner at one hour but end up paying for a three- or four-hour minimum. If it is a union facility find out when their contracts are up for renewal. If it is over the time period of your event how could this affect your event? Do you need to build into your budget an anticipated increase in labour rates? Check your contract. Union costs are often estimated subject to the "prevailing" rate. Build in a buffer. Have them provide estimated union costs in writing based upon your requirements. Ensure any overtime costs are factored in.

Q & A

What are the access routes in and out of the building like? Will freight elevators be required, and can they be booked for specific times? Are there any charges?

Find out where and how items will be moved in. Where are the loading docks? Are there any height restrictions? If there are freight elevators what are the dimensions? How wide are the hallways? Are they cluttered or are they clear? If you will be moving in something bulky like a car display are there weight restrictions? Do the freight elevators work? How often are they out of service for repair (you might be surprised by the answer at some facilities)? When do you have access to them? Can you book specific times?

Q & A

Does the facility have any particular requirements?

For example, suppose you were doing a fund-raiser that offered a new car lease as a prize, you would want to have the car on display where your guests arrive, especially if the car manufacturer was one of the lead sponsors of your event. Find out what the facility requires you to do to move the car. You might have to lay down plastic runners on the carpet and have the car rolled into place by hand. If so, who supplies the plastic runners—the facility, the car manufacturer or you? Will there be a cost involved? Perhaps they will want you to "diaper" the car to ensure no oil drips onto their carpets and floors. If these are damaged could you be charged? Do you need to have insurance to protect you? Discuss with venue managers in detail when you will be arriving, what they can assist you with and where you need to bring in additional help. How do you arrange for that help? Are you limited to specific suppliers? Do you hire the help or does the union? What perks, such as meals for the crew, are part of their contract agreements and need to be included in your budget? Find out everything that needs to be done.

Q & A

What are the electrical requirements?

Know your electrical needs in advance. At one fund-raiser set-up, they wasted countless hours running to buy extension cords and changing the layout to fit their electrical needs. Figure out in advance what has to be plugged in and where the plugs are located in the arrival, registration or the main event areas. Will there be enough power? Do you need back-up generators? Do you need to hire a professional electrician? Does the venue have one? Are you limited to using specific companies that have been approved by the facility? And when you are doing events out of country, check what voltage they use and how their plugs are configured. North American equipment will not work in Europe, for example. Don't assume that you can simply bring your own props and decor with you. Lava lamps for your 70s theme party may not work everywhere. Find out in advance. Check and double check.

Q & A

What will your power cost be?

What costs, such as labour for installation, will you know upfront, and what costs should you budget for that will be billed back at the end of your event based on actual usage? Read the fine print on your contracts. It may say that power charges will be billed based on the amount used during your event. You need to include this in your budget projections. Ask the facility to provide you with an estimate based on similar events. You need to know where, when and how many cables or power bars you will need.

Q & A

Ask if there are any additional costs that you need to budget for.

If you are using special effects such as indoor or outdoor fireworks, lasers, confetti or snow bursts, what costs could apply? What insurance do you need for property damage?

Are there any charges for clean-up or key personnel? For example, if using fireworks who pays for a fire marshal or someone on fire watch? (Note: Consider this position absolutely essential!)

Q & A

What permits will be needed for delivery, set-up and tear down for your suppliers?

These need to be factored into your budget as well. Drop-off locations may be different from the parking for the limousines, and you may need permits for both. You may also have to bring in additional traffic control—separate from what you may require for your event—if suppliers will be dropping off items during peak traffic times. For example, you may be removing existing furniture from a venue and storing it in a moving van parked nearby. You may need a permit for this and another for the area where suppliers pull up their trucks and offload their material. This, of course, depends on the venue and accessibility.

Q & A

Are there any safety or fire regulations that must be followed?

Make sure you know all regulations that apply both inside and outside the building.

At one high-profile celebrity event, many media were on hand to cover guests' arrivals and, because there was danger of them stepping further into the traffic as they sought to capture the perfect shot from their designated area, police had to be hired and barriers erected to create a buffer between the media and the oncoming traffic. The traffic barrier was one of the conditions of the street permits.

Q & A

Are there any zoning laws, noise, time or other restrictions that will affect your event?

Do local by-laws and other regulations restrict you in any way? Do regulations apply outside the venue and inside as well? Are there any time restrictions? Can music be played outside the venue to greet guests? How late can the band play? For example, if your venue is in a residential area your band may not be allowed to play past 10 p.m. How loud can the music be? Is any type of music restricted— hard rock but not classical? At hotels, if you are considering doing a party poolside, you may not be able to have it continue past a designated time as it could disturb other guests. What can and cannot be displayed? You may not be permitted to display banners or company products outside the venue. Certain facilities named after corporations may not allow competitors access, and they may also have a permanent display of their products.

REGISTRATION: GUEST PASS SECURITY AND TICKET PICK-UP

Your guests have arrived and have been greeted and welcomed to your event. All the cars, limos or buses have been parked. People are standing by directing guests to the coat check and restrooms. Staff is easy to identify by uniform colours or with visible ID such as a name tags or logoed security passes that can be worn around the neck. The next stop is guest check-in. Here they'll display their event tickets or VIP identification passes and have their names checked off a guest list and pick up tickets or hotel room registration at a private check-in.

If your event is a fund-raising auction, there may also be a table set up for guests to register their credit cards for bidding. Here, you can have confusion and congestion if the table is not staffed adequately by professional, well-briefed people who are knowledgable about the event. The same applies for those registering for their hotel rooms for a meeting or convention. A credit card imprint is generally required for personal incidentals, taxes and porterage, the main charges going to the master account. This is generally handled by the hotel staff at a satellite check-in set up exclusively for the group.

As you start to plan your event consider what will be needed at arrival. How many tables will be required, and will they have to be draped and skirted? What about chairs? Will you need electrical outlets and phone lines for computers or credit card processing? Will there be display tables requiring outlets as well? How many extension cords will be required, what length should they be, and will the facility supply them? Is there a charge or are they free? Do you need to bring your own? Is the area well lit? Is there more than one access point?

> At one fund-raiser event planners apparently overlooked the fact that there were two entrance points. Guests arriving from one went directly into the ballroom without registering, and there was no one positioned to direct guests to the check-in table. This is what you want to avoid.

Once guests have checked in will they be receiving programs, floorplans, a seating plan or information kits? Do you need a table for these to be displayed on with extras stored underneath? Will you need display easels for signs? Will you be using banners? Do you require telephones, outlets for computers or tables for media kits or take-home gifts? Can tables serve a dual purpose? For example, once all guests have arrived can the registration tables be used to display the take-home gifts? Not all facilities are created equal. Not all have sufficient quantities of tables and chairs and other equipment on hand. When you have to rent additional material you have to factor in the extra time and money.

REGISTRATION: Q&A

What is the ideal layout of the tables and chairs, the stage and the other elements for the needs of the event and the dimensions of the room?

Work from a blueprint or room layout chart, which you can usually obtain from the facility. There are reproduction houses that can shrink blueprints down to a more manageable size. Make sure that you make several copies—for yourself and your suppliers as you begin to sketch out proposed room layouts. Some venues, such as hotels and convention centres, can provide you with plans showing the actual configuration of the placement of the tables, staging and so on as you have laid it out. This will help you to see things more clearly. For example, you may want to have the stage moved to a more central location, or to set up three staging areas or hang a large screen with live video coverage so everyone can see what is happening on stage.

Avoid having the stage at one end of the room with the guests in the back unable to see.

Seeing everything laid out on paper will help you to decide which design will best meet your needs. As you start to look at your proposed requirements make sure that they will all fit into the space provided. What you ideally want and what will actually fit are not always the same thing. Think about how the area can best be laid out to avoid congestion. How many tables will be required, and will they be six- or eight-foot long or round? How many chairs will you need?

Welcome refreshments for arriving guests should be set up away from the registration area for two reasons—to avoid congestion and confusion and to draw guests into the area where you want them.

Are the tables, chairs and such provided free of charge?

Is there a maximum number that can be requested? Facilities do not have unlimited tables and chairs and not all provide them free. Make sure that you ask, and reserve what you need in advance. Make sure they are in good condition. You may have to arrange for extra tables to be brought in, which will add to your costs and involve extra work.

Q & A

Is draping and skirting provided for all the tables free of charge? (Draping covers the top, and skirting covers the legs).

Not all facilities provide draping and skirting—they may provide only draping, leaving the table legs exposed—and even when they do there may be an additional charge. If you are bringing in your own draping and skirting, the facility may have regulations on how it may be attached—no pins, nails or tape—and you could find yourself charged for damaged tables if the proper anchor clips were not used. You will need to find out the depth of the table top to make sure that the proper size clips are ordered. Do you need insurance coverage to protect you against damage at the venue—if a chair breaks, a display item is chipped or the silk wallpaper damaged?

Q & A

Do you have any choice in the colours for the drapes and skirts?

If the facility does provide draping and skirting find out what colours are available. Sometimes you will be able to use the hosting company's corporate colours or the event's theme colours to tie in at no additional charge. One company's colours were red, white and blue and the hotel had all three colours available in draping and skirting. It brightened the room and tied in perfectly with all of the print material and banners at no additional cost.

Q & A

Are the table covers in good condition?

Whether they are owned by the facility or rented, you want to ensure that the draping and skirting does not have any cigarette burns, stains or visible mending. Be very specific about this in the function sheet you send outlining your requests. As you are doing your site inspection take note of the condition of the table coverings that they are using. If you are not satisfied with the quality and condition, you may demand they be replaced or rent replacements from another establishment. This would have to be added to your budget. Another possibility is to place colourful over-lays or runners on top of the existing table draping as accent pieces. Overlays are contrasting pieces of material laid on top of the table cloth, and runners are strips of material placed on the table top. For example, with a black and gold theme you could have the draping black with a gold lamé runner over top.

Q & A

How many chairs will you require? Are they provided free, or is there a cost involved?

In your planning estimates carefully calculate how many chairs you will need. Are they standard banquet chairs, or does the facility offer only heavy bulky chairs that are difficult to move? This could be a problem at the registration table where you need to be able to move around quickly.

Again, don't assume that every facility has a surplus of chairs or that the ones they have would be acceptable to be out on display. A theatre, for example, may only have a few chairs for the manager and the ushers to use for their breaks. They may simply not have enough to set up a registration desk and the ones that they do have may be mismatched and in disrepair, particularly if you are using an older facility.

Q & A

How many easels or sign holders will you require?

Your signage is an important aspect of your event. How many signs or posters will you be having made up, and will they require easels or sign holders or will any be free-standing? Will any need to be hung? Will they be standard size or will there be a variety of sizes and shapes?

Q & A

Are sign holders provided, or is there a charge? Is there a maximum number that can be reserved? What about flip charts?

Find out in advance the number of sign holders and flip charts available. Will they have any other events going on simultaneously, and will they have sufficient on hand to handle everyone's needs? Are the holders provided free and, if not, what is the cost? Do you have to arrange to rent sign holders from an outside supplier? At registration and for meetings flip charts are commonly used. There can be rental charges for the flip charts, the pads of paper and the markers. Factor these into your budget.

Q & A

What condition are the sign holders in?

Are they all similar, or are they mismatched? Are they beat up and battered with missing pieces? Do they just need a little loving attention, or are they in such poor condition that it would be more efficient to bring in good ones? Do the dimensions of the holders match your signs?

Q & A

Will there be banners? Can they be displayed? What is the cost to have them installed and taken down?

It can be very expensive to have banners hung if it involves cherry pickers and three- or four-hour minimum labour charges to put the banners up and to take them down. Find out the cost in advance and budget for it. What are the dimensions of the banner, and where can it be hung? Will the banner require aircuts to let the wind blow through? Will they require grommets? Are these banners that you want to use again, or are they single-use throwaways? Will the banners be hung inside or outside? Do they need to be weather resistant? It will make a difference in the material you use.

Q & A

Does anything need to be attached to the walls, and will the facility allow you to do so?

One of the first questions to ask is whether anything can be attached to the walls. In five-star hotels, exclusive restaurants and private venues the answer very likely will be no, and you will need to come up with creative ways to display your material. At art exhibits paintings are often hung on chains that are attached to the ceiling or on moldings with the use of S-hooks, on large wooden easels or on pieces of furniture that lend themselves to the type of artwork and enhance the painting. Signs can be made to be free-standing, furniture or props can be rented, and walls can be completely draped, which would allow you to change the look of a venue and affix any items you needed displayed to the draping. For an artistic theme, for example, signs could be made up to fit into ornate picture frames—flea market finds that have been spray-painted—that could be propped up against a wall. Light refreshments could include an assortment of dips in different colours set out on artist's palates, with a can of used brushes, their tips painted in matching colours, set out beside them. Do something a little bit different that will draw people's eyes.

Q & A

Does the facility have extension cords, and is there a rental charge? Are there any restrictions on installing electrical cords?

These are not always available free of charge. You will need to know the length you will require, the number and how they can be best laid out. Tape the cords down to avoid having anyone trip over them. Try to get tape that blends in with the carpet and is not unsightly. Find out if the facility has any objections to tape or has other specific requirements. For insurance purposes, the venue may need to have their staff install and tape all electrical cords to ensure that it is done to their standards.

Q & A

What will be your communications requirements with regard to telephones, cell phones and walkie-talkies?

You may need to have telephone lines installed. Never depend solely on cell phones or walkie-talkies because you may find that they do not work inside the building. And even though you may have tested them previously, they may be affected by other events near yours. Always test your cell phones and walkie-talkies in all areas you will be using them. If possible, try a few different models to see which works best where, and make sure you have fully charged back-up batteries that will last from set-up to tear-down, often 24 hours or more. And know, just know, that if one person sees you using the cell phone there will soon be a line-up waiting to use it for "only a moment" or for "a quick call"—and there go your batteries! So, bring lots of spares or practice saying "no" a lot. Know where the public phones are, and have a supply of change on hand—it is less expensive than having guests use your cell phone. Tell them nicely that your batteries are low, but the public phones are just over there and if they don't have change, you do. (Unlike hotels with gift shops and check-out counters, other venues, such as convention centres, may not have areas where you can quickly obtain change.)

Q & A

What are the costs for telephone installation, daily charges, charge per local call, long distance, cell phones, walkie talkies and batteries? How much notice is required to install the telephones?

Most hotels and convention centres do charge for telephone installation. The telephones can be set up for local calls only, limiting the damage if guests manage to get hold of your phone. Most phones can be unplugged and stored out of sight if you need to be away from the table and can be stored in a secure room if you will be away for an extended period of time. Find out if there is a charge per local call and what that is, and—most important of all—find out where the closest pay phones are located to direct people to them.

Q & A

Will you have any special electrical requirements such as outlets and modems for computers?

List all areas where you will need access to electrical outlets. Know exactly where you are going to need them and how many you will need in total. On your floor plan be sure to make note of where electrical outlets are located. Include everything. Will the musicians playing at the reception require outlets? Will the photographer need one for lighting or other equipment? Will the bartender be serving frozen beverages, and, if so, how many blenders will be used? Will you be bringing in an ice cream machine, for example? Where will it be stationed? Is there an outlet there? How many outlets will each person need? Don't wait to find out on the day of the event that there are not enough outlets to go around.

Once you know all your electrical needs, the next thing you need to know is can the facility handle all your power requirements if everything is taking place at the same time? You may have all the electrical outlets you need to power up your event, but if the venue cannot handle the capacity you need to know it at the planning stages and not find out on the day of the event. Has the facility ever experienced blackouts? How have they handled them? Is there a back-up generator? If you are holding your event in a private home, do they have a supply of fuses, candles and flashlights on hand?

At one resort in the Caribbean, when they had an unexpected blackout, their staff sprang into action and within a matter of minutes had candles lit everywhere, and they had enough on hand to give some to guests making their own way back to their guest rooms. The staff was fully prepared, and they had a plan of action in place of what to do should such an event occur.

6
VENUE REQUIREMENTS

STAGING, AUDIO-VISUAL, LIGHTING

Before you can find the ideal location for your event, you need to consider all of your room requirements. For example, if you were planning for 1,000 guests and were considering a ballroom with a capacity of 1,000 for a sit-down dinner but wanted to have a rear-screen projection (which has a clean, professional look), you would need extra space. You need a minimum of 18 to 26 feet behind the screen for projection equipment, which means that you would lose seating for about 250 guests. In this case, you would have to cancel the rear-screen projection idea, reduce the number of guests or get a larger room. Do your plans include any front-of-room set-up by the audio-visual company? Do you need sound booths, translation booths or a dance floor? All these will take away more seating space. It is essential that you know all of your requirements before starting to check the availability of venues. What may seem initially to be the perfect fit may turn out to be inadequate once you take into account all of your needs. Go in with your wish list and know where you are willing to compromise and where you are not. Keep in mind the feeling you are going for. You want your event to have a vibrant energy, and you won't get that if the room is too small or when people are too close together, too hot and uncomfortable.

It is better to seat eight comfortably at tables that can accommodate 10 (10 at tables for 12) and have breathing room, than cramming everyone in elbow to elbow to save a few dollars. Make sure that tables are not too close together and that people can manoeuvre between them with ease. But you don't want the other extreme where a few tables are lost in a massive space. Once again, you will have lost the energy of the room. You want the room to be comfortably filled, vibrant and alive. In one way, you are better off with too much room rather than too little, because you can always reduce the size of the room with decorating tricks, but why spend unnecessary dollars if you do not have to?

Space Requirements

Type of Event	Space Required
Cocktail Reception	8 square feet per person
Cocktails with Food Stations	12–15 square feet per person
Seated Dinner	20 square feet per person
Dance Floor	3 square feet per person
	20 square feet per instrument for the band (room to move around)

Consider not only all your space requirements but also your time requirements as well. Before you proceed, consider how much time is required for staging, audio-visual and lighting to move in, set up, do sound checks, rehearsals and tear down. Will the musicians need a change room or a room for breaks? Do you need any storage space? Look at the total picture before you sign a contract and find that you have neither enough space nor time in which to work.

If you are considering holding your event at a hotel or convention centre find out who is booked in before you.

Questions to ask are:

- When are they tearing down and moving out?
- What are they tearing down and moving out?
- Could they run into any delays?
- When do you have access to the room?
- Who else is moving in and setting up the same day?
- Are there any conflicts with the timing or with competitors or competing events?
- What else is scheduled to take place at the same time you are holding your event? What time are they scheduled to begin and end?
- Will the other events be having any breaks that could cause noise, disruption or congestion to your event? You will need to adjust your timing accordingly.

If you are using only a section of the ballroom, schedule your site inspection at a time when the whole room is empty. Request that the airwall—the retractable wall that divides the ballroom into sections—be put into place. Have someone go into the adjoining section and test the soundproofing. In one five-star luxury hotel the test of the dividing wall revealed that you could hear every word that was being said in the next section of the ballroom. As a result, the contract stipulated that the adjacent section of ballroom remain unused during the event, ensuring no music, speeches or noise from the next room. This is not a common problem in many hotels, but the one time you don't take the time to check can't be undone.

Are there any noise factors to consider? In Las Vegas, in one of the theatres where a car launch was taking place the air-conditioning vents needed to be redirected so that the sound of the tinkling of the crystal chandelier did not distract from the speeches. Are you working with any obstacles? What about sight lines, ceiling heights, pillars or hanging chandeliers that will block views? Can they be raised or removed, and what will it cost? Can the lights be dimmed? Are there window drapes, and can they black out the room if an audio-visual presentation is taking place? Where are the fire exit doors? These have to remain accessible and cannot be blocked or locked. If they are covered with draping you must ensure that an exit sign is clearly posted and that there is a part in the draping that will allow easy access to the doors. How is the layout? Can staging be set up so that there are no bad seats in the house? Can TV monitors or large screens be hung in the room so that everyone, no matter how far away, can see what is taking place on stage or in the audience with live video coverage. Live video cameras project what is happening onto the TV monitors or screens that have been positioned around the room. This is what you see on award shows where the cameras pan the audience to show the winner make his or her way to the stage. Can lighting be hung? Can projectors be suspended from the ceiling? Are there hanging points in the ceiling from which this can be done? These are all things to consider when you are selecting your venue.

> **T I P**
>
> If you are doing live video coverage at your event, it is essential that those operating the cameras know where the VIP guests are seated. Prepare a seating chart and a detailed schedule of events occurring on stage so that the camera operators know when and where to focus their cameras.

Always work with a detailed floor plan. Have the venue provide a layout based on your needs. If they do not have a floor plan work with a copy of the original blueprints, reduced to a more manageable size.

Keep an eye on labour costs. Are there minimum charges, such as on a three-hour or a four-hour minimum call? A minimum call means that you will be charged for a minimum of three or four hours no matter how little they actually do work. Keep overtime in mind, too. Will anything be taking place over a holiday or on a Sunday when overtime might apply? Is the standard overtime time and a half or something else? All of these costs need to be factored into your budget.

STAGING, AUDIO-VISUAL, LIGHTING: Q&A

Q & A

Is the facility unionized or not? How will this affect your program? What additional costs should you budget for? If the facility is unionized, when do the contracts expire?

Always find out the impact the labour situation will have on all areas of your program. How does it affect costs? What regulations do you need to adhere to? Make sure that you have a meeting with union officials to discuss your program, so that you do not incur unexpected costs that should have been budgeted for in the beginning. Before you submit your costing or proposal take all labour charges into account. What would happen if you based your labour costs on regular hourly rates and did not take into account minimum call times, overtime costs and meals for the crew? It can make thousands and thousands of dollars difference to your bottom line.

Tell the union officials what you will be doing, and have them submit an estimate to you in writing including how many people and hours are involved and what it will all cost. Ensure that the AV company that you hire has a technical director who has worked with union facilities before and can monitor the schedule making sure that all breaks are taken and that everyone starts and leaves on time for four-hour calls. Otherwise you could be billed for extra overtime hours. Add a buffer of 10 per cent to your initial budget. For non-union facilities, review your program in depth with management, asking them to put in writing all additional charges that could apply.

Q & A

How high is the ceiling in the facility?

Ceiling height will make a big difference in all your staging, lighting and audio-visual calculations. For example, the recommended minimum ceiling height for rear-screen projection is 22 feet. You will need to set up a site inspection with your staging, lighting and AV suppliers to together decide the best layout for the room based on all your requirements.

Q & A

How are the sight lines?

Check out the room from all angles. Are there any obstacles such as support pillars or hanging chandeliers? Will all guests be able to see the stage or screen clearly? Can the chandeliers be raised or removed, and what will it cost? In many cases this can be done, but you need to know what labour costs are involved. How much time will it take, how many people will be involved and how much will it cost?

Q & A

Will you be having one stage or more?

You need to know where the staging will be set up and how many staging areas you will be having in total, as they can eat up a lot of space in your room and affect the total number of tables or guests you will be able to accommodate.

Q & A

How large or how high does the stage need to be?

What will be taking place on-stage? How many people does the stage need to accommodate? Will the musicians be set up on the main stage or off to one side? Is the height of the stage one that works well if guests are seated at tables or theatre style? It is possible to include elevated seating? Sections of the room can be built up and carpeted, transforming your ballroom into a nightclub or restaurant. You do not have to have everyone seated at one level, but bear in mind that elevated seating is not cheap, and the cost will depend on the room layout and any obstacles such as pillars that will have to be worked around. It also depends on the number of people attending. Amortized over a large number of guests the cost may be acceptable but not for a smaller group.

Q & A

Does the facility have a permanent stage?

Have them provide you with floor plans of the stage including the backstage area. Find out if there are any existing dressing rooms, an area to offload and move in equipment, how wide the aisles are and so on. Will the stage meet all of your needs and requirements?

Q & A

Does the facility have any special effects that you can use?

One of the nice things about doing a product launch in a Las Vegas theatre is being able to use existing props and staging to enhance your presentation. Revolving stages, elevators that will raise your product from below for a dramatic on-stage unveiling of your new product line—all the special effects are already there. You have to work around show times and rehearsals, but it can be done. Find out when the theatres will be dark (no shows going on) and see if a schedule can be worked around that. Restaurants and private clubs may also have special lighting effects, laser shows or bubble machines.

Q & A

What costs do you need to include in your budget for staging?

Will you need any special effects built into your staging, and will they be simple or elaborate? For example, will one of your stages need to revolve, or will you require special ramps or runways? If you are doing a fashion show, will you need to include pipe and draping behind the staging or off to one side to provide change areas for the models? Take the time to think of all the elements that need to be included in your budget.

Q & A

Will there be decor (props, greenery) on-stage?

Will your stage sets be fairly simple, or will they rival those seen on television award shows? How much or how little will be included? How will it work with what will be taking place on-stage? If you are not working with a full production house that can provide both the staging and decor you will need to bring all your suppliers together to best determine your staging needs.

Q & A

Will the stage area require draping?

What will be behind the stage? What will you need as a backdrop? Will it be simply the existing back wall, the more polished look that draping provides or an intricate stage setting? All of these items need to be considered so that you can accurately project your costs.

Q & A

Will there be audio-visual presentations?

If you are including audio-visual, will it be rear-screen or front-screen projection? How many screens do you envision? Does the room have the space for rear-screen projection?

Q & A

Will the presentation be in more than one language?

Will translation booths need to be factored into both the budget and the room layout? If so, you will need to think about where the booths will go and also about an area where the headsets can be distributed. This can be either inside or just directly outside the meeting room. Will you need to provide bilingual (or multilingual) staff to help hand out the headsets and explain how they work? Will you need to ensure that bilingual staff are available throughout the program? Make sure that you count the number of headsets received and have adequate numbers of staff to collect them at the end of the meeting before guests leave the room. You could have guests sign for the headsets but that could cause congestion. Take care in the location of the sign-out table to make sure that it does not block the entrances. Have you included the costs to have the translator there for rehearsals?

Q & A

Will there be any front-of-room set-up required by the audio-visual company?

Find out the needs of your audio-visual company. Do they have equipment, such as teleprompters or live video cameras, that they need to position on or in front of the stage?

Q & A

How much rehearsal time will be required?

Find out when rehearsal time will be needed and for how long. Make sure that rehearsal space has been requested, is available and the time has been blocked off for you. Dancers may need to practice their routines, speakers recite their speeches and video presentations will require review. Everything that will be happening on stage needs to be finely choreographed like any live theatrical stage production. Find out what additional charges for such things as room rental, labour and crew meals will have to be included in your budget.

Q & A

Are there additional charges for cleaning the room?

Once everything is set up you may need to have the room thoroughly vacuumed before the actual event. Some venues will supply people and equipment at no additional cost, others will not. For example, if you were setting up a display in an exhibit hall at a convention centre, you might need to book this service in advance, and there would be a cost involved. Check to see if this needs to be scheduled, and if there will be any additional charges.

Q & A

What sort of access will there be on and off the stage?

How will all those who are involved in the program be getting up onto the stage? Will you need to have stairs leading up from the audience to the stage, or will access be only from backstage? Will it be one or the other or both?

Q & A

Is there an additional cost to rent the stairs, and are there any applicable labour charges?

If you are using an existing stage, the facility may have stairs that you can use at no charge, but if you have a custom-designed stage the cost for the stairs needs to be included in your staging budget.

Q & A

Are the stairs lit?

Strip lighting that runs across the edge of each step can be installed to make each individual stair more visible. If the room is to be in darkness when people are getting up on stage, you may wish to consider adding this type of lighting, or have the stair lit from the sides.

Q & A

Will a ramp or lift be required for wheelchair access to the stage from the audience?

Ramp requirements need to be specific because ramps take a fair amount of space and will affect the layout of the room. Find out how much space will be needed. Some facilities have lifts to raise the wheelchairs onto the stage. When you are positioning the lift you need to keep in mind what else will be on stage and that sufficient room is available to manoeuvre. What additional costs are involved in a lift or ramp?

Q & A

How much time will be required to move in and set up the staging and how much time to tear down and move out?

You need to know how much time is involved in these activities to see how all elements will interact and so you can begin to lay out your initial schedule of events based on the time requirements of all your suppliers. You need to ensure that you have allowed sufficient time for move in. Depending on how elaborate your set is, you could require anywhere from a few hours to two days or more. Then you need to add to this the time you will require for rehearsals and other preparations. If you need more time for set-up expect to pay more for site rental and labour, and factor these into your budget. Doing something as elaborate as a large car launch can require over a week of set-up and rehearsal time.

Q & A

Are there any special requirements or equipment needed for the offloading of material and the set-up of the stage?

Make sure that everything is done to facilitate the move-in, which needs to be done as efficiently as possible with all necessary equipment ready, passageways all cleared and the room empty and ready for the set-up to begin. Avoid any delays that could result in additional costs. For example, make sure that the facility is not just beginning to move tables and chairs out of the way as your set-up crews arrive. Have staff on hand well in advance of the move-in to ensure that preparations are well under way.

Q & A

Have crew meals and breaks during set-up, rehearsals, the event day and tear-down been included in your budget? Have you made provisions to have this billed to the master account? Do you need to have the breaks set up in a separate room, or will they be set up in the room? What other suppliers could be setting up in the room at this time. And will it interfere with their set-up?

Find out what you are responsible for. Do you have to pay the crew for meals and meal time when they are setting up? Will meals for the crew be a separate charge that needs to be budgeted for, or has it been included in the supplier's written estimate to you? In some cases you do not have to pay for this. Find out. Will the crew need a separate room for meals and breaks? If so, has the space been reserved, and is it located close to the set-up area? Will you, as the event planner, need to make the arrangements to book this space, or will your contracted supplier be handling this? Will you be charged for that extra room rental? Who will be making the meal arrangements for the stage crew—you or your supplier? You can work with the facility to have them create menus that will fall within your budget guidelines. Do you need to set up meals for your own staff as well? Will you require additional space for them? If you are using different suppliers, you will need to account for meal and break time for all suppliers. Schedules could differ, for example, between the staging crew and lighting crew. Find out who will be responsible for making all arrangements and overseeing this area.

Q & A

How much time will be required to move in and set up audio-visual requirements? How much time to tear down?

If you are working with two different suppliers, one that is handling the staging and another the audio-visual, you need to make each aware of the other's schedule and time lines so there are no areas of conflict. Ideally, the company that is designing the staging that will also be handling your audio-visual set-up, lighting and stage-decor. Look for companies that are full production houses that can handle all of your needs. However, compare the costs for full production houses versus individual contractors. You may need just a simple stage but an audio-visual and light show that has the intensity of a rock concert. Or you may need an elaborate stage with simple audio-visual and lighting. Find out if the production house owns their own equipment or will rent it based on your requirements. You want to make sure that you have access to what best fits your needs and not what is simply on hand.

Q & A

Are there any special requirements or equipment needed for the offloading of material and the set-up of audio-visual equipment?

Are there any arrangements that need to be made before the AV crew arrives? For example, do any chandeliers need to be removed or air vents turned off to reduce excess noise? Have you made sure that everything is ready to make the move in as easy as possible? What do you need to have for the AV crew so that they can maximize the time available to them? You do not want crew sitting around waiting for rooms or passageways to be cleared. You need to be on-site prior to their arrival to ensure that all has been prepared for their arrival.

Q & A

What additional costs should you budget for?

Find out any and all additional charges that could apply. For example, could charges for labour or power be posted to the master account based on actual usage, or are they firm? Include estimates in your budget from their past events, and build in a 10 per cent buffer. It is better to come in under budget than over. Make sure that you receive written estimates of costs.

Q & A

How much time will be required to move in and set up lighting and to tear down?

Ideally you will have a single contractor for staging, audio-visual and lighting but, if not, you need to work with each one to determine who needs to be in first and what needs to be completed before the next step can begin. Find out what can be done simultaneously.

Q & A

Are there any special requirements or equipment needed for the offloading of material and the set-up of lighting equipment?

Each area of staging, audio-visual and lighting has its own specific requirements and needs. Make sure you review each with the particular supplier so that all is prepared. Will one cherry picker be enough, or will two need to be brought in? Are there any areas of overlap?

Q & A

Have crew meals and breaks for lighting set-up, rehearsals, day of the event and tear-down been included in their budget to you?

Again, as with staging and audio-visual, make sure that you have covered this area with them.

> **T**
> **I**
> **P**
>
> For any changes to the costs for staging, audio-visual or lighting make sure that a revised written estimate is submitted and that all parties approve each change and cost. Never give or receive approval verbally. It can turn out to be a very costly mistake—remember the person who gave their verbal approval may not be there the next day, week, month or next year.

ROOM REQUIREMENTS: Q&A

Q
&
A

Is the room carpeted? Will it require carpeting? What are other options?

Do not assume that all function space in all hotels and convention centres is carpeted, because this is not always the case. Check when you are enquiring about space. Carpeting can be rented, but you need to know in advance how this could affect your budget—it is not cheap. Custom carpets can be made for very special theme parties to tie in with the decor. For example, one car launch considered having the ballroom carpet transformed into a highway (black carpeting with highway markings on it) and having their new cars displayed in various scenes you would find along the highway. For a beach theme party in a production studio or even a ballroom, plastic can be laid down over existing carpeting and covered in sand.

Q
&
A

Will you be having a dance floor?

If you plan on having a dance floor how large does it need to be? How many does it need to accommodate? Will everyone be up dancing at once or just about half at a time? Are your guests traditionally a dancing crowd? If it is a corporate function and spouses are not invited, a dance floor may not be appropriate. Give thought to how much space you will need to accommodate dancing. Allow three square feet per person for the dance floor and 20 square feet per instrument for the band, who move around more than the dancers.

For very special events or theme parties custom-designed dance floors are available. You can have them hand painted to match the motif and pick up on the decor. For instance, for a wedding you could have the couple's initials displayed or the floor could be made into a giant board game with the participants becoming the playing pieces. It could even be a colourful, plastic uplit floor for a disco theme party. You are limited only by imagination and budget.

Q & A

Does the facility you are considering have a permanent dance floor?

Don't assume just because you don't see it that it isn't there. Sometimes a built-in dance floor is hidden under a section of carpeting that can be lifted. Check to see how many the floor will accommodate and what it looks like. Is it in good condition?

Q & A

Is there a rental charge for the dance floor and a labour charge for installation and tear-down?

Find out if any charges will apply. If the dance floor needs to be installed, you need to coordinate the timing with the installation of the staging, audio-visual and lighting. You also need to include any rental and labour charges in your budget.

Q & A

Will you be setting up any major displays such as a car (which is sometimes done at fund-raisers) in the room? Is there a clear passageway from the loading docks to the display area for large items?

Make sure that you work with the floor plans to avoid any areas of congestion. Are you leaving a clear path for the waiters? Will they be able to easily make their way around any items on display? Check the width and the height of all passageways. Will all display items be able to fit comfortably through, and are they free of clutter?

Q & A

Are the ballroom doors wide enough to accommodate large items such as a car?

If you run into any areas of difficulty here, ballroom doors can be removed, but there is usually a labour charge involved. Find out how much that would be, how long it will take and any other constraints. To move larger items into place you may sometimes need to take them through sections of the ballroom that you may not be using for your event. You need to know when these areas will be available, and you need to find out when it is best to have large items moved in so that they will not be in the way of the staging, audio-visual and lighting set-up.

Q & A

Will the floor hold the weight of something as heavy as a car?

Ask the management if the floor will take the weight. A hotel with an orchestra pit by the permanent stage that has been covered over could present a problem. The area may not stand the weight of a car on it. Find out if there are any areas such as this that you need to be concerned about.

Q & A

What are the fire and safety regulations regarding room layout?

Where are the fire exit doors? Are they clearly accessible? Are they hidden by pipe and draping? If so, clearly marked exit signs will need to be posted. Make sure that you adhere to all fire and safety regulations or you may be shut down by the authorities or have problems getting insurance.

Q & A

Will airwalls be in place? Will you need them opened at any point?

At times you may be holding one part of your event in one section of the room and a second in another room. If these areas are adjacent, you need to know if the airwalls—room dividers—are manual or automatic and, if you are having them opened to allow your guests to move easily from one area to the next, how long does it take to open and close them? Who will be operating the walls—can you or your staff do it, or must it be done by facility staff? Are there union rules involved? Discuss this with the account manager who has been assigned to handle your booking.

Q & A

Are you considering any special effects?

Are there any restrictions on indoor fireworks, lasers, dry ice or other special effects? Do any items need to be fire-proofed? What insurance do you need? Will all of the proposed items fall under the fire and safety rulings? Will any permits be required? Speak to management at the facility, the local fire marshal and the company that will be handling the special effects. Do not accept just one opinion. Do your homework and know all that has been attended to.

Q & A

What are the needs of your entertainment?

Are the acoustics in the room good? What are the entertainers' requirements with regard to electrical outlets, rehearsal time, sound checks, dressing rooms, rooms for meals and breaks? Make sure that space is set aside to accommodate their needs, and that you have included all these costs in your budget.

Q & A

How will the room be set up?

Will food be passed or served at buffets, food stations or plated? Will people be standing or sitting? Will there be scattered seating? Will the events take place in one room or several? Will there be smoking or not? Will you set aside a separate smoking area? Are cigar rooms permitted? Are the room and the facilities as a whole wheelchair accessible?

Q & A

Is there anything scheduled to take place at the same time you are holding your event?

What other events are taking place at the same as your event? What time are they scheduled to begin and end? Will they be having any breaks that could cause noise, disruption or congestion for your event? Where will these other events be held? Will their move-in and tear-down be going on while your event is in progress? You don't need hammering and sawing as a background for your presentation, or someone else's coffee break stationed right outside your doors or worse, both of you breaking at the exact same time. This could cause congestion and long line-ups in nearby washrooms. Will anyone else be moving in and setting up at the same time as you are? Will you both require access to the freight elevators and other equipment the facility may have? Have you checked to see how sound-proof the rooms are? Are there any competing events, or are any of your competitors holding events at the same time? Ask management to keep you informed.

At one new product launch, competitors who were staying at the same hotel tried to sneak a peak at the new product that was being revealed in the hotel ballroom. But the ballroom doors had been secured while set-up was going on and security had been posted by the main doors ensuring only authorized personnel with security passes got in.

7
WHO'S IT ALL FOR?

THE GUEST LIST

Who is your targeted audience? Who will make up your guest list? Who you are inviting, and the reasons why you are choosing to invite them can be as varied as the number of events being held. You want to ensure that the "right" people are there and that it is just not a roomful of people. If you send an invitation to a specific person, make sure that you state on the invitation whether it is transferable. In some cases it may be acceptable to have someone else come in the place of your invitee, but in other cases you may have a limited number of spots and you want to prioritize your guests. Therefore, those on Guest List A who cannot attend will be replaced by the next person on your list—Guest List B. In this case you don't really want someone you don't even know coming in place of the original invitee.

Who needs to be there? If it is an event where you are seeking media attention, how many journalists are you inviting? Are government officials being asked? Corporate staff or clients? Suppliers? What kind of energy will be generated if you mix different groups? For example, if a hotel chain does a client appreciation event, it may or may not be appropriate to bring potential corporate clients together with sales staff from competing companies. The potential corporate clients could end up feeling like they have been thrown into a feeding frenzy as sales executives vie for their attention, and sales executives may never leave their side, hoping to keep their competitors at bay. Instead, the hotel could do two different events—one for the potential client and one for the sales executives. Or, if it wanted to showcase its talents, the hotel could do one splashy event for all. What is key is that the hotel know how the guests could interact with one another and make their decision on who to invite based on the objectives of the proposed event.

How Many?

Before you can begin to look for space for your event you need to know the number of guests that will be attending and some ideas of what your event will include.

You need to take into consideration all of your requirements:

- Will you need overnight accommodation? For how many?
- Will the number of rooms be based on single or double occupancy?
- Will you require any suites for VIPs?
- If it is a day event, will you need any accommodation for guests to change in or use for private meetings?
- Will you require any early or late checkouts?
- How many participants will your meeting room need to hold?
- What room set-up will are you considering? Will it be theatre style, rounds of eight, U-shaped, a hollow square? Will it have display areas? How will the food be presented? Will you need to allow space to set up buffet tables or food stations?
- Will you be having rear-screen projection, a stage or translation booths?
- Will you be requiring breakout rooms where guests attending meetings in the main room may break into smaller meetings? For how many? For how long? What will be the room set-up in each? Will any audio-visual equipment be involved?

- Will you be requiring separate rooms for meals or coffee breaks? How many will be attending? Will they be stand-up or sit-down?

- Will you require any rooms or offices for your staff to work from?

- Will you require a private area for set-up? How many people does it need to accommodate?

- What sort of event will you be having? For example, will you be having a silent auction? How many tables will you be require?

- Will your reception be stand-up with some scattered seating? Does it need to be held in a separate area?

- Will your dinner be plated—served at the table—or a stand-up buffet?

- If your dinner is sit-down, will the tables be round seating eight or 10 or perhaps rectangles?

- Will you require a stage, room for a dance band or a dance floor?

Guest profile: Who?

- What are the age demographics?

- Will guests be coming as couples or singles? Is this a corporate event without spouses? (If so, dancing would probably not be appropriate.)

- Are the corporate sponsors attending a funding-raising gala purchasing individual tickets, tables of 10 or tickets for family and friends? Who will make up your guest list—will it be corporate only, social—family and friends—or mixed?

- Will children or teenagers be attending? Will they be accompanied by adults or not? Keep in mind the legal drinking age and the liability of the host to check ID.

- How will guests be handling transportation? Will they all be arriving on their own, by private car or limo, or will accessibility to public transportation need to be a consideration?

For a multimedia event by a major corporate sponsor for 3,000 guests aged 19 to 24, having accessible public transportation was a key factor in venue selection.

Guest List Checklist

List Development   6 Months Before Event

Allow minimum of 8 weeks for the preparation of the guest list to ensure that addresses are current and have been cross-referenced.

Guest List A

Keep in mind maximum room capacity set by fire regulations.
Your event can be closed down if you ignore fire regulations on capacity, fire exits, bathrooms and signage. There are ways of increasing capacity such as outdoor tents, bringing in additional bathroom facilities and the like.

Watch timing of mail delivery and RSVP date.
Will guests be out of the country for school breaks, or will holidays such as Christmas, New Year's, Passover or Easter interfere with the success of your event?

Guest List B

Back-up to replace guests from Guest List A who are unable to attend.
Again, pay attention timing of invitations for mailing and RSVP date.

INVITATIONS

If your event is taking place during a busy social season you may wish to consider sending a save-the-date teaser card. If the event is being held out of country, send post cards showing the location with a printed message saying that you are looking forward to meeting with them here, the date of the event and other pertinent information. Another idea is a letter or teaser invitation, such as a snow scraper with the message "Don't be left out in the cold" sent to participants of an incentive program to spur their sales on. These should include details such as date and time. Location and dress can follow at a later date. This works well for all special events including meetings, conferences, conventions and incentives. It builds a "buzz" of anticipation around your event.

If you state in your save-the-date card or letter that invitations will be forthcoming by a certain date make certain that they are. It will demonstrate to others how your company does business—you deliver on time. When you receive an invitation a month later than the date stated in the save-the-date letter, it demonstrates a lack of professionalism. If the message is going out under your president's signature make sure that you deliver what it says.

If security passes—visual event ID guests wear at celebrity events—or tickets to the actual event are being mailed out once the invitation has been received and the RSVP called in, make sure that you have allowed sufficient time for the guest to receive them. At some events it is necessary to show your security pass, invitation or ticket to the event to gain admittance, and while there will be an official guest list at the front door—should any guests forget to bring theirs—there will be less congestion and the line-ups will move faster if all guests have received theirs in time.

In order to call in food and beverage guarantees and to do a revised costing based on accurate numbers, you must request that your guests RSVP by a specific date and have staff follow up with phone calls to confirm attendance. The phone follow-up is a good time to confirm any name or address changes.

When placing your printing order allow for one invitation per couple and one place card and menu per person. Make sure that you order more than you need and that you have allowed adequate time for printing. For some reason, printers always seem to want a minimum of four weeks. Of course, you will have checked with them to see if they can handle your order and deliver the appropriate quality and quantity of items on time. Make sure that you have all camera-ready artwork ready on time and know the exact Pantone colour to be used for company logos. Have your envelopes printed first so that way you can begin to address them and, if you can afford it, hire a calligrapher. People generally open hand-written invitations first, making them are much more effective than those printed on labels or envelopes.

Whether you are mailing the invitations yourself or using a mail house, always send one to yourself to gauge if you are going to run into any problems. When it does arrive, check to see when it actually went out. If you contracted a mailhouse to have the invitations mailed by a specific date you will need proof when you discuss the matter with them. If the invitation does not arrive by a certain date, you will need to start phoning guests to see if they have received theirs. There could be a problem with delivery, or they could still be sitting on someone's desk. If guests receive their invitation just a couple of days before an event, it makes it difficult to change established plans and could result in a very poor turnout. Not only will it have the effect of making your guests feel as though they were on Guest List Z, it also makes your job planning the event nearly impossible.

- Check mail delivery schedules for first class mail. What are the minimum and maximum number of days for your area? Keep in mind that these times can change without notice and the time of year could have an impact as well. If your invitation is going out over the holiday season, there could be delays. Check with your local post office as you start to plan your event. Check both local and international delivery schedules if applicable.

- Check postage rates for first class mail. Out-of-country mail has a different rate than local. Make sure that mail is separated and the correct postage applied. Oversized and odd-shaped envelopes will require additional postage. It is always best to bring a sample to the local post office to ensure the invitation does not exceed the standard size or weight.

- Check mail delivery schedules for third-class mail. What are the minimum and maximum number of days, and what are the postal rates?

Check both local and international delivery schedules if applicable. Adjust time lines accordingly to accommodate third-class mail delivery schedule if you decide to use this route. You usually have to send a minimum number of pieces to be eligible for third-class mail. Again, out-of-country and oversized, heavy and odd-shaped envelopes will require extra postage. Again, it is always best to bring a sample to the local post office to make sure the invitation does not exceed size or weight standards.

> **T**
> **I**
> **P**
> Never use third-class mail for corporate events. Third-class mail is generally associated with bulk or "junk" mail and is not appropriate for elegant events.

Invitation Checklist

Invitation Design   6 Months Before Event

Issues to Decide:
• Maximum number of guests to attend per invitation.

Things to be Included on the Invitation:
• Number of Guests Invited
• Event Name
• Event Description
• Date
• Time (Beginning/Ending/Schedule of Events)
• Venue
• Directions
• Parking Details
• Dress Code
• RSVP Address, Telephone and Fax Number
• Ticket Order Form (if applicable)
• Return Reply Envelope (optional)

Details to Designer   16 Weeks Prior to Event

• Make sure you have advised designers of your proposed time lines well in advance so they are prepared to handle your order.
• Check to see when they and printers will be closed for holidays.
• Will they require additional time for special orders such as custom paper?
• What will they require from you? Will they want camera-ready artwork? Decide what their needs are and incorporate them into your Critical Path so that you will have everything available to them on time.

Mail House Booked   16 Weeks Prior to Event

• Make sure you have advised mail house of your proposed time lines well in advance so they are prepared to handle your order.
• You may wish to handle mailing in-house for more hands-on control.

First Review of Invitation Design   14 Weeks Prior to Event

Second Review of Invitation Design   13 Weeks Prior to Event
  (if required)

Invitations to Printer   12 Weeks Prior to Event

Envelopes to Mail House   10 Weeks Prior to Event

• Envelopes to be addressed, stuffed and stamped. Allow a minimum of one week for processing. Check their recommended time lines, which could change based on whatever else they may be handling over the same time period.

Invitations Mailed to Guest List A   7 Weeks Prior to Event

• This will vary depending on your area's delivery schedule and where invitations are being sent. A teaser could be sent out earlier letting guests know to hold the event date open, with the invitation to follow.

RSVP Cut-Off for Guest List A   5 Weeks Prior to Event

VIP Guest Passes Mailed to   5 Weeks Prior to Event
  Guest List A

(If applicable—guest passes are generally used as a visible means of security control, and they can be worn around the neck, clipped onto purses or belts or worn around the wrist. At some events there can be two types of guest security passes—one designated "all access" and others that have a more limited access to VIP rooms etc.)

Invitations Mailed to Guest List B   5 Weeks Prior to Event

RSVP Cut-Off for Guest List B   3 Weeks Prior to Event

VIP Guest Passes Mailed to   3 Weeks Prior to Event
  Guest List B (if applicable)

These time lines are based on everything being received and completed on time. Dates should be backed up at least one week if
you have any concerns about artwork being received on time,
imputing of addresses, delivery schedules and such. What you
least expect may happen—mail strikes, computer breakdown—so,
whenever you can, prepare as far ahead as possible.

Invitation Overview

Guest List Development	6 Months Before Event
Invitation Design	6 Months Before Event
Details to Designer	16 Weeks Prior to Event
Mail House Booked	16 Weeks Prior to Event
First Review of Invitation Design	14 Weeks Prior to Event
Second Review of Invitation Design (if required)	13 Weeks Prior to Event
Invitations to Printer	12 Weeks Prior to Event
Envelopes to Mail House	10 Weeks Prior to Event
Invitations Mailed to Guest List A	7 Weeks Prior to Event
VIP Guest Passes Mailed to Guest List A (if applicable)	5 Weeks Prior to Event
Invitations Mailed to Guest List B	5 Weeks Prior to Event
RSVP Cut-Off for Guest List B	3 Weeks Prior to Event
VIP Guest Passes Mailed to Guest List B (if applicable)	3 Weeks Prior to Event

* Depending on local delivery and busy holiday schedules. Keep in
mind that over the holiday season, school breaks, and summer
vacations guests could be out of town and you schedule accordingly
to ensure that Guest List A have sufficient time to respond.

MEDIA

If you are inviting media to your event, you need to look at how and when they will attend. Will they be treated as invited guests? If so, you need to factor them into your food and beverage count. Are you thinking of doing a separate press conference? What are their requirements? It is in your best interest to find out what they need and to do everything possible to make sure that those needs are met. They may need an area to park their film crew's truck, places to run their cables or have a media feed that they can plug into. They could be doing live coverage and need to have a specific interview at a designated time. Take the time to ask what they need—even better, anticipate what they need.

Media people are very busy. Respect their time and never forget what they contribute to the successful coverage of your event. Look for ways you can work together so that both of you come out ahead. They may need access to a room where they can conduct private interviews or have people pose for pictures. It is important to remember that media have numerous events to choose from and if you want them to consider your invitation, you will have to make the experience pleasurable. Work with them. Together you are building working relationships. One thing to always bear in mind though is that they can be called away on a breaking hard news story.

MEDIA: Q&A

Will media coverage be a part of your event?

Decide when and where media will be included in your event. You may choose to hold a press conference beforehand or set up separate media interviews. Consider where these will be best held and if you will need a separate room.

Q & A

Will media be at your event as invited guests?

Have you included them in your food and beverage count? If you are having a cocktail reception followed by dinner, will they be seated at a separate press table or with your guests? At one fund-raiser where media were invited, tables were provided for them but no food. Needless to say, they were not pleased. Imagine the coverage that fund-raiser got, not to mention future relations between the media and the charity and the event planning committee. If you have invited media to be there as guests, treat them as such. If they are invited only to cover a certain segment, be very clear about that in your invitation, so that they know what to expect. If, for security reasons, media are admitted only one at a time to meet key celebrities, a separate media room (with ample refreshments) should be set up for them.

Q & A

Are there any special requirements for media that need to be included such as a separate media room, media feeds or parking for their equipment trucks?

Find out when the media are coming and what they are bringing. What would they ideally like to see happen? What would make their job easier for them? Don't be caught off guard. You don't want a media news team showing up to go live with no news to report. It is a waste of everyone's time if media arrive too far ahead of the celebrities and before the event has truly begun. It is your job to tell the media the best time for them to show up so that the energy of the room comes across on the screen or in pictures. On the hand, keep media deadlines in mind when planning your schedules. For example, if you want coverage of your president's speech on the 11 p.m. news, you have to give the media cameras and editors enough time. To maximize your coverage, you need to work with media wherever possible. That way you both end up winning, and they will remember you at your next event.

Q & A

What is the purpose of press kits?

What needs to be included in the press kits? What can you include that will make it easier for media to report their stories? What do you want to stress? Do media need biographies of any of the attendees or background information on the event or its sponsors? How many kits will you need? Have you added the cost for these into your budget? Who is preparing them? Where will you be handing them out? Will you be setting up a separate registration table for media so that they can sign in? That way you see who has arrived and assign representatives to show them important areas and introduce them to key people. Also, you can keep track of media no-shows and follow up with a phone call and mail them a press kit.

CHILDREN AT YOUR EVENT

If children will be attending your event there are some wonderful properties that seem to be designed just for them. Many cruise ships and hotels have excellent supervised activities. Meals can be arranged at separate times and locations, away from the adults, and experienced babysitters can be arranged. Separate theme parties can be held for adults and children. There are a number of activities for children, such as private excursions, or they can receive expert sports instruction—private beach Olympics can be geared to the children's ages and abilities.

Menus are designed to delight young palates, with small portions that are easily manageable and fun being the order of the day. Entertainment can include acrobats, costumed characters or clowns, face painters, jugglers, magicians, puppet shows, or storytellers.

Sample theme parties that can be set up include:

• Carnival with games and prizes for all. Photo booths and sticker machines (each child's face is put on stickers) can also be rented. Also available are machines for popcorn, candyfloss, candy apples, waffles, snow cones, hot dogs, nachos, pretzels, donuts, ice cream and candy.

- Miniature golf with lessons from the "pros." Older children can actually have lessons on the greens either out on a mini golf course or with simulated golf holes rented and set up at your venue.

- Arcade games can include virtual reality and big screen interactive videos, driving simulators, ski and snowboard simulators, wave runners, foosball, air hockey, and skill cranes filled with stuffed animals of your choice.

- Pool tables with "pool sharks" on hand to teach older children trick shots. (This can also be used for an adult cocktail party theme.) Pool tables can be rented and set up at the venue of your choice.

- Giant inflatables that can include the sticky Olympics (with Velcro body suits and Velcro obstacles), mega mountains to climb, bungee runs, sports games and giant slides and obstacle courses.

If children are taking part in active games, it is advisable to have the parents give their written permission. You will need to know if there are any medical problems such as food allergies, and have professional staff on hand in sufficient numbers to provide proper care. Security is also important. You want to make sure that children are in a safe, protected area. You can also arrange security ID. Make sure that children are accompanied to the bathroom by staff of the same sex so that they can assist them if needed. Name tags on sweaters and jackets do not work as children are prone to take them off and they also allows strangers to call them by name. A wrist band name ID might be a better solution. Make sure that you know how to contact the parents in case of an emergency. Remember, children and parents do not necessarily have the same last names. Make sure you have all pertinent information.

8

FOOD
AND BEVERAGE

Whether your event is a stand-up reception or a formal sit-down dinner, do not feel that you are limited to the menus you are offered. Most hotels, restaurants and caters are willing to work with you to come up with a creative menu that will work within your budget. At one event the dessert was ice cream fruits—ice cream in the shape, colour and flavour of various fruits. Guests left talking about it, and many called the next day enquiring about them. The actual cost of the ice cream fruits was minimal, but the effect was maximum. That is the sort of inspired creativity you are looking for. For example, a well-known caterer does a wonderful fortune cookie cake that contains customized messages. Look for what is different. What can you do that shows flair, creativity, imagination and style?

Give thought to the type of food you will be serving. Remember to always include vegetarian selections. If you are doing a stand-up reception with hot and cold hors d'oeuvres passed around, make sure that they are bite-size and can be handled easily—no dripping sauces or bones. Will people be eating them holding just a napkin, or will there be plates? Does the facility have enough plates for several courses, or will there be delays as they are cleaned and brought back out again? The same applies to glasses for specialty drinks. Does the venue have sufficient glasses on hand or do they have to be brought in and budgeted for? You need to ensure that you ask the questions and are comfortable with the answers. Advertising a martini bar as part of your event loses something in the presentation if you find out the day before your event that the facility does not have martini glasses in stock. You could be scrambling to find rentals at the last minute and paying premium prices. That will play havoc with your budget projections as well.

You will have to tell the caterers exactly how many dinners to prepare in advance. This is known as a food guarantee and it can be a tricky business. If you guarantee 100 dinners and only 50 people actually show up you will have 50 very expensive doggie bags—you will have to pay for all 100 meals. Late RSVPs and no-shows make the guarantee a juggling act. In addition to no-shows you might suffer the opposite problem—unexpected guests. That is where "overage" comes into play. With overage you still have to guarantee a certain number of meals, but the facility will prepare extras in case of last-minute changes. You may be able to cut your guarantee by 5 to 10 per cent less than your anticipated numbers. You are charged on the actual numbers, but should you have last-minute cancellations or no-shows, you may be able to save some dollars.

Decide who are included as guests and need to be included in the food guarantee. Are staff, staging and lighting crew, entertainment, photographers, and media including as invited guests, or will separate arrangements need to be made? If you are feeding them, make sure you have included these costs in your projected budget as well.

Perhaps the first rule of special events is to always have enough bartenders. And, if so, the second rule is to have enough liquor. It is embarrassing to run out. And consider carefully where your bars are placed. You want to avoid line-ups and congestion. Are you being charged per drink, or can a flat rate be worked out? Do you need to obtain any special permits to have a bar or to extend the hours? Do you need to enclose the area where drinks can be served? Do you need to limit the type of drinks served—such as shooters or expensive brandies and wines—when the host is picking up the tab? Guests can quickly become intoxicated drinking shooters, particularly when contests start up, and your bar bill can quickly go through the roof. Rare brandies, ice wines and champagne are expensive and can have a major impact on your budget if everyone decides to sample them. Give precise instructions to the bartenders and waiters about how you want them to handle requests for such items. You may decide guests will be told that they can have champagnes or specialty items, but they have to pay for it themselves. Alternatively, you may decide that while it is not being promoted or offered openly, if a guest makes a specific request it is OK to fulfil it. If wine is included with the dinner, do you want the wine poured by the waiters or the bottles left on the table? Is the quantity unlimited, or is there a set number of bottles per table? How are requests for additional wine above the limit to be handled?

Include a provision for tipping the staff in your budget. Most facilities will calculate the gratuities based on a specific percentage and bill your master account. That percentage varies from venue to venue, so you need to ask in every case. In some areas they also apply a government tax on the amount being tipped. That may not seem like an important consideration, but these pennies can add up. If this applies include it in your budget calculations. Don't assume taxes on food and beverage are one and the same. If you are bringing any items into the facilities find out what the "corkage" charges are. This charge applies if you are providing your own wine or liquor—at fund-raisers a sponsor who is a wine maker may donate the wine for the event, and the facility will charge a corkage fee. If you have an open bar but want to maintain some control, ask the beverage manager to let you know when you have reached the halfway point of your estimated budget so you can decide whether or not to slow service down.

With both food and bar service make sure that tear-down does not begin until staff has received clearance to do so from you. You may have to be flexible. With everything in full swing, guests may not want the party to end, and the client may decide to extend things. Find out about overtime charges—what would apply if you decided to extend the party? Make sure that all staff are aware in advance that this could be a possibility.

In Jamaica on an incentive program, the event planners were sitting in the dining room discussing the schedule and how important it is to be at hand during set-up; you never know what can happen and when you will be needed to step in and make major decisions that could affect the success of your event. At that moment kitchen staff came running to report a fire in the hotel's oven. The gala dinner was up in flames. The fire was quickly put out, but in the process the meat had been doused with fire extinguisher chemicals. Guests were about to arrive, and all there was was chemically soaked prime rib.

The kitchen staff wanted to just wash the chemicals off and serve the meat! Needless to say, this idea was vetoed, but the problem was that the hotel had no more prime rib. In the end the solution was to borrow some from another hotel. The meat covered in chemicals was put aside but in plain sight so that it would not be used by accident or otherwise. That way the result was not a planeload of passengers suffering from food poisoning or worse. Had event staff not been there at that precise moment, would they have been told what had gone on? What would have been the outcome if the chemically soaked meat were served? The event proceeded seamlessly, and the client was not even aware that there had been a problem.

MENU PLANNING

Take the time to do an initial budget before you begin to plan your menu. Start with all of the fixed costs—those that are not flexible—like room rental or bartender charges that could apply if you were taking over a facility exclusively. You can always have a custom menu created to fall within your budget guidelines and switch from a full bar to serving just wine and beer to bring costs in line. Knowing your fixed costs will help you determine what you can afford to spend on food and beverage and where you need to negotiate a better rate. If the facility is receiving extensive revenue from food and beverage, there will generally be no charge for room rental. However, if you require extensive set-up time for staging, lighting and decor, and the facility needs to close to handle your requests, you may be asked to compensate them for lost revenue in the form of room rental charges. These amounts can be negotiated, but you need to know what you are prepared to spend on food and beverage so that the facility can make a fair assessment based on what is coming in from your event versus what could be lost revenue.

A cardinal rule of menu planning is not to run out of food, but that sounds a lot simpler than it really is. Think about what will be put out and when. If you are setting out a lavish display of appetizers for guests to help themselves, you need to consider when the guests are arriving. Will there be anything left for latecomers if everything is put out at once? If you estimate four hors d'oeuvres per person and your guests come directly from work, perhaps having missed lunch, you may have a problem. Famished guests will not stop at four and you will quickly run out. The same applies to receptions where you may have two different groups attending. Group A could be attending a pre-reception event and Group B only the reception, which is scheduled to begin at a specific time. If Group A is delayed and Group B is at the reception first and all the food is put out at once, there may be only slim pickings left for Group A when they do show up. You could request that the food be brought out in staggered amounts, have someone from your event planning committee call to advise you when Group A will arrive so that you can have the tables replenished and ensure that Group A is met with an attractive display ready and waiting for them.

You also need to give consideration to where the kitchen is and how items will make their way to your guests.

At one black-tie event with over 1,000 guests, all the food and drink was coming from only one main area, and it never made it past the first wave of guests who had stationed themselves strategically to ambush the food and drink as it emerged from the kitchen. There were no separate food stations or satellite bars set up that would allow the waiters to approach the guests from another direction. Waiters attempted to move through the crowds carrying trays of wine and beer. It was very difficult for them to move in the congestion, and they had to take extreme care not to spill the content of their trays on the guests. Wine bars placed around the room would have helped to move guests from the one central area and lessened the congestion.

It was also impossible to find a place to lay down empty glasses and dishes. No side tables had been set up. Obviously they had planned to have the staff circulate and clear away used glasses and dishes. Hors d'oeuvres were being passed, but care had not been given to their selection. Items included those served on skewers as well as shrimp with their tails on, and guests disposed of these discreetly in their cocktail napkins. Unfortunately the staff was unable to circulate and clear, so there was no way for guests to dispose of them. The waiters were so busy trying to serve everyone that no one had time to clear the used dishes away. Designated staff to serve and others to clear would have helped to alleviate this.

In the end the waiters came out with bottles of wine in hand and began to try and manoeuvre around the crowds to top up the glasses of the guests who were fortunate enough to have one. To an observer it looked as though they had run out of glasses. To get a non-alcoholic beverage or a glass of water was nearly impossible. Care and attention must not only be given to the selection of the food and beverage but also to room layout, presentation, service and removal as well.

How will you handle early arrivals? Do you have a plan on what to do if you have a line-up at the door half an hour before you are scheduled to begin? If the client has told you to open the doors and serve everyone, are you able to do this? Do you have the bartenders, the waiters, the food and the music ready? Who has the authority to give the staff the official go-ahead? Make sure that all staff are on hand well before the event is scheduled to begin. This is particularly important as staff may be hesitant to open just on the event planner's say-so.

As you begin to plan your menu take into consideration the season, the country, local specialities and how adventuresome your guests are. Not everyone will be open to sampling rattlesnake, alligator or even buffalo meat. In Barbados and Florida they often serve "dolphin," but they are quick to point out that it is not the "Flipper" variety—this is a fish, the other is a mammal—as people begin to turn up their noses. In Morocco, a local delicacy is made from pigeon, which throws westerners, but it can also be made with chicken. Guests will appreciate knowing what they are eating be it rabbit, goat, or anything that may not be standard fare to them. Frog legs look a lot like chicken—and taste like it too—but have a waiter discreetly ask if they would like to try some frog legs. Some will be game and others not. But at least they were free to choose.

How will your guests react to live shrimp being cooked at the table in front of them (drunken shrimp cooked in beer). Will it be a local favourite they will enjoy or not? For events in other countries a good way to experience local cuisine is to have a welcome buffet dinner that includes a sampling of local fare and have staff explain to guests how each dish has been prepared or a description posted by each serving tray. Always make sure that you offer a choice of entrées and a selection of salads and side dishes and an interesting array of desserts, when you are including anything a little on the more "interesting" side.

How will your overall food presentation look? Does each dish complement one another visually and in the choice of selection? Is it vibrant and colourful? How will it look as it is presented? Is it tasty? Do the food choices go together and do they work well together? Have you taken the time to ensure that the menu is balanced and that you have not designed one that is too heavy or not filling enough? If you are planning a heavy entrée, you will want to offer a lighter selection of appetizers, salads and desserts. Foods that are too heavy, too hearty or too rich could leave your participants or guests feeling sleepy and lethargic. It is especially important at a meeting that the mid-day meal leave your participants ready to return to the meeting refreshed, full of energy and ready to continue on for the rest of the day. For this reason it is probably not a good idea to include alcohol at lunch; offer a selection of beverages such as iced tea and lemonade, soft drinks, fruit juices and water instead. Keep the alcohol for the receptions at the end of the day once the meeting has come to a close.

BREAKFAST

You have many options for breakfast at meetings, conferences, conventions or incentives. You may decide to arrange a breakfast buffet so that everyone can eat as a group and give them a chance to interact.

When you are doing a buffet whether it is breakfast, lunch or dinner, try to have a two-sided layout, each set with the same items, so that you have two lines moving at once.

If possible have more than one buffet station so that everyone is not standing in line at the same time. If you require portion control to save money and ensure food for all, have staff members serving. To limit the number in line, move the peripheral items such as juice, cereal and fruit, desserts or coffee to separate food stations. Always make sure that there are sufficient utensils for all. Watch out for areas that could cause congestion. Some resorts have toasters set up for guests to stand and make their own, but they have very limited capacity and are often bottlenecks. One solution would be to have baskets of toast brought to the table instead. And whenever you are in a hot tropical climate make sure that the food is kept at proper temperatures, is not sitting out too long and has a fan or some other device in place to keep insects and birds away.

Generally the hotel offers an array of buffet options at varying prices but read the fine print. What is the minimum charge to set up the buffet? Often the cost for the buffet in the hotel's food and beverage menu is based on a minimum of 50 guests, and there could be an additional surcharge if your numbers fall below that. Surcharges could also apply for a chef to prepare individual omelettes, pancakes and waffles or to carve a breakfast ham. For smaller numbers the venue may be able to create a buffet with fewer choices, or you may need to consider a sit-down breakfast where a set breakfast on a plate is brought to each guest. Wherever possible try to avoid limiting options too severely and offer a menu that has variety and choice for breakfast especially if lunch and dinner menus will be plated, which provides even less choice.

If budget is a concern, and you need to stay within certain parameters, find out if you can work within one buffet budget range but offer different options each day. You will need to work with the catering staff on this. For instance, you may not be able to offer both fruit juices and slices if you are requesting they change the scrambled eggs to something that could be more labour intensive such as omelettes or poached eggs. In order to have offer a variety in the choice of eggs to remain in budget you may need to offer only bacon and sausage and forgo the ham. If your meeting is for an extended period of time you want to make sure that you offer some variety.

People are becoming more health conscious as well. Make sure that along with standard buffet fare of eggs, bacon, sausages and ham that you include yogurt, fresh fruit, juices, cereal and herbal teas and decaffeinated coffee. When given the choice many people are also opting for milk rather than cream in their coffee. Make both available to your guests—and pay attention to future trends; guests have recently begun to request soy milk. Wherever possible have the milk and the cream in servers rather than individual plastic containers. It is a much better presentation. And make sure that the milk or the cream is fresh. Know your client. For example, a nice touch at a breakfast for stockbrokers is to have newspapers such as *The Wall Street Journal* available.

In some areas of the world you can also do fun interactive breakfast buffet events. In Arizona you may want to consider a sunrise trail ride with a cookout in chuckwagons set up as buffet food stations. Guests choosing not to ride horseback can be transported by jeep. (Remember to cost in and arrange for porta potties).

Another breakfast option is to make arrangements for guests to dine at one of the hotel's restaurants, where they can choose anything off the menu, and sign their bill to their guest room. Most hotels offer a full buffet breakfast in their main restaurant, and the cost is often the same as a private buffet and sometimes less. When guests choose just juice, coffee and toast that is all you will be charged for. Remember that planning breakfast is not just about feeding your guests but about your objective. Do you want to bring people together first thing in the morning, or do you want to give them some breathing room because they will be together the rest of the day?

When planning meetings or events never forget that there is a psychology behind everything you choose to do that extends well beyond what you are serving your guests at a particular meal. Take something as simple as coffee. If your guests' internal time clocks are still set on a hectic city pace, and you want to ease the transition to the more laid-back local ways, what can help is delivering a whole pot of coffee—not just a cup—to each guest table immediately. That way guests can relax, serve themselves and adapt to a more leisurely pace. Otherwise they could initially become unhappy with the speed of the service and that unhappiness could spill over into your meeting.

For those choosing the option of having their guests dine at the hotel restaurant their bills will then need to be pulled from their room portfolios and then posted to the master account—leaving guests with their incidental charges such as the minibar or gift store purchases that are not being picked up by the host company. What is and is not included should be clearly outlined in the itinerary of events that each guest is given—make sure that it clearly states what charges, meals and activities they will personally be responsible for. Some companies have even been known to pick up the entire tab, but do not advertise the fact. That is a nice surprise at checkout. At the end of your stay, before the individual room bills are printed and distributed to each guest, sit with accounting to make sure that all authorized charges such as breakfast in the hotel's restaurant have been pulled and do not show on the guest's room bill. The time spent doing this is minimal compared to trying to do it at checkout time, particularly since, as event planner, you will have your hands full with things such as guest luggage collection and transportation to the airport.

You can make arrangements with the restaurant to have block seating for your group and have a staff member on hand to greet them to ensure that they are not left standing in line. If they all have to be out by a specific time advise the restaurant of this in advance so they can plan accordingly. If everyone chooses room service, again let management know in advance so that they can have enough staff on hand. There are ways to ensure that room service staff are not overwhelmed by a flood of orders coming in at the same time. Many hotels have express breakfast cards that can be filled out in advance, and you may be able to design custom ones for your group. To help them adjust to five-hour time differences, one group in Hawaii got fresh orange juice, thermoses of hot coffee and a basket of fresh-baked pastries delivered each morning with their newspaper to enjoy on their terrace, giving them a leisurely beginning to their day before having breakfast in the main restaurant when the rest of Hawaii woke up.

When budgeting for clients allowing their guests to eat off the menu assume that the cost is the same as the breakfast buffet. That is generally the most expensive item, and it builds in a buffer into your costs. Some may only have juice, cereal and coffee. Remember to adjust meal orders and food guarantees on departure days. Depending on flight times you may want to make arrangements for early departures to have just a continental breakfast before heading to the airport, especially if the flight will be serving breakfast on board.

One final option for those staying overnight in hotels is to compare the regular guest room rates to those offered on the concierge floors. These are available worldwide at most five-star hotels and resorts and offer private check-in, upgraded amenities and special services, which can include continental breakfast, afternoon tea and pre-dinner appetizers. It is worth doing a cost comparison. For example, a group had taken over the entire concierge floor of a hotel in Los Angeles. They had all flown in from separate parts of the country, and this was the only time they were all together. The trip had been extremely busy, so they decided that what they most wanted to do was sit around somewhere other than in another restaurant and spend one evening together before heading home. Because they had the entire floor booked for themselves special arrangements could be made. A pizza pyjama party was quickly arranged. Everyone showed up in their hotel robes in the private lounge area, just relaxed, ate pizza and had a great time together.

COFFEE BREAKS

Coffee breaks during conferences can be fun. Milk and cookies was a hit at one meeting with an ice cream sundae bar at another. Remember to keep the season in mind when you are planning. Find out when and where other meetings are holding their breaks so that you can schedule yours to avoid conflict.

LUNCH

For luncheon meetings at a hotel or resort you can have a buffet or an outdoor BBQ or a boxed lunch that is brought to the room or set up just outside. If breakfast has been buffet you might want a plated lunch so that guests can enjoy a different style of service. With lunch, it is easier to choose a menu that will have appeal to all, something for everyone. If you are having a fish-based appetizer or soup, don't repeat fish as the main course for lunch, but go with an alternate like chicken or a light pasta dish instead. If time is a key factor, the table can be pre-set with the salad or appetizer waiting. Have one person in the meeting room ready to alert luncheon staff when the meeting is a close to breaking—the length of the warning will vary depending on the number of guests being served—so that they can start to lay out the salads and fill the water glasses. The waiters will need to know how to handle requests for alcoholic beverages. Will they be available and, if so, will they be charged to the master account or billed to the individual? You have to tell them how to word their reply.

[handwritten margin note: if considering BBQ have backup room un case Rain & shade could be required]

    If you are considering a BBQ or other outdoor function make sure that you have a room reserved for back-up in case of bad weather. It does not matter that it "never rains at this time of year." You will need to make the call on the day of the event, but at least if you have protected yourself with back-up you do have an option available. Something else you need to be aware of for daytime outdoor events is shade. What protection is available and what needs to be brought in?

> **TIP**
> *[handwritten: mentioned earlier]*
> If your hotel has a permanent BBQ area that is close to the guest rooms, take a close look when you are doing your site inspection. Do those rooms fill up with BBQ smoke every time it is used? If so, you will want to exclude them from your room block.

Along with typical casual BBQ fare, include a selection of vegetarian burgers and hot dogs. On your registration forms be sure to include an area that asks about special meal requests and food allergies to help you in planning menus. You will know in advance how many guests are vegetarian, how many have allergies to seafood, peanuts and so on. Special meals can usually be arranged to meet their specific requirements.

At golf tournaments following a morning meeting, box lunches are often very popular because participants are anxious to tee off. Having the box lunches, along with golf balls and the appropriate logoed towels waiting in their pre-assigned golf carts is a great way to get guests onto the golf course quickly. Their golf clubs can be transferred while they are in the meeting and set up in their carts along with any rental clubs that may be required. Arrangements can be made to have a beverage cart assigned exclusively to the group and all beverages and snacks billed back to the master account. The minute their meeting breaks, guests are able to hop on waiting shuttles and head directly over to the golf course. Arrangements can also be made to have the refreshments at the club house at the end of their game billed to the master account. When all have arrived back at the clubhouse return transfers take them back to their hotel.

Whenever possible, try to use different rooms for different meals—using the same room for all meals every day of their stay can get boring. With meeting rooms the opposite is true. What usually works best is having a 24-hour hold on your meeting room so that you can leave everything as is for the next day. The rooms can be locked and secured.

COCKTAILS

Cocktail receptions can last anywhere from one hour to two and a half hours. Generally, though, a cocktail reception is scheduled to take place one hour before a dinner. If you are doing cocktails only, and your guests are on their own for dinner, the reception can be up to two and a half hours long, and the hors d'oeuvres served are usually more substantial. You will need to base your room requirements on the type of food and beverage layout you plan. Will you have food stations set up, passed hors d'oeuvres or a combination of both? Will there be entertainment, scattered seating and tables? As a rule of thumb, have seating for about one-third of your guests, but if a high proportion are elderly, you will probably want to increase that number.

As your guests begin to arrive you need to have an ice-breaker ready. This can take the form of a specialty drink, entertainment or food such as oyster bar, sushi bars or California wrap stations that will provoke interest and comment. That way, the food then becomes part of the entertainment. Have professionals on hand to explain the dishes and their preparation to your guests. Let guests have the opportunity to try something new such as a local specialty. You want your guests to be drawn into the event, relaxed, mingling and entertained. Take care when planning the music. For cocktails you are looking for something low-key: it should be background music—something your guests can easily talk above. You don't want your guests to have to shout at one another. On the other hand, your entertainment should be heard.

For example, at a function for over 1,000 guests the entertainment was a trio, located in the centre of the room. However, with the acoustics of the long and narrow room and the group's inadequate sound system they might as well not have been there. No one could see them and no one could hear them—they were totally lost in the crowd. They actually packed up and left before the cocktail party was finished (which should never be done). Most of the people away from the centre where not even aware that they were there. A more effective and dramatic welcome would have been a strolling violinist, saxophonist or classical guitarist to greet guests or a white baby grand with the pianist in white tux and tails at the entrance where all guests could see and hear him as they passed. Staff could be on hand with silver trays of champagne and canapés to greet the guests as they arrived. The staff could let guests know that the bars are open and that a lavish display of food awaits them inside. All guests would have a moment to enjoy the entertainment before moving further into the room. If you are holding the cocktail reception outside and can time it to take in the sunset, you have added ambience at no additional cost. Do it whenever and wherever you can.

Take the time to look at all the viable options when it comes to selecting where to hold your cocktail party and, in fact, any of your food and beverage functions. You can always hold your

[handwritten margin note: Take advantage of external features that provide no cost el at times very little required extra decor.]

cocktail reception in a traditional room, but if you can do it on the terrace overlooking the ocean at sunset instead, it would be a shame not to utilize what is available to you. The function room can be your weather back-up. Don't pass up a setting that is absolutely magnificent. One resort has a wonderful private courtyard complete with an outdoor fireplace and a working fountain that is beautifully lit at night. Add to this a classical guitarist, some exquisite floral arrangements, twinkle lights in the greenery and you have a beautiful setting for very little cost. It is simple and elegant. There is no need to bring in additional decor.

If you are planning an evening outdoor setting, do your site visit to the area at night. A location may look wonderful in daylight, but you need to see it at the same time that you plan to hold your event to be able to visualize how the area can be best utilized. Will it need extra lighting or heaters? Is there weather back-up? If you don't have dollars to spend on decor take a look at what is around for you to use to create an area of ambiance. Most hotels are more than accommodating in this area. Sometimes you can even borrow items from one of their restaurants that may be closed for the evening you are holding your event.

A Pacific Rim dinner was planned for the ballroom at one of the top hotels in Vancouver. The cocktail reception was in full swing. The drums were beating and the lion dance began to lead guests into the ballroom. An array of children were set to perform between each course featuring local dances and gymnastics to tie in with the particular region of the Pacific Rim whose food was served as that course. It was a memorable evening. The show plates—the plates at each place setting as guests arrive that can be used as a decorative base—were from the hotel's gourmet restaurant. Valued at over $200 each, the plates set off the tables wonderfully. The restaurant was closed and the hotel graciously loaned them at no additional cost. Another time at a hotel in Florida huge potted palms with uplighting—that lights the tree from the base—were moved into the cocktail area for only minimal labour costs. No one else was using the facility that night and the guests had it all to themselves. Moving the palms did not inconvenience any other guests by spoiling the look of the decor in the other sections, but the clusters of palm trees provided a warmer atmosphere.

In the Caribbean, cocktails are often done at poolside. What you need to find out in advance is whether the other hotel guests will have access to the pool area while your cocktail reception is going on. At what time would set-up begin? To open the area up you will have to move the furniture such as the lounge chairs. Will they be moved to a location out of site or simply stacked to the side in unsightly piles? That also applies when you are doing events at restaurant takeovers. You want to make sure that any furniture that has been removed is completely out of sight of guests.

Bathroom facilities are important at any event. If you are taking over one section of a restaurant exclusively for a cocktail reception you need to know where the bathrooms are. How will this affect your set-up? Will you have uninvited guests wandering through your cocktail reception searching for the washrooms? There is one restaurant that is on three levels with washrooms only on the first and third level. When using the top floor for an event, you can get management to direct guests dining on the second floor to use the facilities on the first floor and have staff stationed by the door to make sure that any regular restaurant guests were redirected back downstairs. You could also have signs put up.

One important factor to keep in mind in selecting the best site for your cocktail reception is the layout of the room. Do you have one large area where guests can gather, or is it an area that has multiple rooms and a lot of nooks and crannies? If you want your guests to mingle, you want to have them together in one area. If there are multiple rooms and the space is too large or too spread out, you will lose the energy of your party. Guests arriving will see only a few people and not all those spread out in the various alcoves.

Another consideration in holding receptions is the weather. For a location where guests are cooled by tropical breezes, it is fine to do cocktails and dinner outside. But if you are doing an event at a time of year where the weather is known to be hot, sticky and humid or with extremely intense heat—such as in a desert destination during the day (evenings cool down)—you may be wise to move it inside. This can even work in your favour. For example, suppose guests are attending a convention.

Suppliers are vying to have them attend their individual evening functions. The goal is to make the party interesting, have guests stay as long as possible and thus limit their availability to other suppliers. Two parties are going on. One outside and quite spread out. The other is in a smaller location. It is full of energy, atmosphere, great music, great food and air-conditioning. With temperatures well over 100 degrees Fahrenheit, guests who chose the event with the air-conditioning never made it to the other party. They were in no hurry to leave. Guests who had gone to the outdoor party first were quite appreciative—and very vocal when they arrived at the second party—of being inside in the cool air. They stayed too. The party needed to be extended. Guests and hosts were having a fabulous time. Had both parties been outdoors guests most likely would have showed up at both and then moved on to somewhere cooler.

At another event, the weather was the same—hot, sticky and humid. Guests were attending a convention and suppliers were inviting a very well-travelled and sophisticated crowd out for the evening. The goal once again was how to interest them and keep them at the event. The first virtual reality Olympics at a brand new entertainment complex became exactly the right fit. It was being held indoors and that translated to air-conditioned. It was brand new—the venue had just opened. It was exciting. It was fun. Guests came for cocktails. Rules were explained over drinks and hors d'oeuvres. Teams were sent out with their mission—fun. They were involved in the games for two hours and then met back to hand in their scorecards, relax and enjoy a tempting array of food and beverages. The winning team was announced and then guests were free to use the facility and enjoy all of the games. At midnight guests were still hard at play. It was the perfect choice for this group, and the company achieved their objective. Because the room was large and it was open to the public, what needed to be addressed was how to bring guests together as a group and to spend time with one another without getting lost in the crowds. The upstairs section could be taken over exclusively for groups. It was private but overlooked the activity on the floor below. You could feel the energy around you. By having guests come together for cocktails in a private area, sending them out in assigned teams, bringing them back together at the end of the games to compare scores before letting them enjoy the balance of the evening at leisure, they had a presence even in the midst of a major complex. And having it inside on a hot, sticky night added to their enjoyment and was a definite plus.

> **T**
> **I**
> **P**
>
> It is usually recommended to wait six months with newly opened restaurants or venues before planning an event there to give them time to work the kinks out of the system. If you feel comfortable working with them because of your past experience—have you personally worked with new venues before?—and the quality and calibre of their facility and staff, it could be done sooner, but be prepared to spend the time it will take from both you and the facility to work together to make it successful.

if you decide to use far earlier than 6 mo. recomm. 6 mos.

In addition to room layout and weather, food presentation plays an important part. Pay attention to eye appeal. It is one of the ingredients that adds immeasurably to the success of your event. For example, when you are having appetizers passed, the most visually effective method is to have only one type of food on each tray. This suggests a feeling of abundance and plenty. Instead of one lonely shrimp on a tray mixed in with many other selections, a tastefully presented tray featuring just shrimp stands out. Tray presentation is more pleasing to the eye with garnishes such as fresh herbs, flowers or other items that tie into the theme. Limiting the number of pieces per tray helps to achieve a more elegant presentation. Overall, you can offer an array of choices, but limit it to between eight and 10 items—his is the selection of types of appetizers not quantity per person—in total. Make sure that you have taken the time when planning your menu to balance your choices and include a meat, poultry, fish, dairy and vegetarian selection. Remember not all vegetarians eat dairy so ensure that you include some all-vegetarian choices as well.

Make sure that the pieces served are bite-sized and do not require the use of a knife and fork. At one reception they served shrimp with their tails on, wrapped in noodles. These were passed around with just napkins. The noodles were greasy, slippery to the touch and dripping in the sauce they had been tossed in. Leaving the tails on the shrimp just left people looking for places to dispose of them. The whole thing was awkward and messy, certainly not the best choice to serve to guests in tuxedos and ball gowns. It is also very unappealing to see piles of discarded shrimp bits lying around waiting to be collected. If you are having hors d'oeuvres passed with dipping sauces, serve them on the side so that guests can make their own choices with regard to how much or how little they would like. For formal affairs, it is best to avoid them entirely.

In addition to the hors d'oeuvres you can also set out items on display for your guests to help themselves or have waiters on hand to assist them with their selections. Make sure that these items are replenished often and that each food station is set with appropriate utensils and napkins. Place the tables in different areas of the room to avoid congestion and long line-ups. You may want to set up food stations to feature specialty items or dessert and coffee if you are doing a cocktail reception that is featuring what is referred to as "heavy" hot and cold hors d'oeuvres. When the cocktail reception is taking the place of a dinner, the choices for the canapés will be a little heartier, the quantity per person is increased and coffee and dessert is served. With the desserts, as with the hors d'oeuvres, make them manageable, bite-sized and easy to cut with just a fork. You can make arrangements to have specially trained staff on hand to prepare gourmet coffees at the end of your cocktail reception as a special treat for your guests.

If dinner follows the cocktail reception, calculate on six to eight hors d'oevres per person but if you are not including dinner, the cocktail reception will run longer and the guests will fill up on hors d'oeuvres. Count on guests eating between 18 and 30 pieces per person depending on how substantial the selections are (hence the name "heavy" hot and cold hors d'oeuvres).

Make sure that you give consideration about how guests will be disposing of empty glasses, plates and napkins. Do you have enough waiters to clear efficiently? Have you provided scattered tables—high bar tables or smaller round ones—for guests to set their glasses on? Calculate on using at least three cocktail napkins, glasses and plates per person. For a stand-up cocktail reception, quality paper napkins are acceptable—budget permitting, you could even have them logoed to enhance your theme. For example, in the Midwest at a "diamond and demin" theme party, the napkins were the colour of blue demin and had "diamonds" glued to them. The cost was minimal but people noticed the extra touch.

 At any stand-up reception or buffet, always try to utilize plates that have a slight lip on them. It helps to ensure that the food stays on the plate.

DINNER

There are many options for dinner. It can be a stand-up or sit-down buffet, a plated dinner, formal or themed, fun and casual. The choices are endless. When you are planning a dinner, the purpose is always more than just dinner. As with any event, each time you bring people together you need to look at how you can design your function to achieve your objectives. There is meaning behind the meeting. Guests may be coming from across the continent, and one of your objectives is probably to have them mingle and interact with one another. With this in mind you may want to consider doing a buffet, either stand-up or sit-down, where guests are moving around freely. Seating is not structured, and rather than one long buffet, what would help get people to meet each other would be to have a variety of interesting food stations with entertainment scattered around the room. It is always good to have something to break the ice when standing in line or simply enjoying the event. The objectives you set for a particular event will help to define its content.

In Singapore, guests are led poolside where they are greeted by staff in local costume with tropical beverages—perhaps even a Singapore Sling. The area is filled with the smell of exotic foods being prepared. Tropical flowers are everywhere, candles are flickering, local artisans are at work and entertainers perform at tableside. There is an abundance of things to see, do and sample. All the senses are awakened. There is featured entertainment and then a fireworks finale. Guests are relaxed, open and talking with one another.

Another scenario is in Morocco and for the evening you have taken over a series of fantasy tents. Great care and thought has gone into where which guests will be seated with which. The company wants to make sure that certain guests get to spend quality time with one another and have ample opportunity to talk. Everyone is seated on pillows, leaning back and relaxing. Sheer fabric is draped everywhere, and it billows gently in the evening breeze. Here, the food is brought in on huge platters for guests to sample with their fingers. Entertainment moves from tent to tent and the medina—the old Arab quarter—comes to life in front of you. After dinner guests move outside their tents to marvel at the horsemanship display, and for the finale the company's corporate logo is emblazoned against the black desert sky.

These are two very different events designed with two very different purposes in mind. One aims to have guests mingling with one another, and the other targets specific guests to spend time together.

If the objective of your evening lends itself to a buffet dinner, there are several factors to consider when you start to plan your menu selections. Take into account the temperatures the food is best served at. What has lasting power on a buffet? You want to avoid ending up having food that has crusted over, changed colour or dried out due to the length of time it will be sitting out. Remember to think of food and health safety as well. Avoid dishes such as those with mayonnaise in them unless they are kept chilled. Pay careful attention to how long the food will be on display. Make sure that your dinner foods do not mimic the hors d'oeuvres you have served. Look for variety in your menus. If you can project an image of lavish abundance, say a large display of fresh lush strawberries dipped in chocolate, don't think just chocolate-dipped strawberries, but strawberries dipped in a working chocolate fountain. This unusual conversation piece is inexpensive and will have more of an impact than an endless variety of traditional standard choices (and could actually end up costing less). Choose one standout item that guests will not soon forget. Remember, it does not have to be expensive to stand out.

> **T**
> **I**
> **P**
> When renting an item such as a chocolate fountain remember to include the cost of trained personnel to run it.

If you have designated your buffet to be a stand-up event, make sure that the food can be eaten with just a fork and that your guests are not left wrestling with large pieces of meat, chasing slippery mussels around their plates or attempting to break through deep-fried batter or phyllo pastry that really requires the use of both a knife and a fork. At one black-tie affair the stand-up buffet featured food that was so hearty—thick slices of prime rib, lamb chops, ribs, chicken, spinach baked in phyllo, deep-fried egg rolls, lasagne—it was unmanageable. Guests unwrapping their napkins thought that their knife was simply missing and went back to get another set.

> **T**
> **I**
> **P**
> If you choose to serve a slice of beef at a stand-up buffet, make sure that it is thinly sliced and that bread is available for guests to eat it like an open-faced sandwich.

Always have extra utensils ready.

Make sure that guests are not left waiting in line for clean plates or utensils. One way to ensure that is to have the hotel or facility pre-wrap extra set-ups (knife and fork or other cutlery wrapped in a napkin) and have staff ready to bring in more before they are required. Find out in advance the exact number of forks, knives, spoons, dishes, napkins and glassware that are available to you.

planning ahead allows determination of correct prop plate size.

Consider both the size and the shape of the plates you will be using. As mentioned previously, for a stand-up buffet it is best to use plates that have a raised lip, the better to contain the food on the plate. You will need to decide if you want to go to a full-size dinner plate or something smaller. Keep in mind that a smaller plate could mean multiple trips to the buffet and a fresh plate each time. Planning ahead will allow you to have sufficient quantities of utensils and staff on hand to clear away used ones. If you plan a sit-down buffet or plated dinner, make sure that the facility has extra napkins to replace those that are dropped or soiled. An oversize napkin is recommended for stand-up buffets—should guests find a seat other than at the scattered seating and tables, they can place it in their lap and it will provide better protection. Remember to have seating for at least one-third of the guests and more if your guests are older.

In Mexico, your group can dine on the fish they caught that afternoon when they were out deep-sea fishing. The cost is minute compared with the pleasure it brings. Schedule the deep-sea fishing tournament to take place the same night that you are doing a beach lobster bake and fish fry—it becomes the highlight of the evening—and should no one catch anything you can still have a wonderful dinner. You will have to negotiate in advance with the hotel to clean and prepare the fish and with the fishing boat charter as generally they take home the catch of the day. They may each ask for compensation. Discuss details with the hotel and the charters. One more note about deep-sea fishing—guests will not come in if they have the big one on the line.

If you are doing a sit-down buffet you need to consider how to arrange access to the food. Do you have everyone line up at their leisure, or do you have designated tables take their turns and have the banquet captain and their staff inform guests when it is their turn? Whatever option you choose consider having an appetizer or salad served at the table so that initially everyone has something to eat while they await their turn at the buffet. The number of buffet tables required will vary depending on room layout, menu selection and whether or not you will be having items like the appetizers and salad served at the table. Visualize the feel that you want in the room. Is the buffet set up to move people quickly in and out so they can get back to their meeting, or has it been designed to give your guests an assortment of local specialities?

Sit-down dinners can be handled two ways: open and pre-assigned seating. Open seating allows guests to select their own dinner companions and sit wherever they choose. With pre-assigned seating they are allotted a particular spot. When you choose this route it is imperative that you have a seating plan and a simple, clear way of telling guests where they are seated. You can do this in a number of ways. A seating chart can be posted or table numbers can be included on the guest security passes or given to out at registration. Regardless of which method you select, make sure you have staff who are familiar with the room layout and the table numbers with the seating assignments to help direct guests to their seats. What can help in reducing congestion and confusion is to have signs made up and posted outside the ballroom telling guests which doors to use based on their table assignment.

Make sure the tables are clearly numbered, and think about how you will display the numbers. Does the facility have table numbers and holders? Not all do. If they do, ask to see a sample to make sure they are of good quality and not chipped or broken. How are they displayed? Do they have stands to set them in? Do you need to have tent cards made up? You can have your calligrapher number these stand-up cards, and they can be designed to match the theme decor. If you decide to have them professionally made to tie into the decor make sure the cards will sit securely in the facility's holders. Test it to make sure that it will not slip out.

How do you want the overall table presentation to look? Do you want the table numbers removed once all guests have been seated? Make sure that they are clearly visible and do not get lost among the centrepieces. You will also need to decide on whether or not guests are free to sit anywhere at their assigned table, or do they also have a pre-assigned seat? If the latter, you will need to have individual place cards made up and set at each guest's seat. When one of the objectives of the event is to bring key people together, guests are assigned strategically not randomly. But be prepared to have guests switch place cards so that they can sit next to the person they want to be with. This happens even among senior company executives.

If you are doing a seating plan you have to know when to stop fiddling with the revisions. It will lead only to error and confusion. Flexibility is key when planning events and that includes the ability to handle last-minute changes. But be very aware of when those changes could affect the success of the event and work against it. Table location can be key at an event when you are honouring top suppliers or employees. You don't want to risk offending one group by placing them in a faraway corner at a table that had to be made up at the last minute because ongoing changes muddled the table assignment. Such gaffes cannot be tolerated and reflect badly on the entire organization.

When planning table assignments and layout, the number of people at each table—whether it seats eight or 10—will have an impact on your overall budget. Obviously if you have eight people at a table that could have 10, your guests will be more comfortable but you will need more tables, as well as table linens, overlays—the cloths that are layered over each table linens on an angle that often provide a splash of colour or allow the colour of the table linen to show through—centrepieces, pinspotting (lighting designed so that each individual table is lit), tent cards and waiters. Tables may have to be positioned closer together. Each of these will increase your budget, so remember to factor them in. It is always advisable—budget and room size permitting—to make sure that your guests are comfortable and not sitting on top of one another.

IMPORTANT FLAG

Seating Capacity and Tablecloth Sizes for Round Tables

Seating	Table Size (Round Diameter)	Floor-Length Tablecloth (Rounds)
10–12	72"	132"
8–10	60"	120"
6–8	54"	114"
4–6	48"	108"
4	36"	96"

Waiters

Number Needed	Type of Event	No. of Guests/Waiters
1 Per Two Tables	Informal/Casual Dinner	Maximum 20 Guests
2 Per Table	Formal Dinner	Maximum 10 Guests

When you are in the initial planning stages of your event, try to visualize the room as a whole. What colour are the walls, the carpet, the chairs, the linens, the overlays, the napkins, glassware, the dishes, the cutlery? If you are doing a black-and-white theme dinner, you don't want a hotel to use their signature cobalt blue glasses. How does your menu selection tie in with all of the above? Visualize it. How can you pull in all the colours? The room colours could influence the colours in your centre-piece. Will the menu you have selected compliment the colours you are working with? Does it enhance the total picture presented visually?

Of course—budget permitting—you are never limited to working with the colours in a room. Rooms can be totally transformed with the proper specialty lighting, draping, chair covers—the covers that fit over standard banquet chairs and can totally transform them in appearance—and decor. Some theme dinners have been known to feature food of one colour—either in actual colour tones or in name or both and tie in with special lighting and décor. A menu for an evening "Rhapsody in Blue" could feature martinis with a touch of blueberry, and perhaps grilled blue marlin would be the entrée. Now here the hotel's signature cobalt blue glassware would be an appropriate choice.

A gala dinner being planned to take place out of country had chair covers, linens and napkins all being flown in to the location at a great expense. Customs had to be cleared and local transportation arranged to get everything to the site. It was the first time chair covers had been used in this locale, and staff had to be shown how to put them on. It was important that the event reflect the client's corporate colours, and they were sparing no expense to do so. What someone had neglected to check was the colour of the dinner ware. It was assumed that it was white. It was white but covered in blue flowers, which clashed loudly with the corporate colours. By reviewing the dishes in advance, they were able to find a suitable solution and borrow china from a neighbouring hotel. A detail like checking the colour of the dishes could be thought of as relatively unimportant, but consider the overall effect it would have had on this event.

Find out if there are any areas of protocol that need to be addressed. In some cultures it is appropriate that the VIP table have a more elaborate centrepiece; in others, the colour of ink used to spell out someone's name on place cards could have a negative meaning, the number of flowers in a centrepiece can matter or the colour and the type of flower can be very important as well. Take the time to find out and to explain. For example, in Asian protocol, you need to do everything to ensure that nothing causes another to lose face, and this applies to everyone. Never do anything to cause anyone else to lose face. What may seem ordinary to you could be something new to them. Always take the time to explain anything new you might be introducing.

[handwritten margin note: BE ADWARE TO CULTURAL & CORPORATE PROTOCOLS]

> At one event, chair coverings were being introduced, and a walk through was done with senior officials. As soon as they spotted them, they discreetly asked how they would "unwrap" the chairs to sit down. Of course, you do not have to open them, you simply sit down on them, but this was something new to them and they wanted to know in advance the proper protocol and procedure.

> It is important to honour beliefs and customs of others and to take them into account in any planning. A senior delegate was entrusted to take back home a gift that had been given to the president of his company, but it was lost or misplaced somewhere between the hotel and the airport. It was of utmost importance to the senior delegate that a replacement be found—he would lose face if it wasn't on the president's desk on Monday morning. This was not a matter to be taken lightly. There were urgent calls from the airport, many calls from the plane and many from the connecting airport, but the answer was that there could be no replacement available for another two weeks—the department that handled them was closed for two weeks. They were very sorry, but nothing could be done. When the general manager of the hotel heard about the situation, he informed his staff he had an exact replica of the very item in his office and offered it as a replacement. It was on the next plane and would be on the senior delegate's desk Monday morning. The senior official was greatly relieved. The hotel general manager knew how important finding a solution was.

Sometimes you are just one step away from a solution. Don't stop short. What may seem insignificant to you could be something of major importance to someone else. And always take the one step more to understand customs and protocol. Roger E. Axtell has written several excellent books on international protocol, and are all entertaining and informative, including *Do's and Taboos Around the World*.[1]

If you are taking guests out to dinner in a restaurant as a group, you can do this as a group dinner or as a dine around. The latter allows guests to choose between two or more restaurants on a given night, and the group divides into smaller numbers. This can be done for different reasons. For example, some may wish to try local cuisine, while others want to try a popular seafood restaurant. An added benefit is that one or more representatives from the host company are usually assigned to each restaurant and get to spend quality time with their guests. Dine arounds can also be pre-assigned, the reason being once again to bring certain individuals together for a period of time.

If you take over a restaurant exclusively you can have your guests order off the menu if the numbers are limited, or for larger groups the restaurant will prepare a specially printed menu. Make sure that you work with the kitchen to prepare a menu that offers some choice. Two entrées are enough, but offer variety with the appetizers, salads, soups and dessert. If guests are ordering off the menu go through it carefully to make sure that there are no hidden surprises. At one very upscale restaurant in Miami a very extensive, very special selection of very old brandies were available *starting* at $100.00 US an ounce. Brief the waiters in advance on how to handle the situation if it comes up. This also applies to champagne and other expensive items. Know in advance what can and cannot be offered.

If you are looking at having your event catered be sure to ask for recommendations from the facility—some have a very select list of who they will work with. Get references and talk to staff that were on duty when the caterers handled a function there. Find out what worked and what didn't. If the facility does not have caterers that they recommend, check with quality rental

Get references to caterers

---

[1] Roger E. Axtell, *Do's and Taboos Around the World: A Guide to International Behavior*. (New York: John Wiley & Sons).

companies, florists and other top venues to see who caters their events. The same names often come up time and time again.

Make sure that you do a site inspection with the caterers. Are they comfortable with the layout, the capacity, the size of the stove or fridge? Will their cooking pans or serving dishes fit inside the existing spaces? Do you need to bring in any additional equipment? What are their electrical needs? Will you need to bring in a back-up generator? Will they need a cooking or a food preparation tent? If so, it will probably involve permits. Do they have a liquor licence, or will you need to provide one? Will you need to rent tables and chairs or other items for them? What are they providing, and what are you providing?

mentioned before.

Make sure that you receive all quotes in writing and that these include details on the menu, quantity, price, all taxes and gratuities, delivery charges, how many staff will be on hand, how many hours they are contracted to work and a detailed account of what they are providing. What will the caterers' staff be responsible for? Are they assisting with food preparation, acting as waiters and busboys, passing food, replenishing items from the buffet tables, clearing the tables and taking care of all clean-up including the dishes? Find out what time the caterers will be arriving and where the food will be prepared. Will it be at their premises with final preparations at the site, or will all cooking and food preparation be handled on site? Are there any special arrangements you need to make on their behalf for parking and off-loading of equipment? Find out how the staff will be dressed. How experienced are they?

Wherever you are holding your event, be sure to inform the clean-up staff that when dishes are cleared, the plates are not to be scraped in front of the guests—that looks unprofessional. Make sure that the banquet manager is familiar with the schedule of events. If there are to be speeches, do you want service to stop while the speeches are going on? Make sure that waiters have received clear instructions on how to proceed.

Cocktail receptions can include a full open bar, wine and beer only or feature specialty drinks. With an open bar, you can be billed on actual consumption or on a negotiated flat rate. With the former, you are paying for every drink consumed. When you are paying a flat rate, it is based on an flat hourly rate multiplied by the number of guests attending. The facility may have a rate for one hour, three hours or more. Do you know the guests? What is their history? Do they like to party? Do they enjoy fine wines? The advantage of a flat rate is that you know what your bar bill will be in advance whereas with consumption it can be hard to estimate. One rule of thumb often used to budget is two to three drinks per person per hour, but it will vary from group to group.

If you are paying a flat rate your bar will probably be limited to standard house brands unless you pay a premium. The brands offered will vary greatly depending on the venue and location. And while the pricey drinks may not be visible, guests may still ask for them, and your bartender needs your direction. Shooters will probably not be included in a flat rate. You need to verify that and make a decision as to how to handle requests. Will you be charged for opened bottles or just the number of drinks consumed? Have staff on hand to do an immediate sign off on the cocktail reception bill. If you are concerned with exceeding your proposed spending limit, ask staff to let you know when you have reached your halfway point. The decision is then whether you would prefer to have the service slowed down. Make sure that if there is the possibility of the host wanting the party to be extended that you have an adequate liquor supply and that you are in no danger of running out. Always make sure the bar is stocked with more than you need. One fund-raiser has run out of both food and beverage so often that it has acquired a reputation for it. Think about the image that you are trying to project and how that might affect it.

Count on having at least one bar for every 40 to 50 guests, and ideally not more than 40 guests per bartender. Depending on the room layout you could have a double bar set-up—two bar stations placed side by side—or have several bars set up in various locations. Having multiple bar locations helps to alleviate congestion and long line-ups. You can use the bars to draw your guests further into the room by locating bars away from the registration and check-in area. Take into account the kitchen area and the doors where the waiters will be constantly back and forth, and make sure that the position of the bars will not hinder their service in any way.

Will the bartenders need help with restocking the bar and preparing time-consuming specialty drinks like frozen daiquiris and margueritas? Make sure that your bartenders are professional and experienced. (Six months' experience is recommended.) What is the staff dress code? When will the bartenders be setting up, and what time will they be scheduled to start? What is their break schedule, and how will it be covered? Discuss with them in advance how to handle early arrivals and any other special areas of concern.

At one fashion fund-raising event, the bartenders were giving the models bottles of wine to take upstairs—many bottles of wine. This could have jeopardized the quality of the show, but luckily it was stopped before all the good wine disappeared. Your client may want to extend an invitation to the models or entertainers—depending greatly on who they are and whether it is appropriate—to join the reception, or may send food and drinks backstage after the show. Discuss this with your client in advance and advise your bartenders and banquet manager accordingly. Remember to factor this into your food and beverage counts when you are calling in your guarantees—you do not want to underestimate the amount of food and drink you need to have on hand, and include the cost in your budget calculations.

When you are contracting entertainment be sure to read their "rider" carefully. This outlines their terms and conditions, explaining what needs to be provided for them. For example, it can state specifically what food and beverage must be provided for them backstage, how many encores they will do, if any, if they require first-class air travel and accommodations, and for how many and so on. Riders can affect your budget, so know what needs to be included in advance—food and beverage will be just one of the items.

DISCUSSED BEFORE CHAP. 1 or 2

Make sure that the bar area is kept clear; floral arrangements and candles may look attractive, but they are not practical. Busy bartenders do not need to worry about manoeuvring around the decor. Also it is best to keep open flame away from high-traffic areas where guests could accidently walk into it. Find out the type of bar that is being used for your event and make sure that the area looks as polished and professional as possible—both in front (should you be setting up a banquet table instead of a standard bar station) and behind the bar set-up. Always keep in mind what your guests will be seeing and what you can do to enhance it. If you are having a specialty bar—such as a martini bar—set up and staffed by an outside suppliers, make sure that you have everything that is needed: glassware, garnishes, beverages, spirits, shakers, napkins, tables and all related equipment, and have it all ready when staff arrives. Make sure that you discuss dress code, protocol, break schedule and tipping with them as well.

If you are bringing in specialty beverages with you, or are doing a fund-raising gala where some of the beverages/alcohol may be donated, find out the facility's policy in advance. You may be charged a fee per bottle corkage, and you need to include that in your budget calculation.

With respect to liability find out the responsibility of your client, the facility and yourself. What insurance (host liability) do you need to make sure that everyone is covered in case of an accident on the property or on the drive home? What is the legal drinking age where the event is held? This can differ from country to country and area to area. Make sure that you are aware of local restrictions and age requirements. Will any minors be attending your event? How will you monitor this? You can be held legally responsible for any under-age individuals being served. Make sure to always include an assortment of non-alcoholic beverages, and if you are offering specialty drinks, make them available with and without alcohol so that your non-drinking guests are not excluded from the festivities. It is important to decide how to handle any guests who over-indulge and become a danger to themselves and to others. Be mindful of local laws and customs when doing out-of-country events. How would you deal with a participant of a program who has been arrested? It has happened. Take the time to figure out in advance what should be done. Sometimes the situation may be out of your control, and you need to know in advance how best to deal with it.

Find out how your client would like you to handle such issues as a guest who has had too much to drink or who ends up in a brawl. It can be as simple as having two people—never send out just one person on his or her own—assigned to take the drunk back to the hotel room or home. This is where it is beneficial to have off-duty police hired as security—they have the experience to handle such situations effectively and efficiently. A security company may have certain restrictions with regard to how they would be able to handle a situation such as this—discuss this with them in advance. It is important to know the laws and customs not only at the location where you are holding your meeting but also for any off property venues you may be using—the rules and regulations could be different—sometimes off-property venues can come under a different jurisdiction.

If there is a concern about serving minors a visible means of identification could be used, such as hand stamps, wrist bands or different colour security passes.

Make sure that quality ingredients are used at the bar. Fresh squeezed juices, lemons and limes, garnishes and spices all add to the appeal of the drink, the bar and the event in general. Use quality paper napkins—budget permitting you can have these custom logoed—and avoid plastic glassware wherever possible. Make sure that in everything that you do the attention to detail and quality shows through.

Cocktail Reception:
Basic Bar for 50 Guests—Beer, Wine, and Spirits

Beer

Light/Dark/Imported	Five cases mixed selection (120 bottles)

Wine — Cocktails Only

Red Wines	Five 750 ml bottles (cocktail reception only)
White Wines	Eight 750 ml bottles (cocktail reception only)

Spirits — One Bar Station*

Gin	Two 1140 ml
Rum (Light)	One 1140 ml
Scotch	Two 1140 ml
Tequila	One 1140 ml
Vermouth (Dry)	One 750 ml
Vermouth (Sweet)	One 750 ml
Vodka	Two 1140 ml
Whiskey	One 1140 ml**

Liqueurs can be customized to include any specialty drinks you may want to serve. If champagne is to be offered calculate 12 bottles for 50 guests.

*Specialty Drinks/Blender Drinks/Champagne Not Included.

**Whiskey is usually bourbon in the US and rye in Canada

1140 ml = 40 ounces = 26 x 1 1/2 ounce drinks

Ice	1-1/2 pounds of ice per person, 2-1/2 pounds of ice per person if you will be chilling wine and beer. Additional ice will be required for specialty blender drinks.

Glasses

Napkins/Coasters

Mixers (to be available at each bar station)
  Clamato Juice—Especially for Canadian guests
  Cranberry Juice—All-Natural Whenever Possible
  Cola—Diet and Regular
  Ginger Ale—Diet and Regular
  Grapefruit Juice
  Lemon Juice
  Lemon-Lime Soft Drink (Sprite or 7Up)
  Lime Juice
  Orange Juice
  Sparkling Water
  Tomato Juice
  Tonic Water
  2 litre bottles = 67.6 fluid ounces = eight 8 ounce servings
  Estimate a minimum of three drinks per person.
  50 Guests x 3 Drinks = 150 Drinks x 8 Ounces = 1200 Fluid
      Ounces = Approx. 18 x 2 Litre Bottles

Garnishes (At Each Bar Station)
  Angostura Bitters
  Bar Sugar
  Black Pepper (freshly ground)
  Celery
  Cinnamon (freshly ground)
  Cinnamon Sticks

Cocktail Olives
Cocktail Onions
Grenadine Syrup
Jalapeno Peppers (pickled)
Lemon Slices
Lime Slices
Maraschino Cherries
Margarita Salt
Mint Sprigs (fresh)
Nutmeg (freshly ground)
Orange Slices
Tabasco Sauce
Worcestershire Sauce

Glassware (customize to beverage selections/available at each bar station)
Beer Glasses
Wine Glasses
Cocktail Glasses
Note: You can customize glassware according to your event's particular needs. For instance, you may want red and white wine glasses, martini glasses or brandy snifters and champagne flutes. If you are planning on any glassware being used as serving dishes for desserts order extra and keep these separate from the bar requirements. Calculate on using a minimum of three glasses and three cocktail napkins per person.

Bartending Equipment (available at each bar station)
Bar Spoons (long handled)
Blender
Bottle Opener
Champagne Pliers
Citrus Reamer
Coasters
Cocktail Napkins
Corkscrews
Cutting Boards
Funnels
Garbage Cans and Liners (tastefully draped, covered, lined)
Garnish Bowls
Glass Pitchers

Glassware (Minimum of three glasses per person. In a pinch, a
    water glass can be used for wine and partially filled.)
Hand Towels
Ice Buckets/Tubs (For Wine/Champagne)
Ice Scoops
Ice Tongs
Jiggers
Lemon and Lime Squeezers
Measuring Cups
Measuring Spoons
Mixing Glasses
Mixing Pitchers (large)
Nutmeg Graters
Paring Knifes
Pepper Mills
Plastic to protect area behind the bar
Serving Trays
Shakers and Strainers
Sponges

When serving wine with dinner decide how it will be
poured. Will the opened bottles be left on the table for guests to
help themselves or will the waiters be responsible for pouring
the wine and topping up glasses? Have the waiters fill the wineglasses about a third to half, never more—you want to leave
room for the wine to breathe.

Again, as with the open bar, you must instruct staff to keep
you informed on how the wine consumption is going, and monitor the rate at which it is poured. Staff can give you a count of
how many bottles have been served, and you can make your
decision based on that. Know in advance how you will handle
requests for additional bottles or beverages other than wine.
Clients may decide to provide their guests with their individual
requests and pick up the tab for it, or they may instruct the waiters to say what is being provided is all that is available. How it is
worded is key—it could reflect on your company image. Make
sure that you give them the exact wording you would prefer.

Make sure that you have more than enough wine on hand. You will not be charged for unopened bottles, and if you have purchased them they can be returned in most cases if the seal has not been broken, and the label is intact. If you are doing an outdoor event and chilling the wine on ice, slip the wine into clear plastic bags so that the labels are not damaged.

In certain areas of the world, particularly warm, tropical locales such as the Caribbean, wine may not be as popular as tropical blended drinks, and some hotels carry only a limited number of bottles. They may not be able to meet additional demand and have to substitute another type of wine. This could be an issue in other parts of the world as well and in any restaurant where you have specifically ordered one type of wine.

When calculating the amount of wine per person take into account the rest of the evening. After dinner, will the bars be reopened or will the waiters take drink orders? Will there be speeches and presentations? In the latter case, you may want to increase the amount of wine served and have guests remain seated instead of opening the bar and having the presentation disturbed by guests getting up and down.

Wine with Dinner Following a Cocktail Reception

Wine	Per 50 Guests
Wine (Red)	Eight 750 ml Bottles Based on 2 Glasses/Person
Wine (White)	Twelve 750 ml Bottles Based on 2 Glasses/Person

Wine with Dinner Only (No Pre-Dinner Cocktails)

Wine	Per 50 Guests
Red Wine	Ten 750 Bottles Based on 1/2 Bottle/Person
White Wine	Fifteen 750 ml Bottles Based on 1/2 Bottle/Person

Wine Servings
750 ml = six x four ounce servings

Special Note: These amounts are based on 60/40 white to red
ratio, but will vary based on your menu choices and your guests'
personal preference. Red wine consumption is on the increase
and often goes as high as 60 per cent. If you are planning on
speeches or entertainment after dinner, and you are not
reopening the bar, increase your consumption estimate to one
bottle of wine per person.

An alternative to an open bar after dinner could be liqueurs
and cigars but keep in mind what it will do to the energy of the
main room if some of the guests scurry off to the cigar room.
You want the guests to go and enjoy a cigar but return to the
main area especially if there will be entertainment following dinner. Bear in mind that a quality cigar will take some time to
smoke, so you will lose part of your audience for up to an hour.

If you set up a smoking room make sure that it does not take
away from your overall objective. At one gala fund-raiser they
had an extensive array of items for a silent auction, but the
smoking room became the focal point of the event once dinner
was over. Guests went to the smoking area and stayed because
there was seating, a bar, and monitors showing the entertainment that was going on in the next room. Guests were content
just to sit and relax in the smoking room. Going back into the
cocktail area to revisit the silent auction was the last thing they
were prepared to do. Planners were pulling guests in three separate directions—silent auction area, dinner and entertainment
and smoking room. When planning to include smoking areas,
consider how they can affect the energy level and overall atmosphere of your event.

If you are planning on beginning or ending your event with
a champagne toast make sure that the facility has proper champagne flutes—not saucers—available in sufficient numbers. It
may be necessary to rent some. Corporate clients for special
occasions have also been known to provide their own logoed
champagne flutes, which the guests keep as a memento after
the toast. Arrangements can be made to have them washed and
packaged, but this will be labour intensive and there could be

additional charges to have this done. If you want to add a really festive air to the occasion, you may want to consider ordering champagne in oversize bottles from magnums to methuselahs. You will be ordering the same amount of champagne, but it provides a more elaborate and memorable show for your guests.

Champagne Toast	Per 50 Guests (Allows for 2 Glasses Per Person)
Champagne Toast	18 750 ml Bottles
750 ml = 6 x 4 Ounce Flute Glasses of Champagne	
1500 ml = 12 x 4 Ounce Flute Glasses of Champagne	
1 Case (12 Bottles) = 72 x 4 Ounce Flute Glasses of Champagne	

Champagne Bottle Sizes

Magnum	=	2 Bottles
Jeroboam	=	4 Bottles
Rehoboam	=	6 Bottles
Methuselah	=	8 Bottles
Salmanazar	=	12 Bottles
Balthazar	=	16 Bottles
Nebuchadnezzar	=	20 Bottles

The party is over. The bar has been closed down. Be sure once again to sign off on the bills for food and beverage and take a copy with you. At one event, the venue lost the entire record of charges and had to receive a copy from the event planning company. If there are any areas of dispute you will be able to address them immediately. Always take the time to note specific items on your bill while they are fresh in your mind such as the bottle of champagne that was ordered to celebrate someone's birthday. Three weeks after the event you may not remember why it was ordered and who gave their approval. Making clear notes will assist you with your reconciliation. If the facility is sending a final bill to you after the event you will be able to compare it with your original copy and address any changes or adjustments that have been made.

STAFFING

Let all staff—suppliers, volunteers, in-house staff—know how the event will unfold and what is expected of them (dress codes, protocol, behaviour). They play a major part in the success of your event and need to be—and feel—a part of it. The staff needs to be motivated to want the event to succeed as much as you do. Treat everyone with respect and consideration, including such simple things as saying please and thank-you.

When and where will staff take their breaks and meals? Is there a secure area for them to leave clothes and valuables? What arrangements do you need to make and include in your budget?

> Part of an event was a team-building exercise where the group had to cook dinner and set it out buffet style for 200 guests. This was done in a proper professional kitchen under the supervision of experts who do it every day. The group was divided into teams to prepare and cook certain items. Each was thoroughly briefed. Word came down that the meeting was breaking early and that the buffet for 200 had to be ready an hour ahead of schedule. That announcement galvanized the group, and they worked even faster. The team effort was a success. They managed to prepare the food on time and learned to appreciate and respect the hard work each contributes. The key ingredient in any successful event is the ability of everyone to come together as a team.

Information and communication is key when it comes to having an event without incident. The more the staff are aware of your needs the better they will be able to meet them. When you do a precon it is important to meet with not only your key contact but also the others who will be working behind the scenes as well. If you are doing an event at a hotel, the bell captain will need to know a number of things: What time are the guests arriving? Who is listed on the flight arrival manifest? Is it a local or an international flight? Has customs been cleared in the originating city, or does it have to be cleared upon arrival (this will affect the timing)? Will guests be coming by taxi, limousine or motor coach (each mode of transportation will have its own challenges)? Will the hotel receive a call from the airport letting them know that the guests are on their way?

All of this information will help the bell captain and staff to be in a position to do their jobs to the best of their ability, handle the needs of your arrival and get your guests and their bags to their rooms as fast as possible. They also need to know if they will be delivering any room gifts and when. Do these gifts have to be in the guest rooms before the guests arrive or after? This will affect the number of staff available to handle the luggage and the room deliveries.

The rooms manager will need to know when the guests are arriving at the hotel, if they are to take credit card imprints, if there are any VIPs who will be signing all to the master account, if two room keys must be in each packet in addition to the mini-bar keys and express checkout forms, if there are any room upgrades or special room requirements such as handicapped rooms (rooms close to the elevator for persons with disabilities or for someone who has a heart condition and may need to limit their walking), and accessibility to computer hook-up or fax machine. What is the protocol for VIPs' accommodations? This can be important to Asian clients—where the president is often located on the top floor with no staff or other VIPs on the same level. Will guests require two double beds or just one—may friends or siblings share a room? Will any guests need connecting or adjacent rooms? Will any guests want early check-ins or late checkouts? The location of the satellite check-in is yet another consideration among many.

Housekeeping needs to know arrival times as well to have sufficient staff on hand to turn the rooms around quickly. They also need to know if you will be using any day rooms as group change rooms so that they can have extra towels and other bathroom amenities ready. They will need to make sure that a person is assigned to check on and freshen the room as well. The person who handles the minibars will need to be advised if there are any special requests, such as stocking it with only cola or fruit juice. This can be arranged, but he or she needs to have advance notice.

All these items are covered in the function sheets and the arrival and departure manifest lists you prepare and give to the hotel, but having a representative from each section at your precon gives you a chance to review everything with them to ensure the information has been passed down and you can hear any concerns they might have regarding your planned itinerary. On the day of arrival make sure that you have enough staff to allow you to do a walk through of as many rooms as possible, especially the VIP rooms and the rooms that have special requirements.

> Twice now, in five-star properties, one in California and one in the Caribbean, I have walked into completely empty rooms. In California it was very obvious that the room had not been used or even cleaned in a long while. This was to be a VIP room with access for a computer and was supposedly the only one of its kind in the hotel at the time. An army arrived to put the room right—it was cleaned and sprayed, and furniture was raided from other rooms. It was ready (absolutely spotless) when the client arrived, but had we not checked she would have walked into a room that was empty of everything but cobwebs.

The concept of attention to detail applies not only to meetings, conferences, conventions and incentives but also to fundraising, weddings and any other special events. Success is in the details, someone once said, and they were absolutely right. Effective communication is the key. Sharing information is of utmost importance. Finding out what you *don't* know is crucial. The secret is to never ever assume anything.

Make sure that everyone is aware and knows exactly what is expected, how it is expected, when it is expected, where it is expected, and why it is expected so that you have a successful event that meets everyone's expectations and is without surprises and incident.

CHARITABLE DONATIONS

Loew's Hotels currently has a "Good Neighbour Policy" that makes it easy for organizations holding meetings at their hotels to donate any used or leftover display samples to a local charity after their event is complete. The clients save the time and money of shipping items back to their head offices, help those who are less fortunate and may be eligible for a tax deduction for the donation. In addition, although the purpose of the program is not public relations quite often the organizations donating also receive good press for their efforts.

The same can be done with the abundance of food that is often left over after an event. Check with your venue and local food banks or shelters to see what can be donated. The charity will arrange for the pick-up of items and can advise you of any special requirements. For example, they may be equipped to receive only the non-perishable items.

9 OTHER CONSIDERATIONS

ENTERTAINMENT

Great care must go into choosing your entertainment. Plan it carefully. Know your audience. What kind of event are you holding? Is it social, arty or corporate? Or a mixture of all three? What is the age range? What may be appropriate for one group may be *totally* inappropriate for another. There is a time and a place for everything. Make sure that strict guidelines are given to the MCs, comedians, musicians and performers. Use good judgement.

Does the band have a reputation of being reliable? Will the talent show up? Do your homework. Check references. Get referrals. Make sure they are professional. Read contracts carefully, and check riders for any hidden provisions. What do you need to include in your budget? Will you want encores? It needs to be in the contract. Be specific.

A detailed schedule of events will need to be prepared outlining all that will be happening on stage—the minute-by-minute action that will be taking place—taking into account the MC, the audio, the lighting and what is happening on screen.

Know your entertainment and know all of their act. Andre-Phillipe Gagnon is a fabulous world-renowned entertainer, who was scheduled to appear at an event whose planner had not seen his acts. Doing a final check of the ballroom before dinner and the private performance the planner saw what looked to be the remains of the crew's lunch, fast-food wrappers, containers and beverage glasses were piled in a corner in disarray. Just as a staff member was about to throw out this "garbage," he was stopped. It was actually part of Gagnon's props!

Live entertainment enhances any event as a wonderful ice-breaker. If you are doing an event out of country, find out what is special to the region and would be enjoyable to your guests. A sampling of entertainment to begin or end your event could include: arcade games, acrobats, belly dancers, caricaturists, casinos (complete with slot machines, roulette, craps, baccarat, trained staff and showgirls), church choirs, cigar rollers, magicians, dance bands, dessert chef (waffles or crepes), dance instructors, disc jockeys, chili cookoffs, fire-eaters, ethnic music and dancers, classical guitarists, folk singers, fiddlers, fortune tellers, harpists, handwriting analysts, Hawaiian dancers, ice cream specialty carts/stations, Indian sitar players, indoor fireworks or confetti bursts, interactive games, juke boxes, line-dance instructors, marching bands, mariachi bands, mimes, miniature racetracks, opera performances, oyster shuckers, photo booths, pianists, pool sharks, popcorn maker machines, a one-man band, saxophonists, speciality bars, speciality coffee makers, a square dance caller, reggae, steel drums or calypso music, a string quartet, sushi makers, tea leaf readers and virtual reality games. The list goes on—limited only by your imagination. Look for what is fun, what is new and available in your area. You can have armadillo races in San Antonio. Finding Hawaiian dancers in Nashville to launch an incentive program can be difficult but not impossible.

ENTERTAINMENT: Q&A

What time would the performance take place? Will rehearsal time be required?

In the contract specify what time you want the performers ready and dressed to go on. Always plan to have the music or entertainment begin at least 15 minutes before guests are scheduled to arrive. That way, they won't be greeted with dead air. Emphasize to the performers how important it is that they are ready before your guests arrive. Are they performing elsewhere on the same day? Is there sufficient time left between engagements? Are they scheduled to be anywhere else after your engagement? Do they have a plane to catch, which can be the case sometimes with prominent entertainers and guest speakers.

When you are scheduling rehearsal time, take into consideration what else will be going on in the room. Will the audio-visual crew need to be running sound checks at the same time as the band is scheduled to begin their rehearsal? Will rehearsals be taking place while cocktails are going on in the reception area? Will guests be able to hear them from there? Do you need to adjust the timing in any area?

Q & A

What time would the event end?

What are the chances that presentations and speeches could go on longer than planned? You may want to build in an extra hour as buffer.

Q & A

Would you require the entertainers to extend their hours if the event is in full swing?

In different areas of the world you can arrange for the party to extend pass 1:00 a.m., but you will need to obtain permission and a permit. You may want to have this option available to you should the host want the party to go on. Prepare the band for the possibility of playing longer than contracted. Find out the additional costs involved. Make sure that they know that they are not to start tearing down their equipment until they have been advised that it is OK to do so.

Q & A

When will their equipment be arriving? How long will set-up take?

Find out how the equipment will be arriving. Do you need to make any special arrangements for parking for offloading the truck? Will union crews and fees be involved? Will someone be available to set up immediately? Will the band supply the set-up person, will you or will the venue? How long will it take to set up the instruments and do a sound check? Have they worked at the facility before? If not, schedule a site inspection with them. Are there any areas that could be a concern such as stairs without an elevator, narrow passageways, pillars or hanging light fixtures to work around?

Will they be all ready before the decor and table set-up begins? How will this fit into what else is taking place in the room. What is the order of sequence?

Q & A

Do they have any special requirements for offloading and setting up of equipment?

Will they require the use of dollies? Will they need any assistance to offload? If the hotel is unionized, that help could be mandatory and those dollars need to be included in your budget as they will affect your bottom line. What equipment has to be rented and what costs are involved? Who is licensed to operate them? If you have complicated or extensive staging, lighting, audio-visual and entertainment move-in, set-up, rehearsals, event day and tear-down union costs could be high, in some cases $10,000 and more. That is why it is essential that these items be fully researched and incorporated into your budget. Will they require the use of an elevator, and do you need to schedule a time? Do you know the dimensions and weights of what is being moved in? For example, if you are moving in a piano will it fit in the freight elevator, and will you require a piano tuner? Find out all the entertainers' equipment needs to make the move in as smooth as possible.

Q & A

What is their equipment like?

Is it tasteful, trashy or in disrepair? Does it fit the company image? Are there any areas of concern? Are there any objectionable pictures or words displayed? Don't be surprised by the calibre of the equipment on the day of the event.

Q & A

Will you have anything on stage with the company logo on it?

Check with the agents and review your contracts. Some celebrities will not perform on stage with your product as it could suggest an endorsement. You may have to receive written permission or set up a separate staging area.

Q & A

Will the entertainers require a dressing room?

How many rooms will they need and how large? Are there any special requirements such as mirrors, special lighting, tables, chairs, hanging racks, storage space or refreshments? At one Oscar party one of the entertainers was painted gold from the waist up, and the gold paint needed to be removed at the end of the event. If the entertainment includes animal acts—for example a jungle party theme— what do they and the facility need for the care and safety of the animals and the guests? Visually, it may be exciting to have a live baby elephant or tiger as part of the entertainment, but what food and water or other special requirements will this entail? How hot is the lighting? Will the animals be protected from the guests? Will the guests be protected from them? What is your plan of action should the baby tiger escape among your guests? And who is on clean-up detail?

Q & A

Do meals and refreshments for the entertainers need to be included in the budget? Will they be treated as guests, or will meals be set up in a separate room?

If they are having their meals or refreshments in their dressing room make sure that you arrange for tables and chairs to be set up for their comfort. Performers are often delayed, so select food that will keep well, and do not have the area cleared until you check to see if they have had the opportunity to eat.

At one gala fund-raiser, by the time the performers went to get the food it had all been cleared away and because this happened in a convention centre not a hotel, replacement food was difficult to find. In the end all that was available was leftover hors d'oeuvres. The entertainers give the event their best; it is a sign of respect and appreciation to give them your best in return. And that may be not an option but a condition clearly outlined in their contract rider. Assign a staff person to oversee entertainers' needs.

Q & A

If entertainers are being served a meal, is there a specific time that is best, and do they have any special needs or requests?

Some performers choose to eat after their performance and not before. Find out if there are any special requirements and make sure that someone is responsible for overseeing this area. When a celebrity performer at a gala fundraiser had still not eaten at the end of the evening, it was discovered that he was a vegetarian. The staff managed to put together a suitable meal once his needs were known, but this should have been known and addressed before the event. Entertainers' meals do not need to be same as those being served to the guests.

Q & A

Is the entertainment—bands, models or other performers—permitted to drink or to otherwise join the event at any time?

Make sure that you discuss dress code and conduct with all contracted entertainers. You will need to decide if drinking and smoking are permitted or not. Are the performers to be included as a part of the party? You may want them to be. If you are doing an event with name entertainers you may want them to join in and mingle with your guests after their performance. For instance, at a theatre evening, you may want to invite some of the cast to your private post-theatre event. If the affair is held in a location away from the theatre, make arrangements to get them there and back. Find out what would be required in advance should they choose to accept the invitation. The performers will probably need time to change from costume and make-up, so it is important to know how long you anticipate your post-theatre party will be going on.

Q & A

Work out the band's break schedule in advance.

Does it need to be adjusted to work with the schedule of events? Will there be continuous play with staggered breaks or taped music? If using taped music to fill in at the breaks, do you want it to be the band's own music, or can it be low-key background music?

Q & A

You will need to see the band's repertoire of songs so that you can select a specific song list. Are there any songs that should not be played? Schedule a time to review them. Remember, you are the client and they are the supplier. If they insist on playing songs that are not appropriate for your audience— words or lyrics—they are not the right band for your event. Do you want to work with prima donnas?

Audition your entertainment. Try to see a live performance, and note how they interact with the audience. Many performers have CDs or tapes available, but be absolutely certain—spell it out in your contract—that what you hear on the CD or tape is who will actually be performing at your event. All the band members may not be the same, and the quality of the performance could change.

Q & A

Are they insured? Is their equipment insured?

Find out what insurance the entertainers have. They will need to have enough to cover damage to their equipment or to the facility. Do you need to arrange for additional coverage? Do they? What is outlined in the facility's terms and conditions?

Q & A

What additional costs need to be factored into the budget? These could include things such as music royalties and rights under ASCAP or BMI in the US or SOCAN in Canada, electrical power, rehearsals, overtime, encores, meals, and terms and conditions included in their contracts known as riders. Riders could include items such as air transportation, accommodation, meals, shipping of equipment, dressing rooms, equipment rentals, move-in and set-up costs, rehearsal fees and similar items.

All of the above items have a cost attached and need to be included in your budget. Are cartage or freight costs included in their quote? Is their equipment being shipped to you? What are their electrical power needs? Will they be tapping into the existing sound system, or will they be providing their own? Will you need back-up generators? Is the power at the venue sufficient to meet all of your event needs? Consider not just the entertainers but everything that needs to use power. What else is going on in the room and in the facility? What equipment do you need to provide for the entertainers? Will they require draped tables or chairs on stage, say, for a disc jockey? Do you have sufficient electrical outlets and extension cords? Where are they set up in relation to the available outlets? What do you have to do to avoid having guests tripping over any plugs and wires? Always review terms and conditions of the entertainers and the facility before you begin to prepare your budget so that you know in advance what has to be included.

Q & A

What are the dress requirements? Have the entertainers been informed?

How will they be dressed? Will they arrive dressed, or will they need to change once they get there? Do they require access to anything special such as a private bathroom or shower (in case of extensive make-up or body paint)? Does their dressing room need to be secure? Can it be locked? Will they require storage space?

**Q
&
A**

What are the home phone and cell phone numbers of the entertainers or their managers and agents in case of an emergency?

Make sure that you obtain home numbers, cell numbers or pagers. If something unexpected happens on the day of the event you need to be able to know who to reach, where to reach them and how best to do that. Keep in mind that entertainers generally perform in the evenings and may be difficult to reach first thing in the morning. (They could be sleeping.)

**Q
&
A**

How are requests to be handled?

Make sure this is reviewed with all involved. For example, if you are doing a low-key jazz reception designed specifically so that people will mingle and talk, and a request is made for something else (like hard rock), how do you want the DJ to handle this? For example, the DJ could say that the host has pre-selected the music and that all that is available to play is jazz then ask if there a specific jazz artist they would like to hear. Different music will change the whole tone of the evening, and it will be difficult to get the mood you want back. The purpose of your event may be to have people interacting with one another as opposed to being up on a dance floor. It is hard to mingle and chat if you can't hear one another above the music or if everyone is on the dance floor.

PHOTOGRAPHER

At a top hotel in Puerto Rico, the evening was festive and everything was moving along very well. The photographer had been doing a wonderful job until the presentation began. The moment was now at hand to take photos of key individuals receiving their awards, and his camera batteries went dead. No problem! He had been requested to have a back-up battery and camera. Problem! Both the back-up camera and battery gave out. As fate would have it there was a dance club at the hotel, and it was Valentine's day. The photographer who was on hand to take pictures of the happy couples quickly agreed to help out. He was *very* well compensated for snapping a few pictures of the presentation before he returned to his happy Valentine couples in the dance club. The original photographer adjusted his bill to compensate for not being able to complete his job.

If you are doing special events in a port of call, always budget for staff to fly in ahead of the ship to advance each event and to make sure that all is in readiness.

You can plan, you can prepare, and have Plan B (the backup cameras, batteries and assistant) at the ready, but you still have to be able to think on your feet and think fast to find the solution. Sometimes it's just down the hall on Valentine's Day. Another answer could have been to have the remaining official photos taken back on ship, by the ship's photographer while everyone was still dressed up. A near-disaster could be turned into a triumph—a VIP moonlight champagne reception—as the ship set sail. What would have been missing though would be the beautiful themed decor in the background that was important to the client to capture.

PHOTOGRAPHER: Q&A

How many photographers will you need? Will you want a traditional photographer (posed shots) or a photojournalist-style photographer (capturing what is going on in the room) or perhaps a video of the event? Will you want one photographer stationed in a central spot for specific shots of celebrity guests, for instance, and another to cover the ongoing events in the room as they are happening?

What are your needs? You may miss a priceless photo opportunity if there are not enough photographers on hand. For gala fund-raisers a fabulous photo can be of tremendous value and result in more media exposure. In what areas will you need to station photographers? You don't want your photographers to be continually pulled in all directions, which can happen if you have a number of committee members all issuing different directives. Imagine what would happen when an celebrity pops in for a quick hello unexpectedly, and you miss the chance for a wonderful endorsement of your cause because your photographer was tied up in another part of the event. The moment is gone and so is the celebrity. While the media may bring their own photographers, it is still a good idea to have your own on hand. You will want specific pictures taken and can't expect the media photographers to be at your beck and call. The media's focus would probably be on the celebrities, and they may not include the sponsor in their shots of well-known stars. On the other hand, you want the sponsor's name to appear with that of the star especially if you hope to have this sponsor back again next year and to attract others. It is a good marketing move for them and for you. Name recognition is key. With your own photographer, you will be able to ensure that specific shots are taken and are sent out to the media.

Q & A

When do you want the photographer to arrive? How long do you want him or her to stay?

Will you require pre-event shots to be taken to show the room set-up and decor? Will the photographers have to stay to take pictures of the final addresses or of the winners of door prizes? Do you want them to stay for a set time period or until the very end? What will best fulfil all of your needs?

Q & A

Will you want black and white prints, colour or both? What about slides or video?

Where will you be using your photos, and what will work best? Will they be submitted to the media, used in company newsletters or shown at staff meetings? Will you be sending out a copy to each participant or hanging them on your company's hall of fame? Consider the areas where they can best be used and what will best fit your needs and your budget. You will also need to discuss with the photographer the cost of having the prints produced. Will you be able to purchase the negatives (some photographers will not sell them), and, if so, at what cost? Does the photographer retain copyright? Will the photographer need to be credited for all shots sent to the media? You will need to know this in advance.

Q & A *What size and quantity of prints will you want?*

On incentive programs photographs are often taken and sent out later in custom frames or albums as a record of the event. If time permits, these can be prepared and left as a farewell pillow gift on the last night of the event. Purchase your frames and albums in advance so that you know the exact dimensions of your prints. It is easier to order pictures to fit the perfect frame than trying to find a frame that will fit the perfect picture.

Q & A *Will you want photos shot vertically or horizontally?*

Does the venue have locations that are ideal for photographs? As you do the site inspection of the property think about what area would visually lend itself to the photographs you want taken? Where would you like the photographs taken? At the Opreyland Hotel in Nashville, they have a wonderful staircase, a beautiful atrium area and delightful fountains. In all three of these spots vertical pictures would be preferable. Because of the height of each locale, you would lose much of the beauty of the background if you were to do a horizontal picture. Look at each area as if you were looking through a camera lens. Is there anything hanging, like wires, that would interfere with the picture? Sure, the picture can be cropped, but that might throw the balance of the picture off, and cropping isn't cheap. If you need a professional eye to scout locations, get the photographer to advise you. You will have to pay for this, but it may pay off in the long run. If the photographer has not worked in the location before, he or she may need to do a site inspection, particularly if you are doing specialty shots, to assess what lighting and equipment will be needed.

Q & A

How will the photographer be paid? If charging by the hour, what is the rate? Is there a minimum number of hours? Is there a flat rate? Does that rate include film, contact sheets, negatives, prints? What are the rates for black and white and for colour film? How much are prints?

Make sure you receive a quote in writing and have all costs itemized. Some clients choose to simply pay for the photographer's time, film use and a contact sheet, preferring to have extra prints made at home. If you are purchasing the exposed, undeveloped film only check with the photographer on how best to transport it through the airport X-ray machines. Once you have the film in your possession it is your responsibility, and you have no recourse if it is lost or stolen.

T I P

Most professional photographers guard their creative rights. If your event is a celebrity event it is unlikely that the photographers will release the film and the negatives to you. They will work with you to send them to the media, but they will want their work credited.

Q & A

What is the turnaround time? How quickly will the photographer be able to provide you with contact sheets or prints?

At some events, photographs are taken at the beginning of the evening, developed immediately, put in custom frames and are ready for the guests to pick up on their way out. There are extra charges to do a rush job of this nature, and it can be a real stampede depending on the number of guests in attendance. At a dinner in Portugal, individual pictures of the group were taken during cocktails and by dessert a carton of matchbooks was delivered with the restaurant's logo and each member's personal picture on the front cover. You can come up with many different ideas, but the key is whether your idea is doable logistically and how quickly it can be turned around. It is a wonderful idea to present prizewinners with an album full of pictures at the end of an incentive program, but if something goes wrong with the developing, or there isn't enough time to mount all the photos it could be an expensive and unproductive proposition. Mailing the photo albums to prizewinners after the event is better than nothing but loses the energy, spark and surprise of the original idea.

Q & A

Are there any additional charges to factor into your budget? These would include such things as couriers, meals, refreshments, costs to transport equipment and parking.

Will there be any additional charges if photographers have to take part in a site inspection of the facility? Have you made arrangements for them to be able to eat, either with the guests or in a separate area? Have you factored these costs into your budget? Will any charges apply for transporting equipment? Will you be charged gas and mileage? Find out in advance what costs could apply. For example, on an incentive program while the winners are meeting, it is possible to set up a glamour photo shoot with hair and make-up artists, clothing props and light refreshments to entertain the spouses. Each guest receives notification of their shoot time in advance. A professional photograph can be a wonderful treat and something they might not do for themselves. Costs for the suite, make-up artists, hair-dressers, props and refreshments would all need to be included in your budget in addition to the photographer and film. The guests' spouses will probably be so pleased with the results that they will want copies for their families. How will you handle that request? Will the company be picking up the cost, or are they the responsibility of the guest and billed to their room? Find out in advance.

Q & A

Do photographers have any special requirements? Are they familiar with the venue they will be shooting in? Is there sufficient light, and are there any other areas of concern?

These photographers are experts in their field, or at least they should be—it's your job to find out. Some companies choose to bring their own photographers with them around the world, while others will work with locals. If you do, get referrals. Check with the hotels and florist shops to see whose name keeps coming up. Listen to their advice and suggestions. It is important that the photographers be familiar with the property and, if they haven't worked there before, available for a site inspection. They need to know the locales, what light they will be working in and the equipment they will need.

Q & A

Have you advised the photographers of dress code and protocol?

Be very specific about proper dress and conduct. How do you wish them to be dressed—subdued or flamboyant? You don't want your photographers' mode of dress to become the talk of the evening. Make sure that it is never revealing or loud. You want them to blend in, not stand out from the crowd. As well, discuss their conduct from eating and drinking to the accepted way of speaking with guests.

Q & A

If this is a high-profile event is the photographer you are considering familiar with key celebrities and society guests?

It is imperative to have a photographer who is familiar with who is who. They need to know instinctively who will be newsworthy and make a terrific picture. You need someone who can recognize a dignitary's car and who is well aware of proper protocol.

Q & A

Are you familiar with the photographer's work? Have you seen samples and talked to references?

In local newspapers and magazines study the photo credits on the types of photographs you want. Look at the quality of their work—does it meet your needs? Study the composition, sharpness and colour balance. This is a good starting point when selecting a photographer. Be sure to check references and dig around to find out if there are any unsatisfied customers not mentioned in the references. Keep an open mind, but try to get the complete picture.

Q & A

Do you have specific groupings of photos that you want taken? Who will be preparing the list, reviewing it with the photographer and be assisting them during your event to help identify and bring together the people that you want photographed together?

If you have specific photo groupings that you want taken make sure that the photographer has been provided with a list. Assign a staff member who is familiar with the invited guests to assist the photographer in obtaining the photos.

Q & A

Will you or the photographer be sending copies to the media? Have you included the cost for reprints and couriers in your budget?

Who will have the final say on which photographs are being released to the media? The media of course makes the final decision on what they print or show, but what needs to be established is who will sign off on the prints being released to the media. You may want the photographer's advice on the best pictures, angles, colours, compositions and the like, but you must make it crystal clear that you have the final say. Find out in advance the media deadlines, and make sure that you meet them. Call the media to let them know when to expect the photographs and follow up to ensure that they have received them and find out when the photos will be appearing. Have you included all applicable costs for the reprints, envelopes, letters, couriers and additional time for the photographer in your costing? The same will apply to video footage. Another area to consider is whether you will be using the photographs on the company Web site or posting photos on the Web site so the media can download whatever they want.

THEMES AND PROGRAMS

CENTREPIECES

There are two things to remember when deciding on centrepieces: make sure guests can see each other over them and expect guests to walk off with them. Keep the centrepieces small enough so that guests can see each other across the table when seated. They can be low, raised high on clear pedestals or a mixture of both; they don't have to be one or the other. Have a sample done and test it out beforehand by actually sitting down at a table.

> At an industry function for event planners in Chicago years ago, the guests walked in, sat down, and almost in unison, each table immediately moved the centrepiece; you could not see the person across from you. The centrepieces looked wonderful but defeated their purpose. They became a barrier and an obstacle not a centrepiece that added to the event.

Centrepieces can range from very cheap and simple to very extravagant and elaborate. They can be a dramatic array of orchids or exotic tropical flowers bathed in candlelight or a single, perfect rose. Centrepieces can be beautiful. They can be imaginative. They can be interactive. They can be fun. They can encompass everything from fishbowls with real or blown-glass fish floating around to a beach party theme in the middle of winter to loot bags filled with childhood toys and candies from the past to tie into a theme (for a 50s, 60s, or 70s party).

You create a visually dramatic centrepiece by selecting just one colour and one type of flower. Varying the height and the width of the arrangements provides added interest. If you choose to include an assortment of flowers, remember to take into consideration not only how they will look but also the overall effect of the combined fragrances—do they compliment one another or are they overpowering together? Have you considered all customs and protocol and made sure that no flowers, colours or numbers—white, 13—in a centrepiece will be a breech of what is appropriate? Also, VIPs often demand more elaborate centrepieces.

Find out from the florist the best delivery time. How long will it take the flowers to be fully opened and at their absolute best? Should they to be refrigerated to prevent them from opening prematurely? Are there any special care arrangements? Can the facility accommodate this? How long will the flowers last, and what is the florist's policy on substitutions? Make sure in the written contract they outline what is being sent, the time, the delivery instructions and all costs for delivery and set up.

Suppose you are doing a theme dinner in the Caribbean and the only flowers that will tie in must be pure white. At that time of year there are no white flowers in bloom on the island, so you arrange to have them brought in from Miami. They arrive, but instead of the flowers you expected, they sent a substitution— daisies with bright yellow centres. There is no time to have others flown in, so what do you do? Do you use flowers that would take away from the total effect, or do you get creative? One of the colours in this theme dinner was gold. It is amazing how a little artfully applied gold spray-paint salvaged this situation.

> **T**
> **I**
> **P**
> There is not always a large selection of materials such as gold spray paint on all Caribbean islands, so plan ahead, and, like the boy scouts, be prepared.

At an event in Mexico—flowers were being delivered for a Valentine's Day program—pink roses were to be tied with pink ribbon. The hotel claimed over and over that it had pink ribbon. It did, but it read, "It's A Girl." White ribbon was used. Check and double check.

If you are doing a product launch in your home city you can almost guarantee that the number of guests invited for dinner will increase, sometimes without notice. At one product launch, calls started to arrive at the hotel for instructions on where the dinner was to take place. This was a tad suspicious since all invited guests were staying at the hotel. Senior VIPs had extended last-minute invitations to key suppliers to join them for dinner and the show but had not told anyone. Extra tables were hurriedly thrown together, but that may not always be possible. How quickly could your florist respond to a call for additional centrepieces? Would they have sufficient supplies on hand? Do you need to look at initially building in a buffer and ordering additional centrepieces that could be set out on display tables if they were not required? Check with your client to see if having additional last-minute guests could be a possibility and if they want to order additional centrepieces to cover this. It is important to know in advance if there will be additional guests as the room capacity may not be able to handle more people and there may not be sufficient meals to go around. If the event is open-seating there may be no way to tell who is an invited guest and who is an addition. Your client must keep you informed of any changes. And, as an event planner, it is your responsibility to keep your client informed of room capacity, fire regulations and the effect of having last-minute invited guests.

The second item to remember is to be prepared for your centrepieces to walk away at the end of the night. If they are rented, you could end up with a major unexpected cost added to your budget. If someone has spent $5,000 to purchase a table at a charity event, the last thing you want to tell them is that they can't take the centrepiece. Prepare for it and plan for it in your budget. That way, you avoid unexpected surprises.

You can use the centrepieces as part of your event and reuse them afterwards. You can make them a part of your event by holding a draw having one person at each table win them. If you are doing a meeting the next morning you can use them to enhance the buffet table.

> If you are considering flowers for meeting rooms make
> them potted—that way they can be sent to a nursing
> home or hospital after the event. Little cards can be
> printed stating that they are being donated.

The client may want the flowers or centrepieces sent to their guest rooms or to those of the VIPs. In these cases, arrange for a bellman to deliver them. Don't have your clients carrying them around in evening dress; have it done with finesse. On one two-stage incentive program the client and guests were so enchanted with the floral arrangements that they had to be shipped from one hotel to the next. Advise the facility in advance what you will be doing with the centrepieces. You don't want them to clear them away and discard them if you are planning to use them again the next morning or to send them on to a nursing home or hospital. Make sure you know what is yours when you are pricing your centrepieces. If the base or the vase is rented, donated or loaned you will be charged if guests take them home. The same applies to decorative props.

There are centrepieces that involve indoor pyro (fireworks that are designed for indoors), but they can be very dangerous and should be handled with extreme care. At one event where centrepieces with pyro were used at each table, they were set off by a charger that was located in the service passageway. Afterwards the charger was left unattended and caught on fire, which was discovered by a waiter who just happened to be walking by. Anything involving fire and fireworks requires extreme care. Know the risks and what insurance, permits and safety precautions you need. What is the facility's policy? Some venues will not allow even candles. Whenever indoor pyro is used make sure that you work with professionals who are specialists in this field. Ask them for suggestions that will dazzle your guests. There are some other wonderful alternatives to centrepieces with indoor pyro you can use instead—pyro can startle guests if they are not expecting a firework display coming from their centrepiece and once guests have been seated and placed items on the table top you have no control over what can be leaning up against the pyro. An airburst of indoor pyro over the service doors as dessert is being wheeled out, specialty firework candles in a cake or an indoor fireworks display with a custom logo as the grand finale are alternate suggestions to consider. Other ideas for centrepieces can include water fountains and wet rock gardens. The important thing is to be creative.

DECOR

The term decor includes all of the furnishings and decorations in the room, but just what you include can be a problem. Look around at your selected venue. What colour is the carpeting? What colour are the walls? What about the chairs? Look at the dishes, the silverware, the glassware. Do they all come together? What needs to be done to make it feel more "special"? Will it have an impact or be lost in a sea of hues? Look carefully at the dollars you are spending on decor. Will you be better off spending them all on one area rather than spreading them around and not getting the same results? For example, are you better to use the venue's linens and spend more money on the floral arrangements, or would bringing in something special be more fitting? Picture black linens, oversize black polka dot overlays, black chair covers, red glass plates, black-stem wineglasses, black napkins with red trim or black and white polka dotted with red trim and a bouquet of fresh full red tulips. Alternatively, think about plain white linen, china, silver and crystal with a striking centrepiece. What is the look, the feel, the mood you want to create? What do you remember most from the events you have attended? At one dinner event in Singapore everything was very elegant and traditional until the end. Then, all at once, the floral centrepieces were removed and baskets filled with truffles descended from the ceiling to land precisely in the middle of each dinner table. People walked away talking about that for some time to come. The dinner, the dishes and the food were all excellent but it was the presentation of the truffles that was memorable.

Another part of decor is the print material—custom menus, place cards, table number signs, programs and signage—that need to be included your budget. All of these could be tied together, part and parcel of the total picture. Know how long it will take to have everything prepared. There have been events where the programs arrived after the guests, and custom designed T-shirts showed up literally hot off the press—they were still hot to the touch.

You may be surprised at the endless number of items that are available for rent—everything from hangers and coat racks to elegant serving pieces and silver candelabra. You can rent tables and chairs in any number of combinations from formal elegance to casual and fun. You are not limited to the banquet chairs the facility offers and, even if you choose to use them, they can be covered for greater impact. Along with chairs, tables and chair covers you can rent linens, overlays, napkins, high-top bar tables, banquet tables, registration tables, half-moon tables and serpentine tables.

> **T**
> **I**
> **P**
>
> **Make sure that the tables you will be using are a solid unit in the size requested. Some facilities and rental companies put plywood over smaller tables, which, if not properly attached, can easily tip if someone leans on them.**

Find out if the rental prices include set up, or if the company will just drop off the items. You need to know this in advance because it could take some time to set up, and you may need to bring in additional help.

Schedule a time to meet with the rental company to see the quality of goods they offer. Look beyond their display area. Ask to see samples of what is in back. Spot-check items. You need to make sure that their linens are free of cigarette burns, stains, and visible mends. It is important that the linens are delivered to you in pristine condition.

Table settings for rent run from designer selections to those more appropriate for a company BBQ. You can rent show plates, dinner plates, salad plates, dessert plates, side plates, flat plates, rimmed plates, soup bowls, consommé cups and saucers, regular cups and saucers and demitasse cups and saucers. Cutlery can range from gold plated and sterling silver to plastic, and each has an appropriate use. There are dozens of types of dinner knives, fish knives, butter knives, dinner forks, fish forks, salad and dessert forks, dessert spoons, soup spoons, teaspoons and demitasse spoons.

Glassware can be rented in everything from the finest crystal to everyday glass, both plain and coloured, and you can rent glasses in every conceivable shape—highballs, old fashioneds, martini glasses, wineglasses in a variety of sizes, brandy snifters, liqueur glasses, champagne saucers, champagne flutes, sherry glasses, shooters, pilsner glasses, beer steins and water goblets. Glassware can be used for beverages, desserts and to hold individual floral displays at each place setting. Make sure that you have more than enough on hand.

What you need to find out in advance is how they are being delivered, when they are being delivered, who will be unpacking them, who will be setting them out, who will be collecting them, who is responsible for cleaning them and who will be repacking them and sending them out. Know clearly what the rental agency will be doing, what the facility staff will contribute and what you will be responsible for. Make sure that it is clearly listed on your invoice and contract who is supplying what number of staff for the move-in, set-up and tear-down. Make sure all special requests are noted and that the supplier confirms in writing (known as "signing back") items, pricing and timing. Find out if they are licensed and insured, and who incurs what costs should any items be broken or damaged?

Along with rental companies, check with decor companies, prop houses that work with theatre or movies, florists, antique shops, art galleries, specialty lighting and furniture stores and even nurseries for new and interesting ideas. Be sure you discuss rental costs, delivery charges and insurance with each of them. Check the rental costs against the cost to buy. Sometimes it can be less expensive to purchase the item, but the question then is what do you do with it when the event is finished? You could ask the hotel or venue if they are interested in purchasing them from you, or once again you may want to have the items donated.

Fountains (actual working ones), water art (walls of water that can be lit, waterfalls and an array of other items) and fibre optics through which colours of light shine—(the lights can be programmed to change colour throughout the evening—walls and ceilings can be done this way), are all very dramatic enhancements that can be rented in a variety of sizes. What will be of extreme importance is how much time will be required for set up and if suppliers have any special requirements.

SPECIAL EFFECTS

Special effects are well named—they are not called special for nothing, and they can have a spectacular effect at any event. Imagine walking into a ballroom that has been turned into a forest with the scent of pine reaching into the lobby, or perhaps the room is transformed into an ice-skating rink with "snow" falling.

You can fill a room with sound coming at you from all angles (surround sound) instead of just the stage area. You can fill a room with scent. You can light up the room with a laser show, fireworks or robotic lighting and bring in sweeps of colours. You can create high energy with fast-rolling light beams or have undertones of light crawl across the floor. Smoke (dry ice) can be brought in to give more effect. Custom images or logos can be inserted on clear walls or floors. Events can be cybercast live. You can touch all of the senses—sight, sound, smell, taste and touch—and seek to stimulate all of them.

Special effects can be extremely complicated, so it is essential that you find out how much set-up time is required and know all costs involved including labour and power. Are there permits required, any safety regulations to be aware of? Are the materials being used flameproof? Find out what can go wrong, and what can be done to prevent it. Let your suppliers know what else is going on in the room. Consider the consequences of having candles burning on the tables during a confetti shower. That sounds like a recipe for diaster. The confetti is supposed to be flameproof, but is it? If not, you could end up with a little more excitement than you bargained for. Check to make sure your special effects meet and exceed all safety regulations. Again, you may need to budget for a fire watch to be on duty during the event. A fire marshal and the hotel may have to approve all proposed plans. They will advise you of what needs to be done for your event to move ahead. They may require detailed floor plans, a schedule of events and a show flow chart.

PARTING GIFTS

Parting gifts are always a nice way to mark the culmination of a special event. Make them meaningful. Make them a part of everyone's take-away memory. They don't have to be expensive, but they should be memorable.

> A pre-theatre party was held by the reflecting pool at the Westin Century Plaza in Los Angeles. Guests were then taken to see *Forever Plaid* and after the performance they returned to the hotel's incredible presidential suite with balconies that wrap around the entire floor. The view was spectacular. The cast of the play arrived and mingled with the guests, and when guests returned to their rooms waiting on their pillows was a CD from *Forever Plaid* tied with a piece of plaid ribbon. It was simple and inexpensive but it captured the memory perfectly. It was very well done.

> On one incentive program the welcome gift arrived as all the guests were heading back to the airport. The client had been advised but had not sent them out in sufficient time. Items can and will be held up in customs, and that needs to be factored into the logistics and timing. Find out well in advance what customs will require, what your broker will require and how much time is needed to get the item there well in advance of the guests' arrival. The hotel will store all shipped parcels in a secure area until you arrive.

FINAL TOUCHES

You have chosen the site, you have selected the food and beverage and you have worked with the facility, staging, lighting and audio-visual people to make sure that the room layout and timing logistics will work. There is also decor and entertainment to take into consideration before you are ready to sign contracts. If you are doing an elaborate decor set-up you need to factor in their move in set-up and tear-down time. You need to know that all the pieces will fit together and how, because each is linked and can have an impact on one another. You can't have the tables moved into position and set up if the entertainment and decor need room to bring in their equipment. Planning ahead helps eliminate the need of doing things twice. You lose time, energy, money and sometimes even patience if proper thought and planning have not gone on beforehand.

First consider what atmosphere you are looking to create and how you go about doing that. Then work out the logistics behind it. What will it need to achieve it? Each event is different, but what you learn from one you can often apply to the next.

Are you looking to achieve a warm, welcoming ambience, or are you searching for something of a decidedly different nature?

A *Ghostbusters* theme event was held in the dungeon of a real castle. Candles flickered in the darkness, eerie sounds emanated from the background and an unexpected laser show greeted you as you made your way through the narrow damp tunnels. Then you suddenly emerged into the old stables where a lively party atmosphere enticed you. The planners had wanted a dramatic entrance to their party, and they exceeded everyone's expectations.

If you are doing a theme event as part of your meeting, you can set the party mood from the moment guests leave the meeting and get into their hotel rooms. Glow-in-the-dark hands can hold an invitation to the evening's events for a party that is taking place over Halloween. Inflated dolphins can be placed in the room—or even in a bathtub filled with water—with an invitation to an exclusive dinner set in an aquarium. Children's in-line skates can hold fun candy and an invitation to a day event that will include in-line skating lessons. Deliver one skate to each room as part of the invitation prop. (The next day a skate exchange can be held at the hospitality desk and guests with young children, nieces and nephews, grandchildren can exchange sizes, find a match and the rest can be donated to charity).

You want guests to feel a sense of anticipation, a sense of celebration as they arrive. What will they see first when they arrive? Will it have visual impact? Will there be someone on hand to greet them and welcome them into the event? Does the room have the feeling of all details being attended to in advance of their arrival, or are people running around trying to pull together last-minute changes? At one restaurant opening they kept changing the time and announcing it with a hand-written sign. Guests arriving at the appointed hour peered through the blinds, saw that nothing was ready and left. How is the room temperature—is it too hot or too cold? As more people arrive this is something that needs to monitored. How long does it take for the air-conditioning to kick in and cool down the room?

Is the food and drink readily at hand? Does it look and smell inviting? Is it nicely presented? Is there enough staff to properly service the event? One facility that was attempting to showcase its capabilities underestimated the number of cooking staff it would need for the number of guests invited. Inevitably they rushed things and tried to turn everything around too quickly. They served mussels that were undercooked and unopened. They attempted a too-intricate dish for a buffet. The line-ups were long, and there were not enough other foods available. One yacht cruise being launched had set up a casino to show what could be done on board. There was taped music, but this was a crowd of business people coming together, without spouses, for the first time and dancing was not appropriate. The yacht provided only enough casino chips to last each person about 10 minutes. The cruise was over three hours long, and there was no other entertainment on board. This was only fun play, not for money or prizes, and there would have been no more added expense to have brought along sufficient tokens to allow for unlimited play for those guests who wanted to partake. To top things off, the yacht ran out of food. They had a television crew aboard and instead of an air of excitement and fun, they got fizzle.

> **T**
> **I**
> **P**
> With private yacht charters determine the plan of action should the boat run into difficulties. One yacht simply stopped mid-cruise, and it took hours to get it going again.

Take the time to visualize all aspects of your event. Put yourself in the room. What does it feel like? What does it look like? In your mind walk through the entire event from the moment guests arrive until they leave. What do you need to make it the absolute best? Go through contracts with a fine-tooth comb making sure that all costs have been included in your budget. Read the terms and conditions—have they all been met? Do you have all appropriate permits? Take the time to do a check. And if you can, it is always advisable to have someone else double-check your contracts and costings. A fresh pair of eyes may catch something that has been overlooked. If the proper research and development has gone into your costing and creative, the operations on the project will fall easily into place. If it hasn't, and you have already signed off on contracts, it can have a tremendous effect—financially and operationally—on your proposed project.

CONCLUSION

IT'S A WRAP!

The last guest has departed. Your event has concluded. At the end of the day remember, only you and the people involved in the planning and operations will know if it all came about exactly as planned. Your evening may have had some unexpected twists and turns, but isn't that what life is all about? If you have managed to meet the challenges calmly, serenely and with a smile, no one will really know what actually took place backstage. Keep in your mind the image of a swan gracefully gliding on water while underneath feet are paddling furiously. And during the event try to take time to savour it, if only for a moment before moving on to the next item in your function sheets. Remember to make note of any observations directly on your function sheets. They will refresh your memory when you have your wrap-up review.

If you can, plan to do nothing but pamper yourself the next day. There is always an emotional impact the day after an event. You have put your heart and soul into it, worked day and night to bring it about and now it's over. Sometimes it can be a year in the planning and other times three weeks but, either way, you are probably exhausted. It's a time to reflect and bask in the success of a well-orchestrated event. Take the time to review your event with all those involved, but don't schedule it for the very next day. Give everyone time to review their notes, gather their thoughts and get some rest, but hold the review while the event is still fresh in everyone's mind. When you do the event evaluation make it clear that you are not looking at areas of blame but areas of learning and growth. What worked? What would you do differently next time? To this day, there is not one event where I haven't learned something that I can bring to the next one. Take the time to prepare a wrap-up report, and make a copy for your files that will go with the stored material once your event and final reconciliation have come to a close. Were your objectives met? If not, what could be done differently to bring about different results? Did you come in on budget? Did you spend more in one area than anticipated? What were the reasons? Were they valid? What was the feedback? Record all relevant thoughts and observations. They will be valuable to you later when you begin to plan your next event.

APPLAUSE! APPLAUSE!

Remember to schedule time to say thank you. The best time is in the days immediately following your event, when everything is still very fresh in your mind. Be as specific as you can be. If there were people who went above and beyond to make sure that your event was successful, let them know how much you appreciate their efforts personally and mention them by name in your letter to your main contact.

> **T I P** Take care with the wording of your letters and how much confidential information is in them. They may be seen by others and could be used as reference letters to other potential clients so do not name your client but talk specifically about the event and their involvement in making it a success.

At all costs, avoid form thank-you letters. It destroys the whole message if two or more people discover they have received identical letters. Put the same thought and care into your letters that you want them to put into your event. You never know when you may find yourself working together on another project.

Use your function sheets as a tool to remind you who needs to be thanked. Collect business cards as you go along so you can refer to them for the correct spelling of names, titles and addresses. And, once again, remember to include in your budget an estimated amount for cards, letterhead, envelopes, postage, couriers and any thank-you gifts you may be sending. Put some thought into the thank-you gift you send. Ideally, it will be a reminder of the event. If you had a featured singer, you could have a CD personalized and signed for them. If in conversation you learn what their interests are, perhaps by what they display in their offices, take the time to use that knowledge to make their thank-you gift special. The gift doesn't have to be expensive, but it must be thoughtful. You may even want to come up with a signature gift. I have always loved to give miniature inukshuks, which are the traditional stone built by the Inuit as directional markers, leading the way for others. They are symbolic of our responsibility to each other and our dependence on one another. They are the perfect symbol for event planners. When you do an event you are dependent on one another, and each of us is responsible for leading the way for the others who follow behind.

YOUR NEXT EVENT

The skills learned to plan successful meetings, conferences, conventions or incentives transfer over to other special events. What you learn from one event can help you with your next one. While it may not be exactly the same scenario, what you learned and experienced may trigger an interesting twist you can bring to your next event.

You now have an invaluable record of suppliers, phone numbers and key information. Take the time to record all of these numbers and contact names, organize your files and transfer all the information to one central place. Leave no messy files, no bits and pieces of paper floating around. As you take apart your files, secure them with an elastic and place each section in a separate unsealed envelope that is clearly labelled. Then place them in order—bound together again—in a larger container such as a box or envelope, that has been clearly labelled with key information. You will find that you will go back to this information and refer to it for a variety of reasons as you begin to plan your next event. Having the majority of the event planning stages organized and easily available makes it so much more effortless when you need to find something that is critical to the success of your next event. *What was the name of that balloon company? They were wonderful. You want to include them in your next event, but you just can't remember their exact name.* Store all your related material with it—cost breakdowns, payment schedules, critical path and function sheets with a back-up copy of your computer disk.

Start fresh with each new event. Set up new files. There will be a new set of logistics to consider and work your way through. Start at the beginning and begin to fill in the detail. There is magic in the detail, the magic of memorable events.

APPENDIX A:
SAMPLE COST SHEETS
–GALA FUND-RAISER

A cost sheet is a detailed breakdown of the costs related to your specific event. It is used to provide an overview of items that you will need to include to produce a successful event. It shows you clearly what each item will cost and helps you determine whether or not it is an expense that you wish to include. Once you've had an opportunity to review the total estimated costs as listed you may decide that the money being spent on centerpieces would be better applied to one lavish memorable "WOW" item like a chocolate fountain. Itemizing your costs allows you to see all the elements that must be included in each area and laying them out "storyboard fashion" allows you to do a visual walk through ensuring that you do not miss a step. For example, if invitations are being included in the costing, items you would need to consider and account for under invitations would include: the quality, the size (has a bearing on postage), the printing, the special touches, the quantity required, etc. Envelopes for the invitations would also need to be considered. You would need to detail all the elements and costs that could apply to them: the quality, the quantity (have you costed in sufficient envelopes to cover any addressing errors or damage) or the printing (return address), how they are being addressed—by hand, printed labels or will the addresses be printed directly on the envelopes. All of the items mentioned above have a cost attached to them—be it the actual cost of the item or the cost of labor. All these cost items must be accounted for in order for your projected budget to be based on realistic costs. No one wants to be presented with a $100,000 costing error after contracting—it can and has happened. By taking the time to lay each item out and factoring in all possible costs that could be incurred you can avoid costly errors. Walking through your event step by step on your Cost Sheet with the same detail and thought given to each item, no matter how seemingly insignificant, will help you to fine tune your budget and reduce/eliminate mistakes.

The Cost Sheet is the foundation on which your event is built and it is a multi-purpose tool. You can use it as the base for your Critical Path because many of the elements that need to be handled are outlined in both. The same applies for your Payment Schedule—your Cost Sheet can be copied and reformatted to work out your Payment Schedule, reducing the time spent re-inputting the same information. As your event progresses and items are continually updated and subtracted and final costs are input—what was once your original Cost Sheet becomes your Final Reconciliation—and you will be going into your event knowing exactly where you stand.

The following sample Cost Sheet for a gala fund-raiser includes three columns at the top. This is just one example of how a Cost Sheet can be laid out (a second example is provided in Appendix B). Here the headings displayed are LOT COST, P.P., and # of PAX.

The LOT COST is the total cost of the line item. This can be based on either a flat rate cost, i.e., room rental charge; the total cost, i.e., the cost of table linens based on x number of tables multiplied by the per table linen cost; or a cost that has been calculated on a cost per item multiplied by the number of guests attending.

P.P. refers to the Per Person cost. This is calculated by dividing the LOT COST by the # of PAX (the number of guests attending). A formula can be worked out in either Excel, Lotus 123, or any other accounting system. This formula can be used to calculate the Per Person cost which is based on the LOT COST divided by the # of PAX. The LOT COST when based on a per item cost such as dinner and multiplied by the number of guests attending may also be calculated using the same formula.

Having formulas in place allows you to quickly see the impact on your budget should you increase your guest list, for example, from 72 guests to 100. But when you are changing the number of guests remember to pay attention to line items where the cost has not been based on a flat rate or a rate based on a per item cost multiplied by the number of guests. In the case of rented table linens—if you were doing tables of eight you would have multiplied the cost of the rented linens by nine tables—changing the number of guests to 100 would increase the number of table linens required to 12 (providing 2 of the tables of 8 then became tables that could accommodate 10), you would need to ensure that you have gone in and made the change.

SAMPLE GALA FUND-RAISER—TRIBUTE	LOT COST	P.P	# OF PAX
ESTIMATED SPONSORSHIP DOLLARS REQUIRED			
Special Note: Items have been laid out in "menu format" so that they can be added and subtracted to meet your budget guidelines. A detailed payment schedule will also be provided.			
PRE-EVENT			
Invitations (Estimated based on 4,000)			
Detail			
Envelopes (Based on 4,000)			
Detail			
Order Forms (Based on 4,000)			
Detail			
Mailing			
Addressing/Labels			
Mailing – Estimated			
Couriers – Estimated			
Ticket Sales			
Ticket Coordination			
Ticket Processing			
Liquor Licence			
Special Occasion Permit.			
Special Event Insurance			
Host Liquor Liabilities/Property of Others. Estimated.			
Charitable Event Licence/Permit			
ROOM RENTAL			
Room Rental Access from 5:00 am onward			
Based on the proposed number of guests there is no room rental charge.			
If numbers drop below 700 guests the following rates will apply: $2,000.00 Room Rental 500-700 Guests $3,000.00 Room Rental 300-500 Guests			

	LOT COST	P.P	# OF FAX
AUDIO-VISUAL/STAGING **ONE WAY TRANSMISSION** **SATELLITE REQUIREMENTS** Detail Inclusions			
VISUALS Detail Inclusions			
IMAGE MAGNIFICATION Detail Inclusions			
COMPOSITE SWITCHING KIT Detail Inclusions			
AUDIO Detail Inclusions			
LIGHTING Detail Inclusions			
MISCELLANEOUS Detail Inclusions			
SET-UP (6 HOURS) Detail Labour			
OPERATE Detail Labour			
STRIKE Detail Labour			
TECHNICAL PHONE LINE AND AUDIO **CONFERENCE LINE** Detail			
ON LOCATION TECHNICAL SUPPORT, **VIDEO, LIGHTING, AUDIO SUPPORT** Detail			
FILMED FOR TELEVISION/FILM EDITING **COSTS** Detail			
DELIVERY AND TRANSPORTATION Detail			

	LOT COST	P.P	# OF FAX
CHARGES FOR USE OF FREIGHT ELEVATOR Detail			
COSTS FOR TWO-WAY TRANSMISSION Detail			
STAGING Detail			
FILM CLIPS Editing of Film Clips – Estimated Film Clips – Transfer to Toronto. Estimated. *Special Note: Additional costs involved to secure rights to show film clips.* Script Writing – Introductions, Speeches, Show Flow, Visual Aids (Slides/Power Point) Estimated Power & Power Distribution Charges Estimated Award for Presentation *Special Note: All labour is estimated, actual hours to be invoiced. Prices subject to change* *based on final staging, lighting, audio visual requirements.*			
PARKING Valet Parking. 6:00 pm Start Parking Costs			
CROWD CONTROL Pay Duty Officers. Estimated.			
RECEPTION Estimated based on 2 drinks per person.			
ENTERTAINMENT Detail SOCAN (Paid to the Hotel – Music Royalty/Rights)			
SILENT AUCTION Signage, Bid Sheets, Item Numbering, Pens, Etc. Estimated.			
SIGNAGE FOR THE FOUR DOORS FOR TABLE ASSIGNMENTS IE DOOR ONE TABLES 1-200 ETC Signage, Floor Plan, Table Assignment Floorplans for Hostesses to Distribute. Estimated.			

	LOT COST	P.P	# OF FAX

PLACE CARDS
Place Card Settings. Estimated. Based on 700

TABLE NUMBERS
Table Numbers Cards. Estimated.

MENU
Menu.
Colour output 2 sides, laminated to cover stock.

DECOR – TABLE LINENS
Based on 70 tables of 10. Maximum room capacity 700 for a sit down dinner. Ticket sales cannot exceed 700 guests.

DECOR – TABLE NAPKINS
Based on 700 guests 2 napkins per guest.

DECOR – CHAIR COVERS
Based on 700

CENTREPIECES
Centrepiece. Based on 70 tables of 10

DINNER
Menu
Detail
Food. Estimated. Based on 700
Tax
Gratuties

BEVERAGES
Wine. Estimated. Based on 700
Tax
Gratuties

PHOTOGRAPHER (2)
7 Hours
Tax

Colour Contact Sheets (Estimated 20 Rolls x 36 Print Exposures)
Tax

Delivery of Contact Sheets for Media Distribution
Tax

	LOT COST	P.P	# OF FAX
Return Delivery of Contact Sheets for Processing			
Tax			
Estimated Colour Reprints to Media			
Tax			
Delivery of Colour Reprints to Media			
Tax			
MEDIA Meals for Media			
ADVERTISING Full Page Ad Camera Ready Artwork. Estimated			
PRESS KIT Detail Inclusions and Organization.			
TAKE AWAY GIFT Custom Memento. Estimated.			
CUSTOM T-SHIRTS FOR VOLUNTEERS (FOR ID PURPOSES) Estimated.			
COMMUNICATION COSTS Couriers, Site Inspection Costs/Parking, Function Sheets etc. Final Reconciliation to be based on actual costs incurred.			
PROGRAM DIRECTORS Onsite Program Directors/Set Up/Rehearsals and Day of Event Final Reconciliation to be based on actual costs incurred. Walkie Talkies. Estimated.			
ESTIMATED SUBTOTAL IN LOCAL CURRENCY			
MANAGEMENT FEE			
ESTIMATED TOTAL IN LOCAL CURRENCY			

APPENDIX A:
SAMPLE COST SHEETS
—MEETING

I n the sample Cost Sheet for a Meeting you will see the addition of a grid. When an event encompasses more than one day it is helpful before costing to lay all your requirements out on a grid. This grid has a dual purpose—it can be used to help you visualize and capture all inclusions for your Cost Sheet and it can be used to send to the hotel or venue as an outline of the function space you will require.

CLIENT NAME:

DESTINATION: JAMAICA

TRAVEL DATE:

BASED ON:

PROGRAM OUTLINE	DAY ONE Saturday	DAY TWO Sunday	DAY THREE Monday	DAY FOUR Tuesday	DAY FIVE Wednesday	DAY SIX Thursday	DAY SEVEN Friday	DAY EIGHT Saturday
BREAKFAST		Breakfast at leisure	Breakfast Meeting 8:00 am – 10:00 am	Breakfast at leisure	Breakfast Meeting 8:00 am – 10:00 am	Breakfast Meeting 8:00 am– 10:00 am	Breakfast Meeting 8:00 am – 10:00 am	Breakfast at leisure
MORNING ACTIVITIES		Private Sail Dunn's River by Catamaran Pickup at the pier.	Activity Allowance Choices could include: Deep Sea Fishing Horseback Riding Scuba Diving Helicopter Ride (1.2 hr)	Morning Meeting	At your leisure	Activity Allowance Choice could include: Deep Sea Fishing Horseback Riding Scuba Diving Helicopter Ride (1/2 hr)	At your leisure	Return Transfers will commence
LUNCH		Included At Your Leisure	Included At Your Leisure	Included At Your Leisure	Included At Your Leisure	Included At Your Leisure	Included At Your Leisure	
AFTERNOON ACTIVITIES	Private Transfer Hotel Refreshments Motor coach	The Spa Golfing Watersports The Choices are endless ...and included.	Choices continued Blue Mountain Bike Tour Shopping Shuttle Golf Tournament	Late Beach Olympics	At your leisure	Choices continued Blue Mountain Bike Tour Shopping Shuttle Golf Tournament	At your leisure	
COCKTAIL RECEPTION	Welcome Reception 7:00 pm – 8:00 pm				Private Sunset Sail Cocktail Reception		Farewell Reception 7:00 pm – 8:00 pm Military Band	
EVENING ACTIVITIES	Caribbean Buffet 8:00 pm – 11:00 pm Mento Band	Included at your leisure	Private Dinner in the Spectacular Green Grotto Caves 7:00 pm - 9:00 pm Folkloric Show Steel Band 9:00 pm – 11:00 pm	Lobster Bake & Fish Fry On the Beach 7:00 pm – 9:00 pm Reggae Band	Included at your leisure	Included at your leisure	Farewell Dinner 8:00 pm – 9:30 pm Cabaret Singer with Back-Up Band 9:30 pm – 11:00 pm	

* All meals are included during your stay. The hotel is an all inclusive resort— all meals and beverages have been included. Unless group functions, guests are free to enjoy their meals at their leisure at any of the hotel's four restaurants.

SAMPLE COSTING: CONFERENCE/MEETING JAMAICA ESTIMATED LAND COSTING IN US DOLLARS	LOT COST $US	COST P.P $US	# PAX
JAMAICA – ALL INCLUSIVE RESORT			
SPORTS * RECREATIONAL FEATURES Detail all activities available to guests at the hotel where there is no additonal cost ie:			
Tennis		Included	
Basketball		Included	
Golfing		Included	
Squash		Included	
etc.		Included	
		Included	
		Included	
		Included	
		Included	
		Included	
		Included	
		Included	
WATERSPORTS FEATURES Detail all activities available to guests at the hotel where there is no additonal cost ie:			
Watering Skiing		Included	
Banana Boat		Included	
Jet Skis		Included	
Paddle boats		Included	
etc.		Included	
		Included	
Scuba Diving		Additional	
SPA SERVICES			
Full body massage ***		Included	
Neck and back massage ***		Included	
Reflexology ***		Included	
Dry sauna		Included	
Wet sauna		Included	
Whirlpool		Included	
(Appointments necessary for all services and treatments)			

	LOT COST $US	COST P.P. $US	# PAX
*** One complimentary per person per stay. Repeats available at a modest surcharge. Choice of 25 minute full body massage, 25 minute neck and back massage or 25 minutes with the reflexologist.			
OPTIONAL ACTIVITIES AND/OR SERVICES SUBJECT TO SURCHARGES			
Skin Care Treatments/Facials/Waxing/Styling Salon		Additional	
OTHER RESORT FACILITIES			
Night Club		Included	
Piano Bar		Included	
Carbaret		Included	
Nightly dancing and entertainment		Included	
Large Screen TV in Game Room		Included	
Library with books and newspaper		Included	
Video Library		Included	
Currency Exchange		Included	
Gift Shop		Included	
DINING * LOUNGES * REFRESHMENTS			
Six restaurants on property.		Included	
Selection of international wines at all resort restaurants.		Included	
ACCOMMODATION			
Seven nights accommodation.			
Hotel Taxes		Included	
Porterage at the hotel		Included	
Maid Gratuties		Included	
DAY ONE: SATURDAY			
ARRIVAL TRANSFERS One way transfer by air-conditioned motorcoach based on group arrivals.		Included	

	LOT COST $US	COST P.P $US	# PAX
Airport porterage at $2.00 US per person, based on two pieces of luggage per person. Beer and soft drinks onboard motor coach. Special Note: The hotel is a scenic one and one half hour transfer from Montego Bay Airport			
ARRIVAL AT THE HOTEL Welcome rum punch upon arrival.		Included	
WELCOME COCKTAIL RECEPTION AND DINNER Native Bamboo Stalls will be set up on the lawn to display the tempting array of local food. Pepper Lights and Candlelight provide added ambience.			
COCKTAIL RECEPTION One hour open bar. Standard Bar to include volka, gin, rum, rye whiskey, bourbon, scotch, cuevo white, triple sec, sweet vermouth, napoleon brandy house wines red and white Red Stripe Beer		Included Included Included Included Included Included	
HOT AND COLD HORS D'OEUVRES Assorted Canapes		Included	
PRIVATE WELCOME DINNER *Caribbean Buffet* *Salads* *Buffet Platters* *Basket* *Entree* *Desserts* Surcharge for private dinner.			

	LOT COST $US	COST P.P. $US	# PAX
BEVERAGES Standard Bar to include Volka, Gin, Rum, Rye Whiskey, Bourbon, Scotch, Cuevo White, Triple Sec, Sweet Vermouth, Napoleon Brandy House wines red and white Red Stripe Beer		Included Included Included Included Included	
ENTERTAINMENT Mento Band			
DAY TWO: SUNDAY			
BREAKFAST AT YOUR LEISURE			
MORNING ACTIVITY Private Sail. Dunn's River by Catamaran. Pickup at the hotel pier. Beer and soft drinks onboard Catamaran Tipping of guides at Dunn's River Fall *Special Note: Embarkation and Disembarkation is done in the water.*			
LUNCH AND DINNER AT YOUR LEISURE		Included	
DAY THREE: MONDAY			
BREAKFAST MEETING Breakfast served in meeting room.		Included	
ACTIVITY ALLOWANCE Deep Sea Fishing * Horseback Riding Shopping Shuttle Scuba Diving * Special Note: Should any of your guests catch a fish we can make arrangements to have the fish prepared and served at tomorrow night's Lobster Bake and Fish Fry.			

	LOT COST $US	COST P.P $US	# PAX
LUNCH At your leisure.		Included	
PRIVATE DINNER IN THE SPECTACULAR RUNAWAY CAVES Green Grotto Caves – Round trip transfers Hotel catered 5 Course Meal Folkloric Show Steel Band			
DAY FOUR: TUESDAY			
BREAKFAST At your leisure.		Included	
MORNING MEETING Coffee, Tea and assorted cold drinks and ice water.		Included	
LUNCH At your leisure.		Included	
AFTERNOON ACTIVITY Beach Olympics Beer and Soft Drinks during Beach Olympics Fun Prizes			
LOBSTER BAKE AND FISH FRY ON THE BEACH *Lobster Bake and Fish Fry* *Salads* *Buffet Platters* *Basket* *Entree* *Desserts*			
Lobster Bake and Fish Fry Surcharge Reggae Band			

	LOT COST $US	COST P.P. $US	# PAX
DAY FIVE: WEDNESDAY			
BREAKFAST MEETING Breakfast served in meeting room.		Included	
DAY AT LEISURE TO ENJOY THE HOTEL'S FACILITIES Special Note: A golf tournament could be an optional enhancement to your program, but it will require more money for refreshments, prizes etc. For the non-golfers you could look at putting on a private shopping shuttle or additional spa treatments being made available to them.			
LUNCH At your leisure.		Included	
SUNSET SAIL Sunset Cruise (2 Boats) Cocktail Reception			
DINNER At your leisure.		Included	
DAY SIX: THURSDAY			
BREAKFAST MEETING Breakfast served in meeting room.		Included	
ACTIVITY ALLOWANCE Deep Sea Fishing Horseback Riding Shopping Shuttle Scuba Diving River Rafting Up the Martha Brae			
LUNCH At your leisure.		Included	
DINNER At your leisure.		Included	

	LOT COST $US	COST P.P $US	# PAX
DAY SEVEN: FRIDAY			
BREAKFAST MEETING Breakfast served in meeting room.		Included	
LUNCH At your leisure.		Included	
COCKTAIL RECEPTION One hour open bar.			
ENTERTAINMENT FOR COCKTAIL RECEPTION Miltary Band (1Hr)			
HOT AND COLD HORS D'OEUVRES *Assorted Canapes* *Hot*			
PRIVATE FAREWELL DINNER *Menu*			
ENTERTAINMENT Cabaret Singer with Back-Up Band			
DAY EIGHT: SATURDAY			
BREAKFAST At your leisure			
RETURN TRANSFERS Delivery of departure notices. One way transfer by air-conditioned motor coach based on group departure. Airport porterage at $2.00 US per person based on two pieces of luggage per person. Beer and soft drinks onboard motor coach. Airport Departure Tax (Current rate – subject to change)			
ROOM GIFT ALLOWANCE Estimated Costing			

	LOT COST $US	COST P.P. $US	# PAX
OPTIONAL SUGGESTIONS FOR ROOM GIFTS			
Beach Wraps with Logo			
Beach Bags			
Golf Shirts			
Ray Chen's Jamaican Book			
Jamaican Plantation Hamper (Blue Mountain Coffee, Jamaican Cigars, Liquors)			
Jamaican Pastry Platter			
Sunrise Deluxe (Coffee, 2 Coffee Cups, Tia Maria, Preserves in a basket)			

PROMOTIONAL

Three rigid bag tags per person with your company logo based on two colours.
PST
GST

One soft vinyl ticket wallet per couple. Logo'd based on two colours.
PST
GST

One itinerary booklet per couple. Estimated costing.
PST
GST

Customized airport/hospitality desk signs. Estimated costing.
PST
GST

Screen Charges included in above costing. Estimated costing. Camera ready art to be provided. Final Reconcilation will be based on actual costs incurred.

SITE INSPECTION

Based on one (1) company executive and (1) J.A. Productions executive
Estimated costing. Final Reconcilation will be based on actual costs incurred.

	LOT COST $US	COST P.P $US	# PAX
PROGRAM DIRECTORS Two Program Directors to co-ordinate all onsite aspects of your programme. Estimated costing. Final Reconcilation will be based on actual costs incurred. **COMMUNICATION** Communication costs. Estimated (Long Distance, Faxes, Couriers, Walkie Talkies)			
SUBTOTAL LAND IN US FUNDS			
MANAGEMENT FEE			
ESTIMATED PER PERSON LAND TOTAL IN US FUNDS			

APPENDIX A:
SAMPLE COST SHEETS
–INCENTIVE PROGRAM

I n the sample Cost Sheet for an Incentive Program you will see an example of where the costing shows both local (destination) currency and the currency the program will be contracted in. It is helpful to be familiar with local currency and to include it in your Cost Sheet. You will have a copy of your Cost Sheet with you onsite and you can use it to compare costs for any bills that may be presented to you for signoff in local currency.

As seen in the sample Cost Sheets for a Meeting, a grid is included here to help you visualize all your requirements.

CLIENT NAME:
TRAVEL DATE:
DESTINATION:
BASED ON:

BANGKOK – 6 NIGHT PROGRAMME

PROGRAM OUTLINE	DAY ONE Friday	DAY TWO Saturday	DAY THREE Sunday	DAY FOUR Monday	DAY FIVE Tuesday	DAY SIX Wednesday	DAY SEVEN Thursday	DAY EIGHT Friday	DAY NINE Saturday
BREAKFAST				Full American Breakfast	Full American Breakfast	Full American Breakfast	Full American Breakfast	Full American Breakfast	Full American Breakfast
MORNING ACTIVITIES	Depart Toronto	Enroute Crossing International Date lines	Arrive Hong Kong 6:45 am Depart Hong Kong 9:25 am Arrive Bangkok 11:25 am	Halfday Bangkok Klongs and Grand Palace Tour	Activity Allowance Choice of: City&Temple Tour Rice&Barge Cruise Shopping Safari	Full Day Tour Chiangmai Elephant Camp in jungle	At Leisure	At Leisure	Depart Bangkok
LUNCH				Buffet Lunch at Tiara Supper Club	On Own	Buffet Lunch Mae Su Valley	On Own	On Own	
AFTERNOON ACTIVITIES			Private Transfer to Hotel Light Refreshments in Guestroom	At Leisure	At Leisure	Handicraft Village Return Flight to Bangkok	At Leisure	At Leisure	Arrive Hong Kong 2:00 pm Depart Hong Kong 3:30 pm Arrive Toronto 5:45 pm
COCKTAIL RECEPTION								Rose Garden Farewell Reception and Dinner	
EVENING ACTIVITIES			At Leisure to relax, settle in and adjust to the time change.	On Own	Thai Dinner & Classical Dances	On Own	Cash Allowance (or possible Dine Around)	BBQ Dinner Music Boat Along River Firework Display 30 Minute Show Loy Krathong Festival	

SAMPLE COSTING: INCENTIVE PROGRAM BANGKOK ESTIMATED LAND COSTING IN US DOLLARS (THAI BAHT TO US$ $1.00)	LOT COST THAI BHAT	LOT COST $US	COST P.P $US	# PAX
ACCOMMODATION Six nights accommondation at the Royal Orchid Hotel – Bangkok				
DAY ONE:ARRIVAL TRANSFERS One way transfer by air-conditioned motor coach based on group arrivals. Welcome Flower Garland by girls in Thai costume				
PRIVATE CHECK-IN A private check-in will be provided for your guests. Welcome drink upon arrival				
WELCOME REFRESHMENTS IN THE ROOM Light refreshments including finger sandwiches, fresh tropical juices, mineral water will be waiting in each guest room. (Estimated costing) Guests will be arriving in Bangkok late evening if arriving by Northwest or Korean Airways. Cathay Pacific would arrive in at 11:25 am. We recommend a light beginning to your programme to allow your guests to adjust to the time difference.				
SUGGESTED ROOM GIFT Ramayana mask with stand and box. One set per room. Enclosure provided by client Delivery of room gift. (Estimated)				
DAY TWO:				
FULL AMERICAN BREAKFAST AT THE HOTEL At your leisure.				

	LOT COST THAI BHAT	LOT COST $US	COST P.P $US	# PAX

HALF DAY BANGKOK KLONGS & GRAND PALACE TOUR

BUFFET LUNCH
Buffet Lunch
Local Beer/Soft Drinks based on (2) per person.

DINNER AT LEISURE

SUGGESTED ROOM GIFT
Thai Silk Shirt for the Men/Thai Silk Sarong
for the Women — silk can be customized at
an additional cost with company logo)
Enclosure inviting them to wear this to dinner tomorrow night delivery of room gift.
(Estimated)

DAY THREE:

FULL AMERICAN BREAKFAST AT THE HOTEL
At your leisure.

ACTIVITY ALLOWANCE
Guests can pre-select their optional tour.
City and Temple Tour
Afternoon Rice and Barge Cruise
Half Day Shopping Safari
Shopping tour will include visits to stores
offering Thai Lapidary (Gemstones),
Thai Silk or Casual Wear / Imitation Goods.

*Special Note: For costing purposes only I have
based your costing on the highest possible
option to present you with an idea of total
budget costs should all guests choose this
option. Final reconcilation will reflect costs
based on actual tours selected. Until registration forms are received in we will not know
the guest's preference. It is better to cost on
the highest price tour and make sure that we*

	LOT COST THAI BHAT	LOT COST $US	COST P.P $US	# PAX

still fall within budget guidelines than to average them out and possibly end up exceeding budget projections should all guests decide to take the most expensive tour.

EVENING THAI DINNER & CLASSICAL DANCES
Roundtrip transfers to/from hotel.
Thai Dinner including cocktails and wine with dinner

SUGGESTED ROOM GIFT
Silk Photo Frame size 3" x 5". One per couple.
Enclosure
Delivery of room gift. (Estimated)

DAY FOUR:

FULL AMERICAN BREAKFAST AT THE HOTEL
At your leisure.

TOUR OF CHIANGMAI
Duration: 12 hours (6:00 am – 6:00 pm)
6:00 am   Transfer to Bangkok Domestic Airport
7:30 am   Depart Bangkok for Chaingmai.
8:30 am   Arrive Chaingmai. Transfer to Elephant Camp.
10:00 am See elephants at work in teak forest.
10:40 am Depart for Mae Su Valley for lunch. Garden setting – lush green lawns and garden brilliant with colours of cassias, dahlias, daisies, and poinsettia. Your guests will enjoy lunch overlooking Mae Sa Valley.
11:30 am Buffet Lunch.
12:45 pm Visit to the Handicraft Centre and gain insight into the making of teakwood furniture, Thai silk, silverware and Thai umbrellas.

	LOT COST THAI BHAT	LOT COST $US	COST P.P $US	# PAX
3:30 pm Transfer to Chiangmai Airport				
4:45 pm Return flight to Bangkok				
5:45 pm Arrive Bangkok				
6:00 pm Arrive Hotel				

DINNER AT LEISURE

SUGGESTED ROOM GIFT
Thai Cookbook
Enclosure
Delivery of room gift. (Estimated)

DAY FIVE:

FULL AMERICAN BREAKFAST AT THE HOTEL
At your leisure.

AT LEISURE FOR PERSONAL ACTIVITIES OR SHOPPING

LUNCH ON OWN

CASH ALLOWANCE FOR DINNER

SUGGESTED ROOM GIFT
Brass Elephant Paperweight with base and plaque. One per couple.
Custom Invitation to Farewell Dinner (Estimated)
Delivery of room gift. (Estimated)

DEPARTURE NOTICES
Delivery of departure notices.

DAY SIX:

FULL AMERICAN BREAKFAST AT THE HOTEL
At your leisure.

	LOT COST THAI BHAT	LOT COST $US	COST P.P $US	# PAX
AT LEISURE FOR PERSONAL ACTIVITIES OR SHOPPING				
EVENING: ROSE GARDEN				
Included in the evening:				
Roundtrip Transfers				
Fresh Flowers in Company Logo				
Garland Welcome and Cold Towels				
Welcome Fruit Punch				
Elephant welcome with custom banners				
Elephants for VIP couple				
Elephant Show and Rides				
Fruit & Vegetable Carving, Garland Making Demonstration				
One hour open bar with hot and cold hors d'oeuvres				
30 Minutes in Handicraft Village				
Klong Sabatchai procession to riverside lawn for dinner barbecue and stalls				
Barbeque Buffet Dinner and Food Stall				
Music boat along the river				
30 minute show (3 dances, sword, short/long pole fighting, wedding ceremony)				
Loy Krathong Festival				
Fireworks and Logo, Farewell Message				
Rose Garden Dinner as outlined above				
One half bottle of wine per person				
Police Escort (Estimated)				
SUGGESTED ROOM GIFT				
Thai Raw Silk Robe (Solid Colour). One per person. Logo'd or with guest's initials at additional cost.				
Enclosure				
Delivery of room gift. (Estimated)				
DAY SEVEN:				
FULL AMERICAN BREAKFAST AT THE HOTEL				
At your leisure.				

	LOT COST THAI BHAT	LOT COST $US	COST P.P $US	# PAX

DEPARTURE

Departure Transfer from the hotel to the airport will be by River Jet Cruise. The River Jet Cruise is non-exclusive.* The River Jet Cruise can be bought out on an exclusive basis but based on 300. Alternate option would be to transfer by motor coach.The River Jet Cruise offers one final look at the city before flight. The minimum check-in time at Don Muang Airport is two hours prior to flight departure time. The Program Directors will assist with check-in and pre-departure formalities. All checked luggage will be transferred to the airport by separate van with a baggage master.

There will be other passengers on board who are not with the group. To have the transfer exclusive to the group we would need to purchase 300 seats.

International Airport Departure Tax
(Current rate – subject to change)

PROMOTIONAL/COMMUNICATION

Three rigid bag tags per person with your company logo based on two colours.
Taxes
One soft vinyl ticket wallet per couple.
Logo'd based on two colours.
Taxes
One itinerary booklet per couple. Estimated costing.
Taxes
Customized airport signs. Estimated costing.
Taxes
Screen Charges Included in the above pricing.
Camera Ready Artwork to be supplied.
Final Reconcilation will be based on actual costs incurred.

	LOT COST THAI BHAT	LOT COST $US	COST P.P $US	# PAX
SITE INSPECTION Based on one (1) Company Executive and (1) J.A. Productions Executive Estimated costing. Final Reconcilation will be based on actual costs incurred.				
PROGRAM DIRECTORS Two Program Directors plus Sales Executive to co-ordinate all onsite aspects of your programme. Estimated costing. Final Reconcilation will be based on actual costs incurred.				
COMMUNICATION COSTS Communication costs. Estimated (Long Distance, Faxes, Couriers, Walkie Talkies)				
SUBTOTAL LAND IN US FUNDS				
MANAGEMENT FEE				
ESTIMATED PER PERSON LAND TOTAL IN US FUNDS				

APPENDIX B:
SAMPLE PAYMENT SCHEDULES
–CORPORATE EVENT COSTING

The first form in Appendix B is another example of a sample Cost Sheet. Here the event is a Wine Appreciation Evening. Remember that your Cost Sheet is the basis from which you generate your Payment Schedule. Here the client wanted to know exactly what they were spending in Food and Beverage, Décor and Entertainment, Miscellaneous Costs (such as Doormen, Security) and Onsite Staffing Costs, Promotion and Communications. This is just a variation on the original Cost Sheet. You are still dealing with LOT COST—just under different headings—P.P. cost and # of PAX.

In this particular example you will also see a GST column which is a specific tax that must be listed on invoicing in Canada. The GST would be included as a line item cost but a formula line can be included to list the GST under a separate column as well for a quick calculation of total GST costs only for invoicing purposes.

Once the costing has been finalized and the preparation of the contract is to begin you will need to work out a Payment Schedule based on your inclusions.

The Cost Sheet can be saved and copied under a new name. Depending on when your event is scheduled to take place and the payment requirements of your suppliers you may have several different payment dates to adhere to. Work with the various suppliers to bring the due dates of payments into line—you will usually find them more than accommodating—and make sure that they will work within your company/client's specific cheque runs as well.

SAMPLE COSTING: WINE APPRECIATION EVENING
(ALTERNATE COST BREAKDOWN STYLE)

ESTIMATED LAND COSTING	LOT COST FOOD & BEVERAGE	LOT COST DECOR & ENTER.	LOT COST MISC	LOT COST STAFF/CO PROMO.	COST P.P $	# PAX	GST
EXCLUSIVE RESTAURANT TAKEOVER							
DATE 6:00 p.m. – 7:00 p.m. Ice Wine Reception 7:00 p.m. – 10:00 p.m. Gourmet Dinner/Wines 10:00 p.m. – Dessert/ Coffee/Liqueurs/Cigars							
PARKING Parking nearby. Guests to pay their own.							
COAT CHECK Tipping							
DOORMAN Estimated cost							
DJ Estimated cost							
RECEPTION 6:00 pm – 7:00 pm							
BEVERAGES RECEPTION * ICE WINE SAMPLING Based on 2 per person – Estimated. Service Charge Staff Taxes Taxes							

	LOT COST FOOD & BEVERAGE	LOT COST DECOR & ENTER.	LOT COST MISC	LOT COST STAFF/CO PROMO.	COST P.P $	# PAX	GST
WINEMASTER * *** WELL KNOWN WINE-MASTER/CHEF** Speaker's Fee – Estimated pending final confirmation Taxes							
Marriage Between Food and Wine Menu/Wine Coordination Taxes							
WINEMASTER'S DINNER Eight Course Gourmet Dinner – Estimated Service Charge Staff Taxes Taxes							
To include: *Fresh Foie Gras of Duck* *Live Lobster* *Oysters* *Servuga Caviar (Russian or Royal Iranian)* *Prime US Beef* *Various Organic Raised Game* *Fresh Seafood*							
WINE WITH DINNER Appropriate Wines to accompany each course Service Charge Staff Taxes Taxes							
To Include: *Opus One* *Cabernet Sauvignon – Unfiltered Napa* *Pinot Noir – Unfiltered Napa*							

	LOT COST FOOD & BEVERAGE	LOT COST DECOR & ENTER.	LOT COST MISC	LOT COST STAFF/CO PROMO.	COST P.P $	# PAX	GST
Chardonnay – Sauvignon Blanc (or Fume Blanc) A Dessert Wine Plus two others							
PLACE CARDS Place Cards Taxes Taxes							
DINNER MENUS Dinner Menus Taxes Taxes							
TABLE CARDS Table Cards Taxes Taxes							
ENTERTAINMENT (Soft Background Jazz) Trio (Piano/Vocals, Bass, Saxophone or Guitar) Taxes							
Yamaha Digital Grand Piano Cartage $250.00 Taxes							
The Yamaha GT2, a digital grand piano is very small and quite elegant – would be fitting for the evening/ambiance.							
Sound System/Technician and Cartage							

	LOT COST FOOD & BEVERAGE	LOT COST DECOR & ENTER.	LOT COST MISC	LOT COST STAFF/CO PROMO.	COST P.P $	# PAX	GST
Meals for the Musicians – Estimated Service Charge Staff Taxes Taxes							
Souvenir CD – Estimated Taxes							
Music Royalities							
Special Note: I will have them autographed with actual guest's name							
Coffee/Liqueurs Based on 1 per person. Service Charge Staff Taxes Taxes							
Selection of world's finest handmade cigars. Cigars – Estimated ($20.00 – $50.00 each) Based on 1 per person. Service Charge Staff Taxes Taxes							
Cigar Hostess (3) Gratuities							
Lighters and Clippers							
Custom Logoed Banding							

	LOT COST FOOD & BEVERAGE	LOT COST DECOR & ENTER.	LOT COST MISC	LOT COST STAFF/CO PROMO.	COST P.P $	# PAX	GST
ROUNDTRIP TRANSFERS TO/FROM HOTEL Awaiting final decision re limos/motor coach **COMMUNICATION** Communications Costs. Faxes, Couriers, Function Sheets, Cell Phone Misc. Tipping etc. Estimated. **STAFFING** Onsite Program Management							
ESTIMATED SUBTOTAL (IN LOCAL CURRENCY)							
ESTIMATED SUBTOTAL (COLUMNS 1-4)							
MANAGEMENT FEE							
ESTIMATED TOTAL (IN LOCAL CURRENCY)							

APPENDIX B:
SAMPLE PAYMENT SCHEDULES
–PAYMENT BREAKDOWN

As seen in the following sample Payment Schedule for the Wine Appreciation Evening, payments are laid out as Payment A, B, C, etc., and assigned specific dates to each. Rather than re-input all the detailed description of the line items use what the you/your client is already familiar with—the Cost Sheet—and simply change the headings to reflect the payment dates. A supplier may want 50% of costs upon contracting/depositing, 40 % at a specified time prior to the event taking place, and 10% post event. It will vary with each supplier and the terms of their individual contracts. You will need to go in and adjust the formulas but you will be able to cross reference your Payment Schedule total costs with your Cost Sheet easily because you will not be working with two entirely different layouts.

SAMPLE PAYMENT SCHEDULE BREAKDOWN: WINE APPRECIATION EVENING

Cost sheet can be saved under a different name and changed to payment schedule format. Then it can be re-named and used for your reconciliation.

ESTIMATED LAND COSTING	DEPOSIT PAYMENT A	DUE DATE PAYMENT B	POST EVENT
EXCLUSIVE RESTAURANT TAKEOVER DATE			
6:00 p.m.– 7:00 p.m. Ice Wine Reception 7:00 p.m.– 10:00 p.m. Gourmet Dinner/Wines 10:00 p.m. – Dessert/Coffee/Liqueurs/Cigars			
PARKING Parking nearby. Guests to pay their own.			
COAT CHECK Tipping			
DOORMAN Estimated cost			
DJ Estimated cost			
RECEPTION 6:00 p.m.– 7:00 p.m.			
BEVERAGES RECEPTION * ICE WINE SAMPLING Based on 2 per person – Estimated. Service Charge Staff Taxes Taxes			
WINEMASTER * WELL-KNOWN WINEMASTER/CHEF Speaker's Fee – Estimated pending final confirmation Taxes			

	DEPOSIT PAYMENT A	DUE DATE PAYMENT B	POST EVENT
Marriage Between Food and Wine Menu/Wine Coordination Taxes			
WINEMASTER'S DINNER Eight Course Gourmet Dinner – Estimated Service Charge Staff Taxes Taxes			
WINE WITH DINNER Appropriate Wines to accompany each course Service Charge Staff Taxes Taxes			
PLACE CARDS Place Cards Taxes Taxes			
DINNER MENUS Dinner Menus Taxes Taxes			
TABLE CARDS Table Cards Taxes Taxes			
ENTERTAINMENT *(Soft Background Jazz)* Trio (Piano/Vocals, Bass, Saxophone or Guitar) Taxes			
Yamaha Digital Grand Piano Cartage $250.00			

	DEPOSIT PAYMENT A	DUE DATE PAYMENT B	POST EVENT
Taxes			
Sound System/Technician and Cartage			
Meals for the Musicians – Estimated			
Service Charge Staff			
Taxes			
Taxes			
Souvenir CD – Estimated			
Taxes			
Music Royalities			
Coffee/Liqueurs			
Based on 1 per person.			
Service Charge Staff			
Taxes			
Taxes			
Selection of world's finest handmade cigars.			
Cigars – Estimated ($20.00 - $50.00 each)			
Based on 1 per person.			
Service Charge Staff			
Taxes			
Taxes			
Cigar Hostess (3)			
Gratuities			
Lighters and Clippers			
Custom Logoed Banding			
ROUNDTRIP TRANSFERS TO/FROM HOTEL			
Awaiting final decision re limos/motor coach			
COMMUNICATION			
Communications Costs. Faxes, Couriers, Function Sheets, Cell Phone Misc. Tipping etc. Estimated.			

	DEPOSIT PAYMENT A	DUE DATE PAYMENT B	POST EVENT
STAFFING Onsite Program Management			
ESTIMATED SUBTOTAL **(IN LOCAL CURRENCY)**			
ESTIMATED SUBTOTAL **(COLUMNS 1-4)**			
MANAGEMENT FEE ESTIMATED TOTAL **(IN LOCAL CURRENCY)**			

APPENDIX C:
SAMPLE FUNCTION SHEETS
—CONTACT SHEETS

Function Sheets become your onsite "bible" and need to contain as much detail as possible. They must include your instructions to your suppliers, staffing assignments, and the negotiated costs (as your suppliers will not be receiving a copy of your Cost Sheet, only the costs that are relevant to them). If there are any pricing discrepancies it is better to know in advance when they're reviewing your Function Sheets, rather than at the close of the event. They should be clearly laid out and in order of sequence of events.

The Function Sheets are sent to all suppliers. They are what the onsite staff work from. They ensure that everyone is working from literally "the same page." A hotel, for example, may have there own variation for their internal staff—they will review your Function Sheets, note any changes, and send you their version for your sign off and review—but both of you will have cross-referenced each others eliminating any potential problems/conflicts.

A key component of a Function Sheet is a Contact Sheet. It needs to be filled out in great detail, and as seen in the following example, should contain all of the information you need to have for each contact. On the following page is a list of all the different contacts you may need to compile this information for.

Possible Contacts

Limousines (List all drivers)
Media (List all)
Orange Cones
Photographer
Police (Security—List all)
Print Production
Road Permits
Ropes and Stanchions
Skytrackers
Speaker Support
Special Effects
Speech Writer
Street Permits
Staging/Lighting/Audio-Visual (List all key staff members)
Transportation (Motor coach)
Walkie-Talkies
All Other Applicable Suppliers

You should have every possible number to reach a supplier after hours—from cell phone numbers to pagers to after hour business lines. When you have an emergency and need to reach your supplier you need to ensure that you have a means to do so. This means the motor coach driver, the limousine driver, and everyone on up. Your Contact Sheets also become your checklist for sending out thank you letters after the day/event is over.

CONTACT SHEETS

EVENT PRODUCTION COMPANY
Company Name In Full
Address In Full
Contact: *List All Involved (i.e. Creative Director, Producer, etc)*
Title:
Tel:
Fax:
Email:
Cell:
Home:

ON SITE "DAY OFF" STAFFING
Address In Full
Contact: *List All Involved*
Title:
Tel:
Fax:
Email:
Cell:
Home:

VENUE (LIST ALL KEY STAFF MEMBERS)
Company Name In Full
Address In Full
Contact:
Title:
Tel:
Fax:
Email:
Cell:
Home:

AUDIO-VISUAL (LIST ALL KEY STAFF MEMBERS)
Company Name In Full
Address In Full
Contact:
Title:
Tel:
Fax:
Email:
Cell:
Home:

DECOR (LIST ALL KEY STAFF MEMBERS)
Company Name In Full
Address In Full
Contact:
Title:
Tel:
Fax:
Email:
Cell:
Home:

ENTERTAINMENT (LIST ALL KEY STAFF MEMBERS)
Company Name In Full
Address In Full
Contact:
Title:
Tel:
Fax:
Email:
Cell:
Home:

FLORAL
Company Name In Full
Address In Full
Contact:
Title:
Tel:
Fax:
Email:
Cell:
Home:

LIGHTING (LIST ALL KEY STAFF MEMBERS)
Company Name In Full
Address In Full
Contact:
Title
Tel:
Fax:
Email:
Cell:
Home:

APPENDIX C:
SAMPLE FUNCTION SHEETS
— MEETING

In the following Function Sheet for a Meeting you will notice that instructions have been repeated for each day they occur. This laying out of items in storyboard fashion and in sequence avoids you having to continually search through your function sheet for information.

As each element is completed, relevant notes can be made on the page. You will not need to go back and refer to them again until it is time to do the reconciliation. Such items as staffing will change day to day and laid out this way makes it easy to see where these changes occur and how to deal with them.

THE EVENT	Client Appreciation Sales Conference being held in London.
THE GUESTS	All male. They are all each others competitors. They are all from Montreal.
THE ELEMENTS	Inter-active events that evoke feel of play. Sales Conference
THE VENUES	Hockey Hall of Fame Exclusive for the guests. Reception and use of the full facility. Dinner at Wayne Gretzky's The Shot (Railway Station Restaurant with Pool Tables) Pool expert to teach guests trick shots

SCHEDULE OF EVENTS: OVERVIEW

MONDAY

	Judy to pick up walkie-talkies and proceed to Sheraton to advance check-in and room gift distribution.
11:00 a.m.	Liane and Judy to meet at the Sheraton.
11:30 a.m.	Carol to advance Montreal airport.
12:00 p.m.	Guests to arrive at Montreal airport for group check-in
1:00 p.m.	Air Canada 413 is scheduled to depart Montreal.
1:00 p.m.	Liane to arrive at the airport to monitor flight arrival Toronto Airport. Meet with DMC and oversee motorcoach transfer/spotting.
	Room Gift Delivery – Welcome (Large Pretzels & Beer)
	Room Gift Delivery – Hockey Puck Custom Design
	Room Delivery – Invitation to this evening's event.
	Room Gifts to tie in with "Hockey Night in Canada" Reception and Dinner.
	Departure Notices and Baggage Pull Arrangements
2:08 p.m.	Air Canada Flight 413 scheduled to arrive. Liane and Carol to transfer with the motorcoach to the hotel.
	Mr. *** will be arriving by train independently — he is unable to fly due to a medical condition.

3:00 p.m.	Estimated arrival at the hotel. Check in 21st floor.
	Carol to reconfirm arrangements for baggage pull the next morning and distribution of departure notices.
	Liane and Carol to do quick site inspection of Hockey Hall of Fame drop-off point and Wayne Gretzky's Restaurant.
5:00 p.m.	Judy and Liane to advance Hockey Hall of Fame.
5:30 p.m.	Motor coach to spot. Carol to oversee and transfer guests. Liane to meet motor coach and escort guests to the Hockey Hall of Fame.
5:50 p.m.	Motor coach to depart for Hockey Hall of Fame
6:00 p.m.	Motor coach arrival Hockey Hall of Fame
7:30 p.m.	Judy to advance Wayne Gretzky's.
	Carol to oversee motor coach arrival for transfer to Wayne Gretzky's.
9:00 p.m.	Carol and Liane to transfer with guests to the restaurant.
	Guests to make their own way back to hotel.

SCHEDULE OF EVENTS: OVERVIEW

TUESDAY

	Carol to oversee luggage pull
	Carol to oversee motor coach and hotel checkout
	Judy to advance and oversee breakfast.
8:00 a.m.	Private group breakfast
9:00 a.m.	Depart for London to attend conference.
	Guests to be dropped off at conference. Lunch is included.
	Carol and Driver to advance hotel and drop off luggage.
	Departure notice and baggage pull
	Carol and Driver to visit The Shot Restaurant and Pool Hall.
	Return to conference.
5:00 p.m.	Transfer guests to the hotel.
5:45 p.m.	Estimated arrival at hotel.
6:30 p.m.	Transfer to The Shot. Motor coach to remain with group.
9:30 p.m.	Return to the hotel. May want one early shuttle as well.

SCHEDULE OF EVENTS: OVERVIEW

WEDNESDAY

		Carol to oversee Luggage Pull
		Carol to oversee Motor coach and hotel checkout
		Carol to advance and oversee breakfast.
9:00	a.m.	Breakfast
10:00	a.m.	Depart for conference.
10:30	a.m.	Estimated arrival time conference.
		Carol to reconfirm flights.
12:30	p.m.	Lunch included at conference.
1:30	p.m.	Depart for factory (host's company factory)
2:00	p.m.	Tour of factory
3:30	p.m.	Depart for airport
		Check in at London airport.
		Toronto guests to remain onboard and transfer to the city.
5:40	p.m.	Air Canada 1218 is scheduled to depart London to Toronto.
6:18	p.m.	Air Canada 1218 arrives in Toronto.
7:00	p.m.	Air Canada 194 departs for Montreal.
		Carol returns with group.
8:05	p.m.	Air Canada 194 arrives in Montreal.
		Train passenger overnights at hotel and departs in the morning.

FRIDAY

J.A. Productions

Judy to reconfirm all arrangements for Monday for pick up walkie-talkies, headsets and batteries.
(Both walkie-talkies and batteries to be fully charged)
Company
Address
Contact:
Tel:
Fax:
Email:
Cell:

MONDAY

J.A. Productions

Judy to pick up walkie talkies, headsets and batteries.

J.A. Productions: 3

1.   Judy
2.   Carol
3.   Liane

Walkie-talkies to have earphones, belt and channel selector on top.

FRIDAY
HOTEL PRE-CON

10:00   a.m.

Location:
Set Up: Boardroom/Hollow Square
To attend:
Sales
Club Room Check-In Manager
Catering Manager
Banquet Manager
Bell Captain
Please ensure that a list outlining all extension numbers, names and titles of all department heads has been prepared and is available for this meeting. J.A. Productions will require three copies.

11:00   a.m.

Approximate end of pre-con.

HOCKEY HALL OF FAME/MOVENPICK CATERING PRE-CON

1:00   p.m.

Pre-Con with Hockey Hall of Fame/Movenpick Catering
Location:
Hockey Hall of Fame
To Attend:
Hockey Hall of Fame: Contact Name
Movenpick Catering: Contact Name

WAYNE GRETZKY'S PRE-CON

3:00   p.m.

Wayne Gretzky's
Location: Wayne Gretzky's
To Attend:
Wayne Gretzky's: Contact Name

MONDAY
ADVANCE MONTREAL AIRPORT

	Carol to arrive in Montreal August 13 (evening)
	Hotel accommodation has been blocked at:
	Montreal Dorval Airport Hilton
	12505 Cote de Liesse Road
	Montreal, Quebec
	H9P 1B7
	Tel: (514) 631-2411
	Fax: (514) 631-0192
	Reservation: 1664167
	$127.62 inclusive of taxes ($112 base weekend rate)
	Room has been guaranteed.
	No guests will be staying overnight at the hotel.
11:30 a.m.	Arrival at the airport. Seat selection has been arranged for the group. Group check-in has been arranged. Contact Name:
12:00 p.m.	Guests have been advised to check-in one hour prior to departure. They will be looking for Carol. Please display company sign.
1:00 p.m.	Air Canada 413 is scheduled to depart for Toronto.
2:08 p.m.	Arrival in Toronto. Liane will meet Carol at the gate. Look for the company sign.
	Quebec departure taxes are pre-paid.

MONDAY
TORONTO AIRPORT ARRIVAL/TRANSFER TO HOTEL

1:00 p.m.	Air Canada 413 is scheduled to depart for Toronto.
2:08 p.m.	Arrival in Toronto.
	Liane will meet the flight.
	DMC will meet Liane at the Air Canada arrival area (section C).
	Included in transfer cost:
	One-way transfer by air-conditioned motor coach based on group arrival.
	Airport Meet and Greet Staffing
	Porterage at the Airport
	Special Request: French Speaking Staff where possible. Same driver throughout program.
	Liane to transfer with the group back to the hotel. Richmond Street entrance will be the motor coach drop-off point.

Hotel porters will deliver bags to the guest rooms.

Note to Liane/Carol: Please call the hospitality desk prior to leaving the airport to advise you are on your way.

MONDAY
HOSPITALITY DESK HOTEL/PRIVATE REGISTRATION CLUB FLOOR

Daily Requirements	One House Phone/No Long Distance Access
	One Skirted Table (6 x 3)
	Three Chairs
	Two Flip Charts/Easel
	Markers. Two Colours.
	One Waste basket
	One Table Lamp (only if not in a well-lit area)
10:00 a.m.	Registration set-up to be ready. Desk to remain in place for 24 hours.

MONDAY
HOTEL CHECK IN PROCEDURES

Hotel check-in is 3:00 p.m. but early check-in has been requested. The majority of the participants will be arriving as a group. Early arrivals may be the Toronto head office staff who will be overnighting at the hotel. Other guests will be arriving on Air Canada 413, which is scheduled to arrive at 2:08 p.m.. Guests will be arriving by motor coach as a group.

Motor coach Drop-off point and hotel porterage to be arranged: Richmond Street entrance.

One guest will be arriving by train and three by car.

Parking to master for overnight Toronto guests has been arranged. They will be leaving their car at the hotel while they are in London travelling with the group.

A private, satellite check-in desk is to be set up beside hospitality desk on the 20th Floor. This is to be ready by 11:00 a.m.. Check-in to be manned by staff exclusively for group. **French-speaking staff requested. All guests are from Quebec.**

Please ensure adequate staff scheduling has been provided for the private registration desk, the bell desk and the lounge.

All check-ins are to be pre-registered and rooms to be pre-assigned.

No room rates are to appear on individual folios.

Express check-out forms to be included in each key packet along with room key, mini bar key and hotel information.

Separate key packets to be prepared for each guest. Two keys per packet.

Key packets to be ready and waiting in alphabetical order prior to guests' arrival at the satellite check-in desk.

Upgrades or changes of room are not permitted unless authorized by J.A.\Productions.

Four copies (both alpha and numeric) of rooming list will be required.

Scheduled welcome room gift deliveries to be in each guest room at least one hour before guest arrives.

MASTER ACCOUNT

Client # 1

All to master (room, taxes, all meals and incidentals signed to the room) including valet parking *

Client # 2

All to master (room, taxes, all meals and incidentals signed to the room).

Client # 3

All to master (room, taxes, all meals and incidentals signed to the room) including valet parking*

*   Their cars will remain at the hotel while the group is in London. They will be returning late Wednesday evening to pick up their cars. All parking charges to go on the master account.

Judy Allen Productions

1.   All to master including valet parking
2.   All to master including valet parking
3.   All to master

Balance of Guests

All guest room charges and taxes are to go to the master account, but participants are to give a credit card imprint to cover incidentals such as room charges for meals in restaurants, room service, laundry, health club and mini-bar. Unless specified the client will not be responsible for participants incidental accounts.

AUTHORIZED SIGNATURES FOR THE MASTER ACCOUNT

Client

1.   Name and Title
2.   Name and Title
3.   Name and Title

Judy Allen Productions

1.   Judy
2.   Carol
3.   Liane

ACCOUNTING

Judy Allen to meet with hotel's accounting department on August 14th (approximately 10:30 p.m.) to review all individual room charges (guest folios). This must be done prior to the folios being delivered to any guest rooms.

All bills to be posted to the master account must be signed off by an authorized member of J.A. Production staff. Judy Allen will meet with accounting Tuesday, August 15 once guests have departed for London. Please have two copies of all bills and folios available.

ROOM BLOCK
Please see attached rooming list.

City Hall view and all guests to be located on the same floor have been requested.

Guest room rate $000.00 Commissionable at 10 %.

Special Note: Every room must have two beds. A bed and a pull out couch is not acceptable.

SHERATON CLUB ROOM EXCLUSIVE SERVICES AND AMENITIES
These include:
- Complimentary local calls
- Dataports in room
- Separate concierge service on 20th floor
- Private lounge serving complimentary:
    Continental Breakfast (6:30 a.m. – 10:30 a.m.)
    Afternoon Tea & Cookies (3:00 p.m. – 6:00 p.m.)
    Evening Hors D' Oeuvres (5:00 p.m. – 7:00 p.m.)
- Guest rooms with bathrobes, valet stand, skirt hangers, specialty lotions, mineral waters and extra bathroom amenities
- Complimentary access to the Adelaide Club, featuring squash, aerobics and weight equipment.

FUNCTION SPACE
Conference Room D&E
Breakfast August 15   Sit Down   Double-Sided Buffet
                                            7:00 a.m. – 9:00 a.m.

MONDAY
ROOM DELIVERIES
ROOM GIFT – WELCOME
Giant Pretzels with condiments (mustard) –two per person.
Iced Beer – two per person.
Both items to be provided by Sheraton.

Bill To Master Account

Pretzel and Condiment $0.00 + + +
Iced Beer $0.00 + + +
Delivery Charge $0.00 + 0 % taxes

MONDAY
VIP ROOM GIFT DELIVERY

Judy Allen will bring gifts with her. To be delivered to:

1. Name
2. Name
3. Name

MONDAY
TRAIN TRANSFER

Mr. *** is unable to fly due to an inner ear problem.

He will be arriving by train. He will be met by limo driver at the station and transferred to the hotel. Client has advised him that he is being met.

Train 57 departs Montreal 10:00 a.m. and arrives Toronto 3:30 p.m..

Limo driver to call hospitatlity desk upon departure from the train station to advise Liane that he has met the guest and they are on their way to the hotel. Liane to meet guest at the front door with porter and transfer him to check-in.

Limo driver's name:
Cell number:
License number:
Description of limo:

MONDAY
HOTEL ARRIVAL

Arrival Schedule:
Air Canada 413 departs Montreal 1:00 p.m.
Air Canada 413 arrives Toronto 2:08 p.m.
Guests will be met at the airport and transferred to the hotel by motor coach as a group.
Luggage will be transferred with the group.

2:30   p.m.

Hotel staff (French-speaking requested) to be in place at the satellite check-in.

Hotel staff members to take credit card imprints when guests arrive with the exception of those whose expenses are going on the master account.

1. Name
2. Name
3. Name

Participants will be arriving at the Richmond Street entrance.

Upon arrival at the hotel, luggage is to be taken from the participants and delivered directly to their rooms. Their guest rooms are all located on the Club Floor.

Hotel porterage is included in their stay.

Please ensure that valet parking has been advised that parking for:

1. Name
2. Name

be charged to the master account and that their cars will be at the hotel until late evening on the 16th. All parking charges up to and including the 16th are to be put on the master account.

All guest rooms are blocked into the hotel's Club Level accommodation. Guests should proceed directly to the 20th floor via the express elevator for private check-in. A French-speaking guest services agent has been requested.

Bill to Master Account

Room:	$000.00
Taxes:	00%
Porterage:	$0.00 + 0% taxes roundtrip
Valet Parking:	$00.00

MONDAY
LUGGAGE PULL/DEPARTURE NOTICES

Departure notices will be given to the bellmen for delivery this evening while the guests are out for dinner.

Bags are to be left inside the room. Pick-up will be at 7:30 a.m. on the 15th. Motor coach to depart at 9:00 a.m..

ROOM GIFT

Hockey puck (customized) to be delivered to each guest.

Letter/card to accompany gift.

Hockey Pucks will be delivered to the hotel by noon.

To be placed in each guest room once guests have departed for their evening's event. Scheduled departure time from the hotel 6:00 p.m.

Bill To Master Account

Delivery Charge $0.00 + 0% taxes

MONDAY
TRANSFERS FROM HOTEL TO HOCKEY HALL OF FAME
5:35   p.m.   Motor coach to spot.
5:50   p.m.   Departure from the hotel (Richmond Street
                            entrance) to the Hockey Hall of Fame.
                            Carol to travel with group.
                            Liane will meet motor coach at the 181 Bay
                            Street entrance to the Hockey Hall of Fame.

TRANSFERS FROM HOCKEY HALL OF FAME TO WAYNE GRETZKY'S
8:45   p.m.   Motor coach to spot.
9:00   p.m.   Departure from 181 Bay Street entrance to
                            Wayne Gretzky's:
                            99 Blue Jay Way
                            Toronto, Ontario
                            M5V 9G9
                            Guests will make their own way back to the
                            hotel. Motor coach is required to be on
                            standby to extend pending weather condi-
                            tions for return transfer to the hotel. Carol
                            will advise driver before disembarking.

MONDAY
HOCKEY HALL OF FAME RECEPTION
                            Insurance faxed August 10 for their files.
4:30   p.m.   Judy and Liane to advance.
6:00   p.m.   Welcome Reception Esso Theatre located in
                            the Hockey Hall of Fame. Wine and beer to
                            be passed on trays. Hot and Cold Canapes.
                            Mixed Drinks will be brought upon request
                            (served to the guests). Facility exclusive to
                            the group.
                            Attach Menu – Description of Inclusions.
                            Clip-on microphone has been ordered.
                            Briefing on what they will be seeing, doing
                            and experiencing
                            Special Note: Some of the guests do not
                            speak English and French-speaking staff
                            requested. Carol, Liane and Marguerite will
                            be on hand to assist with translation.

		Details about the departure for Wayne Gretzky's to be given at this time. Also guests to be advised that the store will remain open from 6:00 p.m. – 7:30 p.m.. Purchases at their own expense. Maps of the facility will be given out.
6:30	p.m.	Wall goes up.

Guests will be given a quick walk through of the facility. Would like them divided into two groups. Carol to accompany one group to assist with translation. Liane to accompany the second group. Marguerite to help where required.

Be sure to mention how they can have their personal hockey team photos in the Hockey Hall of Fame should they be interested in doing so.

Group to be at leisure to enjoy facility. It is their's exclusively.

Central food and bar station will be set up with a Satellite bar with light snacks Hall. Please ensure both areas are covered on the walk through.

9:00	p.m.	Guests to depart to Wayne Gretzky's.

MONDAY
WAYNE GRETZKY'S

7:30	p.m.	Judy to advance
9:00	p.m.	Guests scheduled to arrive via motor coach

Guests will be arriving from the Hockey Hall of Fame. They are taking over the facility for a private reception. They will be there from 6:00 p.m. – 9:00 p.m..

VIP Line Pass — Tables to be waiting for the group. Group to be seated immediately. No standing in line.

Private section to be reserved for the group. Smoking Section. Number of guests:

Tables not to be positioned too tightly to allow waiters to manoeuvre between chairs and guests can easily get in and out.

Menu to be specially printed for the group. Notice to be placed on the bottom of the menu that two drinks per person will be compliments of client and that additional drinks will be at their own expense. For example, a group of four could split a bottle of wine but if they wanted more, they would have to pay for it themselves. Carol will be available should the waiter have any questions on how things should be addressed.

Need separate area for J.A. Production staff to be out of sight from the guests but close enough that we can check on them from time to time. If the Studio (adjacent private room) is not in use could a small table be set up there?

Requested waiters assigned to the group be exclusive to the group.

Choice of one of the following two appetizers:
Caesar Salad
Soup of the Day

Bread
Cheesy Garlic Flatbread

Choice of one of the following entrees:
Half Chicken with Fennel, Chilies, Oregano, Cinnamon
BBQ Back Ribs
Atlantic Salmon Grilled with Black Bean Sauce
Linguini with Shrimp, Clams, Mussels, Squid, Garlic, Tomato, Green Onions in Traditional Clam Sauce

Choice of one of the following desserts:
Chocolate "Evolution"
Homemade Apple Cake with Whisky Sauce
Hot Fresh Fruit "Calzone"
Ice Cream or Fruit Ice

Beverages
Coffee or Tea

TUESDAY
PRIVATE GROUP BREAKFAST

7:00	a.m.	Judy to advance breakfast
		Conference Room D & E
		Rounds of 10 but set for eight.
		Double-sided buffet
7:45	a.m.	All to be ready to go in case of early arrivals
8:00	a.m.	Breakfast

Buffet Set Up not Plated
Chilled Apple and Freshly Squeezed Orange Juice
Scrambled Eggs
Choice of Bacon or Sausage Links
Roasted Potatoes
Croissants and Muffins
Fruit Preserves and Butter

Coffee, Assorted Teas, Decaffeinated Coffee.
**Ensure tear down does not start while guests are
still in the room.**
Special Note: Menu to be served buffet style at
no additional cost.

Bill to Master Account

Buffet Breakfast $00.00 + + + per person.

TUESDAY
TRANSFER TO CONFERENCE

7:30	a.m.	Luggage transfer will begin. Porterage has been prepaid.
8:15	a.m.	All luggage to be down and in a secure area.
8:45	a.m.	Motor coach to arrive at the Richmond entrance. Luggage to be loaded.
9:00	a.m.	Motor coach to depart for conference. Smoking in not permitted on motor coach. Carol to advise. The driver will be French-speaking. Same driver as airport transfers will stay with you for duration of the trip. Map to conference has been given to driver. Please review with driver. The number to call show you run into any difficulty is 1-800-000-0000.
10:30	a.m.	Estimated time of arrival at conference. Lunch provided. Carol and driver to continue to London to drop-off the luggage. Carol please give client the phone number of the motor coach. Parking has been requested at the hotel for the motor coach and a room has been arranged for the driver. Room and tax will go the master account. Hotel will ask for credit card for incidentals. Carol and driver to proceed to The Shot to advance. Carol to give driver money to purchase cooler, beverages, ice, glasses garbage bags etc. for drive from conference to hotel. Have him provide receipts for everything. Driver to stock cooler with soft drinks, juices mineral water, ice, cups and garbage bags. Drinks to be offered only on drive from conference to London.

		Carol and driver to return to conference to wait for guests. Advise client when you have returned in case they would like an earlier departure. Cell number: Hotel is approximately 45 minutes from the conference.
		Parking at conference. There is ample parking and a spot has been reserved for you # 123. There is no charge for parking.
5:00	p.m.	Guests scheduled to depart conference for London.
		Beverages to be served onboard.
5:45	p.m.	Estimated arrival time in London.
		Note to Carol: Call hotel to let them know you are en route so that they can ensure all is in place.

To be billed to client

Additional cost for beverages – .

TUESDAY
ADVANCE HOTEL
HOSPITALITY DESK/PRIVATE REGISTRATION
DELTA LONDON ARMOURIES

Daily Requirements	One House Phone/No Long Distance Access
	One Skirted Table (6 x 3)
	Three Chairs
	Two Flip Charts/Easel
	Markers. Two Colours.
	One Waste basket
	One Table Lamp (only if not in a well lit area)
	11:00 a.m. Registration desk to be set up and to remain in place for 24 hours.

Bill To Master Account

Flip Charts

House Phone

Balance of items provided by the hotel at no charge.

TUESDAY
HOTEL CHECK IN PROCEDURES DELTA LONDON ARMOURIES HOTEL

Hotel Check-In is 3:00 p.m.. The participants will be arriving as a group.

Guests will be arriving by motor coach. Carol will drop them off at 10:30 a.m. at conference and will proceed to the hotel with their luggage. Carol will also meet with the front desk manager to review procedure for private check-in. Carol will return to conference to pick up the group and return with them to the hotel.

- Motor coach drop off point will be in front of the hotel.
- Overnight parking for motor coach has been requested.

Overnight parking charges to be billed to the master account for motor coach.

A private, satellite check-in desk is to be set up beside hospitality desk. This is to be ready by 4:00 p.m.. Check-in to be manned by staff exclusively for client. **French-speaking staff requested. Guests are all from Quebec.**

Please ensure adequate staff scheduling has been provided for the private registration desk and the bell desk.

All check-ins are to be pre-registered and rooms to be pre-assigned.

No room rates are to appear on individual guest bills.

Express check-out forms to be included in each key packet.

Separate key packets are to be prepared for each guest, two keys per packet.

Key packets to be ready and waiting in alphabetical order prior to guests' arrival at the satellite check-in desk.

Upgrades or room changes are not permitted unless authorized by J.A. Productions.

Four copies (both alpha and numeric) of clients rooming list will be required.

Scheduled welcome room gift deliveries to be in each guest room at least one hour prior to guest arrival.

MASTER ACCOUNT
Client
1. Name   All to Master
2. Name   All to Master
3. Name   All to Master

Judy Allen Productions
1. Carol   All to Master

Balance of Guests
All guest room and taxes are to go to the master account. Participants are to give a credit card imprint to cover incidentals. Unless specified client will not be responsible for participants incidental accounts.

AUTHORIZED SIGNATURES FOR THE MASTER ACCOUNT
Client
1. Name
2. Name
3. Name

Judy Allen Productions
1. Carol

ACCOUNTING
Carol to meet with hotel's accounting department on August 15th (approximately 10:30 p.m.) to review all individual room bills. This must be done prior to the folios being delivered to any guest rooms.

All bills to be posted to the master account must be signed off by J.A. Production staff. Carol will meet with accounting Wednesday, August 16 before guest departure (10:00 a.m.). Please have two copies of all bills and folios available.

ROOM BLOCK
Please see attached list.

FUNCTION SPACE
Gunnery Ballroom Breakfast August 16 Sit down Double-sided buffet 7:00 a.m. – 10:00 a.m.

TUESDAY
HOTEL ARRIVAL

Arrival Schedule:
Guests will be transferred to the hotel by motor coach as a group.
Luggage will have been delivered to the hotel earlier in the day while guests were attending conference. All luggage to be waiting for guests in their rooms.

	Estimated arrival time 5:45 p.m.. Carol will contact the hotel when they are en route from the show so that staff will be ready.
5:15 p.m.	Hotel staff (French-speaking requested) to be in place at the satellite check-in. Hotel staff members to take credit card imprints when guests arrive with the exception of those where all is to the master account. Participants will be arriving at the Dundas Street entrance. Hotel porterage is included in their stay. **Note to hotel:** Some guests will have an understanding of English but I have been advised that there may be some who speak no English at all.

Bill to Master Account

Porterage	$0.00 + 0% taxes roundtrip
Parking	Motor coach. Reserved Parking

TUESDAY
ROOM GIFT

Welcome gift to be delivered to each guest room. Carol to receive from client prior to advancing the hotel along with a letter from the company to accompany gift. Gift to be waiting in each guest room.

Bill to Master Account

Delivery $0.00 + 0% taxes roundtrip

TUESDAY
LUGGAGE PULL/DEPARTURE NOTICES

Departure notices will be given to the bellmen for delivery this evening while the guests are out for dinner.
Bags to be left inside the room. Pick-up will be at 8:30 a.m. on the 16th. Motor coach to depart at 10:00 a.m.. Bell staff to advise if they will require more time for luggage pickup.

TUESDAY
TRANSFER/RECEPTION AND DINNER AT THE SHOT

6:30   p.m.   Depart Hotel for The Shot Restaurant
(The restaurant is no more than a five minute drive from the hotel)

Enter parking lot. There is a charge for parking. Carol to pay.

The back section of the restaurant and pool tables have been reserved exclusively for the group.

The pool tables as you enter the restaurant will be for the restaurant's other guests.

Guests seated in raised section of dining room. Please ensure that there is sufficient space between tables and seating.

Client would like to have all guests in pool area to see beginning of demonstration first. Drinks and snacks in will be served in this area. Guests will probably be hungry as they will only have had a light lunch at the show.

Need separate area for J.A. Production staff to sit out of sight from the guests but close enough so that we can check on them from time to time. Could a small table be set up for Carol in the patio?

Requested waiters assigned to the group be exclusive to the group.

Pool expert will perform from 6:30 p.m. to 7:15 p.m. and he will stay and interact with the guests. Meals and beverages are included.

7:30 p.m.	Dinner to be served. Two beverages in addition to the beverages (2) served during the reception to be compliments of client Additional beverages to be at guests own expense.
9:00 p.m.	Shuttle to begin.
9:30 p.m.	Last transfer complete.

WEDNESDAY
HOSPITALITY DESK HOTEL OUTSIDE GUNNERY BALLROOM (PRIVATE BREAKFAST)

Daily Requirements	One House Phone/No Long Distance Access
	One Skirted Table (6' x 3')
	Three Chairs
	Two Flip Charts/Easels
	Markers. Two Colours.
	One Waste Paper Basket
	One Table Lamp (only if not in a well lit area)
	6:00 a.m. the registration desk set up and to remain until 10:00 a.m.

Bill To Master Account

Flip Charts

House Phone

Balance of items provided at no charge from the hotel.

WEDNESDAY
PRIVATE GROUP BREAKFAST GUNNERY BALLROOM

8:00	a.m.	Carol to advance breakfast
		Gunnery Ballroom to the right of main dining room.
		Round tables of ten but set for 8.
		Double-sided buffet
8:30	a.m.	All to be ready to go in case of early arrivals.
9:00	a.m.	Breakfast

Buffet

Orange Juice, Grapefruit Juice, Apple Juice, Cranberry Juice

Scrambled Eggs with Chives

Strip Bacon, Peameal Ham, Breakfast Sausage

Home-Fried Potatoes

Grilled Tomato

Fresh-Baked Danish Pastries, Bran and Fruit Muffins, Butter Croissants

Mini Bagels with Cream Cheese

Fruit Preserves and Sweet Butter

Coffee, Assorted Teas, Decaffeinated Coffee.

Ensure tear down does not start while guests are still in the room.

Bill to Master Account

Buffet $00.00 + + + per person.

WEDNESDAY
TRANSFER TO CONFERENCE/FACTORY/AIRPORT/TORONTO

8:30	a.m.	Luggage transfer will begin. Porterage has been prepaid.
9:15	a.m.	All luggage to be down and in a secure area.
9:45	a.m.	Motor coach to spot. Luggage to be loaded.
10:00	a.m.	Motor coach to depart for conference. See attached.
10:30	a.m.	Estimated time of arrival at conference.
		Motor coach Parking pre-reserved.
12:30	p.m.	Lunch included at the conference.
1:30	p.m.	Depart for factory.
		1-519-000-0000

2:00	p.m.	Arrival factory
3:00	p.m.	Depart for airport. Recommend at least one hour for transfer due to traffic. Carol to reconfirm.
4:00	p.m.	Arrival at airport. Carol to handle porterage at airport.

Those departing on the flight to disembark.

Air Canada 1218 departs London 5:40 p.m.
Air Canada 1218 arrives Toronto 6:18 p.m.
Air Canada 194 departs Toronto 7:00 p.m.
Air Canada 194 arrives Montreal 10:05 p.m.
Carol departs with group.
3 head office staff plus 1 guest to continue to Toronto
1 client staff member to be dropped off at Yorkdale Shopping Centre.
Motor coach drops off remaining guests at the Sheraton.

WEDNESDAY
OVERNIGHT HOTEL ACCOMMODATION FOR TRAIN PASSENGER

Overnight accommodation has been blocked for Mr. *** for the night of the 16th. Club Room. Bill to master account.
Liane to meet motor coach at hotel and assist Mr. *** with check-in and head office with valet parking — making sure all costs are charged to the master account.

THURSDAY
TRANSFER FROM THE HOTEL TO THE TRAIN STATION

A driver will meet for Mr. *** in the hotel lobby. He will have company sign.
Note: Liane please ensure that you advise him to be at the front doors at 9:00 a.m. for transfer to the station. Continental buffet included with his stay on club floor.
Driver's Number:
Train 56 departs Toronto 10:00 a.m. arrives Montreal 2:41 p.m.

INDEX

Access routes, 118
Advance planning meeting (precon), 22, 70
Airwalls, 146, 147
Anniversary of the Virgin of Guadalupe, 26
Arrival. *See* Guest arrival
Audio-visual/staging/lighting, 131-144
Axtell, Roger E., 190

Bagging parking meters, 90
Balloon burst, 112
Band (entertainment), 193, 207-215
Banners, 126
Bar locations, 192
Barn-to-barn charges, 77
Bartenders, 164, 165, 192, 193
Bathrooms, 51, 58, 67, 178
Betsy's Wedding, 64
Beverages. *See* Food and beverage
Blackout, 129
Blueprints, 122, 134
Box lunches, 175
Breakfast, 169-173
Briefcases, 109
Budget. *See* Cost/charges
Budget breakdown, 14-16
Buffet, 170, 171, 184, 185
Building restrictions, 53
Buses (motor coaches), 76-78, 81

Car rally, 52
Carpeting, 144
Cars on display, 118, 145, 146
Caterers, 190, 191
Ceiling height, 135
Cell phones, 127, 128
Centrepieces, 223-227
Chairs, 125
Champagne toast, 200, 201
Charges. *See* Cost/charges
Charitable donations, 205
Check-in table, 122
Children, 160, 161
Chocolate fountain, 184
Cigars, 200
Client appreciation event, 6
Coat check, 108-110
Cocktail reception, 175-182, 191-198
Coffee, 172
Coffee breaks, 173
Communications requirements, 127, 128
Complimentary parking passes, 86
Concierge floors, 173
Conferences

objectives, 5
time of day/day of week, 28, 29
time of year, 26
Contact sheets, 22, 23
Contracts, 69-71, 233, 234
Convention centres, 46-49
Corporate events
objectives, 5
time of day/day of week, 28, 29
time of year, 26
Cost/charges
bar costs, 191, 192
centrepieces, 226
changes to original estimates, 144
chocolate fountain, 184
cleaning the room, 139
dance floor, 145
entertainers' meals, 211
entertainment, 214
hotel services, 104, 105
motor coaches, 77
permits, 89, 120
photographers, 220
preliminary cost estimates, 2-4
professional help, 56
set-up view, 141
sign off on bills, 201
staging, 137, 139
street permits, 89
telephone installation, 128
thank-you letters, 237
tipping the staff, 58, 165
unions, 117, 135
Cost sheets, 14, 15
Creative director, 8, 60
Critical path, 17-20
Customs, 231
Cut-off times, 18

Dance floor, 144, 145
Date selection
day of week/time of day, 28-30
long weekends, 33
major holidays, 31
other considerations, 35
other special events, 35
religious observations, 32
school breaks, 32, 33
sporting events, 33, 34
time of year, 25-28
Day of week/time of day, 28-30
Day rooms, 114
Decor, 227-230

Decor companies, 229
Deep-sea fishing, 185
Dinner, 182-201
Disabilities. See Wheelchair accessibility
Disney's opening gala
    (Beauty & the Beast), 39
Do's and Taboos Around the World (Axtell), 190
Donations, 205
Doormen, 106, 107
Double bar set-up, 192
Draping, 124, 138
Drinks. See Food and beverage
Drop-off point, 101

Easels, 125
Eid Festival-Hari Raya Puasa, 25
Electrical requirements, 119, 127-129
Entertainment, 193, 207-215
Entrance, 102-105
Event committee, 9
Extension cords, 127
Eye appeal (food presentation), 180

Fanfare, 111-121
Father's Day, 26
Final touches, 231-234
Fire and safety regulations, 61, 146
Fireworks display, 226, 227
Flowers, 223-226
Food and beverage, 163-205
    bartenders, 164, 165
    breakfast, 169-173
    buffet, 170, 171, 184, 185
    champagne toast, 200, 201
    charitable donations, 205
    cigars, 200
    cocktail reception, 175-182, 191-198
    coffee, 172
    coffee breaks, 173
    dinner, 182-201
    food guarantee, 164
    food presentation (eye appeal), 180
    hors d'oeuvres, 167, 181
    liquor, 164
    lunch, 174, 175
    menu planning, 166-201
    minors, serving alcohol to, 195
    non-alcoholic beverages, 194
    out-of-country specialities, 168, 169
    overage, 164
    specialty drinks, 75, 194
    staffing, 202-204
    utensils, 184, 185
    vegetarian selections, 163
    wine, 165, 199, 200
Food guarantee, 164
Food presentation (eye appeal), 180
Freight elevators, 118
Frog legs, 169

Front entrance attendants (doormen), 106, 107
Function sheets, 20-24
Fund-raisers
    objectives, 5
    silent auction, 31
    time of day/day of week, 28, 29
    time of year, 27

Gagnon, Andre-Phillipe, 208
Gala openings (new venues), 71, 72
Global considerations. See Out-of-country events
Golf tournaments, 175
Golf towels, 6, 7
Good Neighbour Policy (Loew's Hotels), 205
Guest arrival, 97-129
    access routes, 118
    cars on display, 118
    coat check, 108-110
    doormen, 106, 107
    drop-off point, 101
    electrical requirements, 119, 127-129
    entrance, 102-105
    fanfare, 111-121
    "private party" sign, 107
    q&a (arrival/weather considerations), 99-110
    registration (guest check-in), 113, 114, 121-129
    set-up time, 116
    special equipment, 117
    weather considerations, 97-110
    welcome refreshments, 123
Guest check-in (registration), 113, 114, 121-129
Guest day room, 114
Guest list, 149-152

Heaters, 42
Helium balloons, 111, 112
Holidays, 31
Homeless people, 106
Hors d'oeuvres, 167, 181
Hotels, 27, 28, 46-49, 104, 105

Incentive programs
    objectives, 6
    time of day/day of week, 28, 29
    time of year, 27
Indoor fireworks display, 227
Indoor-outdoor events, 69. See also Tents
Indoor pyro, 226
Initial planning, 8-11
Insurance, 52, 213
International considerations.
    See Out-of-country events
Invitations, 152-157

Kyle, Mackenzie, 9

Las Vegas, 114, 133, 137
Lead time, 11
Lighting/audio-visual/staging, 131-144

Limousines, 30, 73-76, 88
Liquor, 164
Live chat room, 7
Location, 37-72, 81. *See also*
    Venue requirements
    contracts, 69-71
    convention centres, 46-49
    gala openings (new venues), 71, 72
    hotels, 46-49
    location requirements, 43-46
    parking lots, 94
    potential problems, 89-93
    restaurants/private venues, 49-62. *See also*
        Restaurants/private venues
    site selection, 37-43
    tents, 64-69
    theatres, 62-64
Loew's Hotels (Good Neighbour Policy), 205
Long weekends, 33
Lunch, 174, 175

Mailings, 19, 155
Major holidays, 31
Making it Happen (Kyle), 9
March break, 26
Media, 7, 8, 91, 158-160
Meetings
    objectives, 4
    time of day/day of week, 28, 29
    time of year, 26
Menu. *See* Food and beverage
Minors, serving alcohol to, 195
Mother's Day, 26
Motor coaches, 76-78, 81
Movenpick Marche, 39
Murphy's law, 1

New car launches, 26
New venues (gala openings), 71, 72
Newly opened restaurants/venues, 180
No, never accept, as answer, 70
Noise restrictions, 52, 120, 121
Non-alcoholic beverages, 75, 194

Objectives, 4-8
Off-duty paid police, 91
Open seating, 186
Orange cones, 90
Organization and timing, 17-35
    critical path, 17-20
    date selection, 31-35
    day of week/time of day, 28-30
    function sheets, 20-24
    time of year, 25-28
Oscar party, 30
Out-of-country events
    alcoholic beverages, 194
    key considerations, 42, 43
    local celebrations, 25, 26

precon, 70
protocol, 189, 190
shuttle buses, 95
specialty foods, 75, 168, 169
Outdoor events, 42, 69
Overage, 164
Oversize napkin, 185

Parking, 78-88, 93-95
Parking lots, 94
Parking meters, bagging, 90
Parting gifts, 231
Partnering with another company, 10
Payment schedule, 16
Photographer, 215-223
Police (off-duty paid), 91
Power (electrical) requirements, 119, 127-129
Pre-assigned seating, 186
Pre-paid parking, 84, 85
Precon, 22, 70
Preferred suppliers, 23
Preliminary cost estimates, 2-4
Press kits, 160
"Private party" sign, 107
Private venues. *See* Restaurants/private venues
Private yacht charters, 233
Product launch, 225
Proms, 24, 25
Protocol, 74, 189, 190
Purpose of event, 4-8

Questions and answers
    arrival/weather considerations, 99-110
    entertainment, 208-215
    fanfare, 112-121
    first steps, 8
    media, 158-160
    photographer, 216-223
    registration, 122-129
    restaurants/private venues, 49-62
    room requirements, 144-148
    staging/audio-visual/lighting, 135-144
    transportation, 80-95

Rain, 102, 103
Recordkeeping, 237, 238
Red carpet, 111
Registration (guest check-in), 113, 114, 121-129
Rehearsal time, 139, 208, 209
Religion, 26, 32
Rentals, 228-230
Requests (band), 215
Restaurants/private venues, 39-41, 49-62
    bathrooms, 51, 58
    building restrictions, 53
    dishes, 57
    experienced staff, 59, 60
    fire and safety regulations, 61
    insurance, 52

kitchens, 54, 55
lighting, 54
noise restrictions, 52
room capacity, 50, 51
sight lines, 54
staff breaks, 59
utensils, 55-57
zoning, 51, 52
Riders (entertainment), 193
Road rally, 52
Room capacity, 50, 51
Room layout chart, 122, 123
Room requirements, 131, 144-148.
    See also Venue requirements
RSVP, 34, 35
Rubber boots, 104

Saturday, 32
Save-the-date card, 152, 153
School breaks, 32, 33
School prom, 24, 25
Scope of event, 2
Security, 194, 195
Set-up time, 116
Shooters, 165, 192
Shuttles, 79, 80, 87, 88
Sight lines, 54, 136
Sign holders, 125, 126
Signage, 125-127
Silent auction fund-raisers, 31
Site inspection (walk through), 57, 115, 133,
    174, 177, 204
Site selection, 37-43
Skirting, 124
Smoking room, 200
Souvenir umbrellas, 102
Space requirements, 131
Special effects, 230
Special equipment, 117, 141-143
Special events
    objectives, 6
    time of day/day of week, 29, 30
Specialty drinks, 75, 194
Sponsorship dollars, 46
Sporting events, 33, 34
Staff parking, 95
Staging/audio-visual/lighting, 131-144
Start time, 82. See also Date selection
Street permits, 80, 89
Street vendors, 90
Suppliers, 23

Table assignments, 187
Table covers, 124, 125
Tables, 228
Taxi stands, 91
Teaser e-mails, 7
Telephones, 127, 128
Tents, 64-69

Thank-you letters, 236, 237
Theatres, 62-64
Theme parties, 160, 161, 223-227, 232
Time of year, 25-28
Time requirements, 10, 11. See also
    Organization and timing
Tipping the staff, 58, 165
Traffic barrier, 120
Transportation, 73-95
    limousines, 73-76, 88
    motor coaches, 76-78, 81
    moving guests between locations, 79
    orange cones, 90
    parking, 78-88, 93-95
    questions and answers, 80-95
    shuttles, 79, 80, 87, 88
    street permits, 80, 89
    taxi stands, 91
    unusual modes of, 76, 88
Tray presentation, 180
Type of event, 9, 10

Unions, 117, 135
Utensils, 55-57, 184, 185

Valet parking, 93, 94
Vegetarian selections, 163
Venue requirements, 131-148
    airwalls, 146, 147
    car displays, 145, 146
    ceiling height, 135
    dance floor, 144, 145
    fire and safety regulations, 146
    other events, 148
    room requirements, 144-148
    sight lines, 136
    space requirements, 131
    special equipment, 141-143
Visualization, 11-13
Volunteers, 23, 24, 56

Walk through (site inspection), 57, 115, 133,
    174, 177, 204
Walkie-talkies, 127
Weather, 97-110, 178
Wedding rehearsals, 41
Weekends, long, 33
Welcome refreshments, 123
Wheelchair accessibility
    entrance, 105
    parking, 86
    stage, 140
Wine, 165, 199, 200
Wrap-up review, 235, 236

Yacht charters, 233

Zoning, 51, 52, 120, 121